LINA BO BARDI

LINA BO BARDI

First published in Japan on November 22, 2017
Second published on December 10, 2023

Editorial Supervision: Etsuko Watari, WATARI-UM, The Watari Museum of Contemporary Art
Cooperation: Instituo Lina Bo e P. M. Bardi

Publisher: Akira Watai
TOTO Publishing (TOTO LTD.)
TOTO Nogizaka Bldg., 2F
1-24-3 Minami-Aoyama, Minato-ku
Tokyo 107-0062, Japan
[Sales]Telephone: +81-3-3402-7138 Facsimile: +81-3-3402-7187
[Editorial]Telephone: +81-3-3497-1010
URL: http://www.toto.co.jp/publishing/

Designer: groovisions
Printer: Dai-Nippon Printing Co., Ltd.

Except as permitted under copyright law, this book may not be
reproduced, in whole or in part, in any form or by any means, including
photocopying, scanning, digitizing, or otherwise, without prior
permission. Scanning or digitizing this book through a third party, even
for personal or home use, is also strictly prohibited.
The list price is indicated on the cover.

ISBN978-4-88706-369-3

LINA BO BARDI

目次

6 　序　アンドレ・コヘーア・ド・ラーゴ

10 　建築作品
12 　ガラスの家
36 　サンパウロ美術館
68 　SESC ポンペイア文化センター
104 　サンタ・マリア・ドス・アンジョス教会
118 　サルヴァドール旧市街修復プロジェクト
136 　テアトロ・オフィシナ
148 　ヴァレリア・P・シレル邸
156 　民衆文化伝承館
164 　エスピリト・サント・ド・セラード教会
172 　サンパウロ・シティ・ホール

180 　建築周辺のデザイン
182 　家具デザイン
190 　キュレーションと会場デザイン
202 　舞台と劇場デザイン
210 　植栽デザイン
218 　都市計画
226 　日本とリナ
235 　対談　妹島和世×塚本由晴

254 　リナ・ボ・バルディの生涯
256 　自伝　1914〜51年
272 　年表
280 　あとがき　和多利恵津子
284 　作品データ
285 　リナ・ボ・バルディ建築作品マップ
286 　参考文献、出典、クレジット

Contents

8 　Preface　　　André CORRÊA DO LAGO

10 　Architectural Works
12 　The Glass House
36 　São Paulo Art Museum
68 　SESC-Pompéia Factory Leisure Center
104 　Santa Maria dos Anjos Chapel
118 　Historic Center of Salvador
136 　Oficina Theater
148 　Valéria P. Cirell's Home
156 　Solar do Unhao — Popular Art Museum
164 　Espírito Santo do Cerrado Church
172 　São Paulo City Hall

180 　Around the Architecture
182 　Furniture Design
190 　Curation
202 　Stage and Theater Design
210 　Botanical Design
218 　City Planning
226 　Lina in Japan
235 　Interview Kazuyo Sejima & Yoshiharu Tsukamoto

254 　The Life of Lina Bo Bardi
262 　Literary Curriculum by Lina Bo Bardi
276 　Chronology
282 　Afterword　　Etsuko Watari
284 　Data on Works
285 　Architectural Works Map
286 　Bibliography, Sources, Credits

序

アンドレ・コヘーア・ド・ラーゴ
駐日ブラジル大使

本書をご覧になれば、リナの手掛けた建築とデザインがいかに質の高いものであったか、いかに多様であったかが手に取るようにお分かりになるでしょう。むしろ彼女の作品が国際的な評価を得るまでに、これほど時間がかかったことに驚きを覚えます。本書の読者には自明のことですが、何しろ彼女は1992年に他界するまで、実に40年の長きにわたってブラジル文化の中心人物であり続けたのですから。

イタリアからブラジルへ移住した時、リナは32歳でした。そのブラジルで、彼女は輝ける世代の若手建築家（ルシオ・コスタ、オスカー・ニーマイヤー、アフォンソ・レイディ、ヴィラノヴァ・アルティガスほか）と出会います。当初は、そんな彼らが自らの知識や努力よりも直観や衝動を当てにしているように、彼女の眼には映りました。けれども彼女自身は次第にブラジル文化の深みにはまり込んでいくうちに、この新しい文化を吸収していきます。そもそも彼女は母国イタリアで優れた学識と実務経験を積んでおり、それもジオ・ポンティ、ブルーノ・ゼヴィ、夫のピエトロ・マリア・バルディといった戦前の当代一流の思想家たちが身近にいるという環境でしたから、さすがに呑み込みも早かったのでしょう。

経験豊富で何事にも一家言をもっていた彼女は、ブラジル建築の2大流派――いわゆるカリオカ派（リオ・デ・ジャネイロ）とパウリスタ派（サンパウロ）――のいずれにも与せず、我が道を行きました。そしてブラジル建築に新たな系譜を誕生させます。まだサステイナブルな建築が普及していなかった時代に社会・環境問題を取り上げ、実際に低所得地域の住民や多方面のアーティストと膝を突き合わせて対話をしながら、従来の建築観を塗り替え、ある時は教育者として、またある時は執筆者として、そうした建築観を世の中に伝えていきました。そんなリナのことを知れば知るほど、もっと知りたくなることでしょう。

サンパウロ空港に到着したリナ・ボ・バルディと夫ピエトロ・マリア・バルディ。(1947年)
Lina Bo Bardi and husband Pietro Maria Bardi arriving at São Paulo Airport. (1947)

デザイナーとしてのリナは、美術館の展示や会場構成では既成概念を打ち破り、また数々の素晴らしい家具や舞台装置に加え、アクセサリーまで手掛けました。もちろん最大の功績を果たした建築の分野では縦横無尽の活躍ぶりで、たとえば「サンパウロ美術館（MASP）」（1968、p. 036）の非常に洗練された建物を設計したかと思えば、「サンタ・マリア・ドス・アンジョス教会」（1987、p. 104）のようにひどく地味な建物もつくりますし、あるいは「民衆文化伝承館」（1959、p. 156）では歴史的建造物を、「SESCポンペイア文化センター」（1982、p. 068）では古い工場を大胆に改修しています。

このようにリナは第2の母国でかなりの影響力を与えるまでになりますが、それは何も彼女が建築とデザインの分野で数多くの作品を手掛けたからというだけでなく、ブラジル大衆芸術の編集者、批評家、学者、プロモーターとして活躍したからでもあります。彼女はその強い個性、博識、旺盛な好奇心、才能ゆえに一目も二目も置かれましたが、どんな論争にも尻込みしなかったので周りから恐れられもしました。

リナの生涯と作品を紹介する日本初の展覧会が2015年に東京のワタリウム美術館で開催されるということで、これを企画なさった和多利恵津子さんにお声掛けいただきました。何しろ私はリナ作品の大ファンですから、この企画は願ってもないことでした。しかも妹島和世さん――日本を代表する女性建築家――が会場デザインを監修してくださる、言うなればブラジルを代表する女性建築家の仕事を日本の皆さんに向けて「翻訳」してくださると聞き、喜びもひとしおでした。さらに本書を通じて、きっと日本でもリナの建築とデザインに対する評価が高まることでしょう。

Preface

André CORRÊA DO LAGO
Ambassador of Brazil in Japan

This book shows very clearly the quality and diversity of Lina's contribution to architecture and design. It is therefore surprising how late the international recognition of her work happened, even more when it is clear for the reader that she was a central figure in Brazil's culture for four decades, until her death in 1992.

Lina arrived in Brazil from Italy when she was 32 years old. She discovered Brazil's brilliant generation of young architects (Lucio Costa, Oscar Niemeyer, Affonso Reidy, Villanova Artigas and many others). At first, she thought they seemed to rely more on intuition and impulse than knowledge and hard work. But little by little she became immersed in different dimensions of Brazilian culture, absorbing influences that she integrated to her strong academic background and professional experience in Italy, where she was surrounded by some of the pre-war most influential thinkers such as Gio Ponti, Bruno Zevi and her husband, Pietro Maria Bardi.

She had such a particular viewpoint and rich background that she found her own way, beyond the two main directions of Brazilian architecture - generally described as the Carioca (Rio de Janeiro) and Paulista (Sao Paulo) schools. She developed an influential new lineage for Brazilian architecture, introducing social and environmental dimensions well before sustainable architecture became relevant, exploring, teaching and writing about new perspectives for architecture through real dialogue with low income communities and different artists. There are, therefore, many reasons to learn more about Lina.

As a designer, she pushed the boundaries of museum displays and exhibition arrangements and created a series of brilliant pieces of furniture, theatre sets and even jewelry. Naturally her greatest achievements were in architecture, where she navigated comfortably between highly sophisticated structures, like the Art Museum of Sao Paulo (1968, p. 036), extremely modest buildings, such as the Santa Maria dos Anjos Church (1987, p. 104), and innovative restoration of historic buildings, like the Solar do Unhao (1959, p.156), and industrial buildings, like the SESC Pompeia (1982, p. 068).

Lina's influence in her adoptive country was therefore not only strong because of her creations in architecture and design, but also as an editor, a critic, a scholar and a promoter of Brazilian popular art. Her strong personality, knowledge, curiosity and talent allowed her to be highly respected and even feared, since she did not shy away from debates.

As a great admirer of Lina's work, I was extremely happy to colaborate in 2015 with WATARI-UM, The Watari Museum of Contemporary Art, Tokyo, in showing the first ever exhibition in Japan about her life and work, curated by Watari Etsuko. It was an additional pleasure that Sejima Kazuyo - the best woman architect in Japan - participated in the supervisor of the exhibition, "translating" the best Brazilian woman architect to the Japanese public. I am sure this new book will strengthen the recognition of Lina's architecture and design in Japan.

建築作品
Architectural Works

ガラスの家
The Glass House

São Paulo, 1951

The intention was therefore to
situate the house within nature,
bringing it into contact
with its 'dangers'
without fussing too much
about the usual 'protections'.
Lina Bo Bardi, 1953

そこでのねらいは、住宅を自然の中に置くことでした。
建物に対するありがちな「保護」をいろいろ考えることはせず、
あえて「危険」に晒すということでした。
リナ・ボ・バルディ、1953年

完成当時の外観。(1951年)
The exterior at time of completion. (1951)

リナの処女作である「ガラスの家」は、1951年、リナが36歳で内装や家具も含めてデザインした自邸である。傾斜地に建つこの住宅は、眺望の開けた側を全面のガラスファサード、山側を伝統的なデザインの居室部分として、周囲の風景との一体化を図りながら、リナ作品の特徴のひとつである「現代建築と土着的建築の融合」をみごとに表している。アプローチからピロティへ入ると鉄製の階段が現れ、階段を上がるにつれて風景が広がり、自然の中に溶け込むかのように迎え入れられる。建物を貫くような一本の木を中心にもつ中庭が内外のバランスを取り、自然と一体化した建築を実現している。この自邸の完成と同時にリナはブラジル国民となり、ブラジルで生きることを選んだ。そして、1992年に亡くなるまでこの自邸で過ごした。

繊細な美しさと大胆なボリューム感をあわせもつこの自邸は、単なる優雅さを超えた包容力や活力を感じさせる。間仕切り壁のないリビングルームは家具で緩やかに区切られ、中庭を中心にモダンなリビングルームからヴァナキュラーな居住部分へと滑らかに一周する動線計画となっている。床面まで延びるガラス窓からは、窓際に立つと森の中に落ちてしまうように感じるほど、外の環境が迫って見える。内部空間は、色彩が効果的に用いられている。水色のハンドメイドのガラスタイルを全面に用いたリビングルームの床は、ガラスファサードからの光を反射して輝き、椅子や小さな壁面にも同様の水色を用いて空間に統一感を与えている。キッチンは白と緑、浴室は濃い青、洗面所は黒と、各室に異なる色のタイルを用い、寝室はダークブラウンのフローリングと白壁とするなど、空間ごとの色彩に変化を与えている。タイルの質感やシンプルで多様な建具、リナと夫ピエトロが集めた美術品や民芸品、そして生い茂る植物が、理性的なデザインに血を通わせている。

当時、住宅の建つモルンビ地区は新興住宅地ではげ山だったが、リナは自身で周囲の植栽デザインを練り(p. 212)、土を抑える石壁と、石や陶器を敷いた小道を巡らせた。60年を経て植物が大きく成長し、今では全体がジャングルに覆われたみごとな環境となっている。敷地内には、後年リナが自分のために建てた小さなスタジオもある(p. 227)。

初期の外観のドローイング。ガラスのファサード、カーブしたアプローチのアイデアは当初からあった。
Early drawing of the exterior. Ideas for the glass façade and curved approach were there from the start.

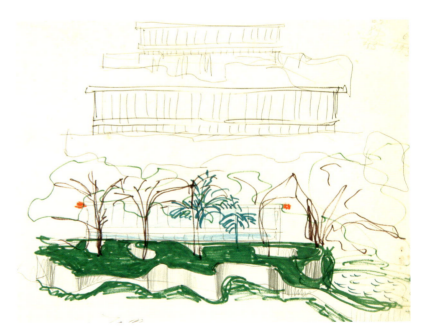

緑に囲まれた住宅というイメージが描かれた、外観のドローイング。
Drawing of the exterior depicting an image of a house surrounded by greenery.

In 1951, at age 36, Lina designed her own house, including the interior decoration and the furniture. The residence, known as the "Glass House", is her maiden built work. A glass facade stretching the whole frontage faces the side with the view afforded by the building as it sits on a sloping plot of land. With its legendary design, the living area facing the mountain side outlines a desire to integrate with the surrounding landscape, and offers a prime example of a "fusion of modern and indigenous architecture", one of the characteristics of Lina's work. Moving from the approach between the pilotis, an iron staircase appears, revealing with each step the landscape that lays ahead, as if being greeted by nature and becoming embedded in its midst. In the residence is a courtyard that allows a tree in the center of the garden below to grow up into the heart of the house, thus striking a balance between the interior and the exterior in an example of architecture integrated with nature. Lina became a naturalized Brazilian citizen the same year she completed her home in São Paulo where she lived the rest of her days. Lina died at the "Glass House" in 1992.

The home combines subtle beauty and bold volumes to give a sense of inclusiveness and vitality beyond mere elegance. Devoid of partition walls, the living room is instead loosely partitioned by pieces of furniture. Moreover, the courtyard at its center creates a subdued looping line of flow between the modern living room and vernacular living quarters. The outside environment appears to close in through the glass windows which extend down to the floor, giving the impression that one could fall into the forest when standing by the window. The interior of the residence showcases an effective use of colors. For example, blue handmade glass tiles covering the living room floor reflect the natural light coming in from the glass facade, while the same blue color is echoed in the seats and small wall surfaces to impart a sense of unity to the whole space. Every space is imparted a

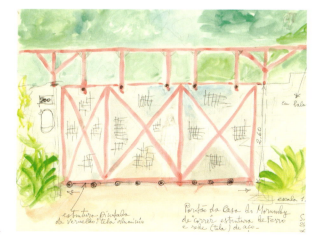

敷地のゲートのドローイング。
ここから入りアプローチの坂を上がった先にガラスの家がある。
Drawing of the gate to the site.
From here, the "Glass House" is located ahead of the hill approach.

different color scheme by installing a dark brown flooring against off-white walls in the sleeping room and by using tiles of different color in every other room —— white and green in the kitchen, deep blue in the bathroom, and black in the restroom. The tile textures, the simple yet versatile fittings, the artworks and articles of folk craft collected by Lina and her husband Pietro as well as the luxuriant vegetation surrounding the residence, all contribute to give life to this rational design.

At the time, the Morumbi neighborhood where the house is built sat on a bare hill in a newly-developed residential area. However, Lina took it upon herself to establish a botanical design of her surroundings (p. 212) and to build stone walls to retain the soil as well as a path flanked by stones and ceramic vessels. The vegetation has thrived over the past 60 years and now offers a fantastic environment completely reclaimed by the jungle. In her later years, Lina would go on to build a small studio for herself on the property. (p. 227)

完成当時、丘のふもとから見る。まだ樹木が育っておらず、街を見晴らすように建つ。(1951年)
Looking from the base of the hill at time of completion.
There are still no trees, and its position thereby affords a panoramic view of the city. (1951)

リビングルームからサンパウロの景色を望む。リナによるデザインの「金属球の椅子」が置かれた。(1951年)
Gazing at the São Paulo scenery from the living room.
The "Bola de Latão Chairs" (Brass Ball Chairs) designed by Lina were placed here. (1951)

The Glass House

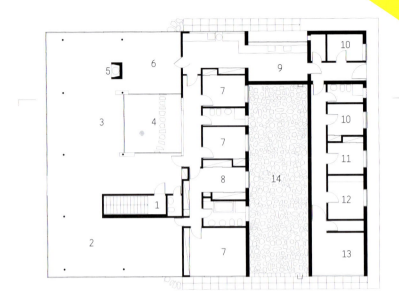

1F Plan

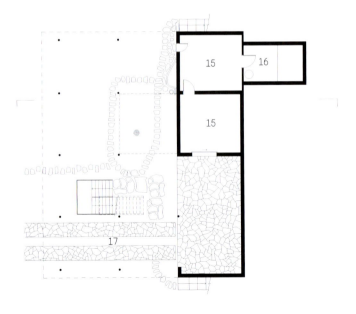

GF Plan

1. Entrance
2. Library
3. Living Room
4. Patio
5. Chimney
6. Dining Room
7. Bedroom
8. Dressing Room
9. Kitchen
10. Maid's Room
11. Service Room
12. Laundry Room
13. Veranda
14. Courtyard
15. Storage
16. Machine Room
17. Parking Space

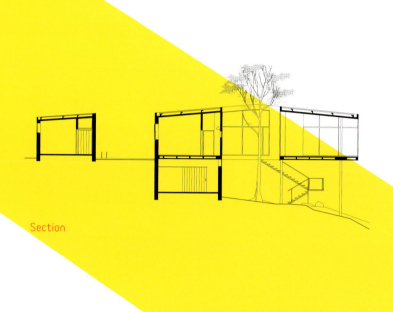

Section

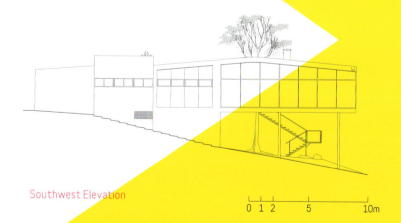

Southwest Elevation

0 1 2 5   10m

The Glass House 022

アプローチからピロティを見る。
Looking at the pilotis from the approach.

リビングルームへと続く階段。
The stairway that connects to the living room.

階段を上がり、
リビングルームへ続く入り口。
The stairway leads to this entrance connected to the living room.

リビングルーム。カーテンを外したオリジナルの状態。
The living room. In its original state with curtains removed.

リビングルーム。リナとピエトロが集めたブラジルの民芸品がたくさん置かれている。
The living room. Many Brazilian folk art pieces collected by Lina and Pietro are displayed.

（上）木が茂る中庭、周囲を緑に囲まれたイメージが描かれた、内観のドローイング。
(top) A drawing of the interior depicting an image of a thickly-wooded courtyard and surrounding greenery.

（下）絵画や民芸品がたくさん置かれたリビングルームのドローイング。
(above) A drawing of the living room where many paintings and folk art are on display.

リビングルーム奥の書斎スペース。
A library at the back of the living room.

建物の中心に位置するパティオを介して各室が向かい合う。
パティオを通り、ピロティの樹木が上へと伸びる。
Each room faces the others via the patio positioned in the center of the building.
Across the patio, the trees extend above the pilotis.

The Glass House

パティオに面したダイニングルーム。リビングルームとプライベート空間をつなぐ。
壁にはヨーロッパから持ち込んだ絵画が飾られている。
Dining room facing the patio. It connects the living room and private spaces.
The walls are adorned with paintings brought back from Europe.

キッチン。落ち着いた緑のタイルによりリビングとは大きく印象が変わる。奥に見えるのは裏庭へ続く扉。
The kitchen. The impression contrasts greatly with the living room because of the calm green tiles. The door connecting to the backyard is visible in the background.

浴室。濃い青と白、グレーのモザイクタイルが使われている。
The bathroom. Deep blue, white and gray mosaic tiles were used.

プライベート空間が面する中庭では亀が飼育されている。
Turtles being raised in the courtyard that faces the private space.

裏庭。右手にあるのは料理用の釜。プライベート空間は高さが抑えられている。石の歩道が建物の周辺や中庭へと続く。
The backyard. On the right is a kiln used for cooking.
The height of the private space is limited. A stone footpath connects to the building's surroundings and courtyard.

リビングルーム。
The living room.

ファサード正面。ピロティの柱が樹木に擬態する。
The front façade. The piloti pillars mimic trees.

サンパウロ美術館
São Paulo Art Museum

São Paulo, 1968

A corner for memories?
A tomb for illustrious mummies?
A deposit or an archive
for human works? None of this.
The new museums should throw
open their doors,
let in the fresh air and light.
Lina Bo Bardi, 1952

記憶のための場所？　それとも有名なミイラを納める墓？
人類の遺産をしまっておくための倉庫？　いいえ、そうではないのです。
これからの美術館は、扉を開け放ち、
フレッシュな空気と光を採り入れるべきなのです。
リナ・ボ・バルディ、1952年

リナの夫、ピエトロ・マリア・バルディが館長を務めた「サンパウロ美術館（MASP）」は、市民ホールや講堂をもつ半地下の基壇部分と、パウリスタ通りに面し、巨大な支柱でガラスの箱を浮かせた地上部分の、ふたつの層に分かれたモニュメンタルな建築だ。柱梁で建物をもち上げることで、通りにつながる1階部分を「ベルヴェデーレ」（見晴し台）という名のオープンスペースにした。リナは、美術館は「知の霊廟」ではなく生き生きとした教育的な場所であるべきと考え、サンパウロ市を一望できるこの場所を、あらゆるアートの屋外展示や、市民活動のための開かれた場所になるよう設計した。「MASP」は、パウリスタ通りのランドマークとしてだけでなく、世界中から多くの人びとが訪れる美術館として、サンパウロ市における重要な場所となっている。

ブラジルのメディア王シャトーブリアン氏が立ち上げ、ピエトロを館長として1947年にオープンした「MASP」は、ビルの数フロアを借りた小さな美術館だった[*1]。コレクションの増加に伴う新築計画がもち上がった頃、現在の敷地にあった見晴し台を広場と地下トイレに改築するという市の計画を聞いたリナは「まったくナンセンスだ」と感じ、街の歴史の一部であるこの土地を美術館として生かすことを考えた。まずブラジルメディアへの影響力が強いAP通信のエドムンド・モンテイロ氏の協力を仰ぎ、当時サンパウロ市長で大統領選に出馬していたアデマール・デ・バロス氏に交渉、大統領選をメディアが支援する代わりに市の計画を撤回させ、美術館計画を承認させた[*2]。MASPの財政問題や市の行政の影響で何度も工事が休止したが、着工から11年後の1968年に完成した。落成式には英国のエリザベス女王も来館している。

構造システムは巨大なプレストレスト・コンクリートの赤い柱梁が支えている。最上階の天井は上から2本の赤い梁に、スラブは2階天井の梁により下から支えられ、各梁は4本の赤い柱に支えられている。さらに2階のスラブを梁からワイヤーで吊り下げる

1階の「ベルヴェデーレ」を描いたドローイング、「夕暮れの影（L'ombre della sera）」。（1965年）
"L'ombra della sera", a drawing of the ground floor "Belvedere". (1965)

ことで、1階のオープンスペースを含むすべての階を完全な無柱空間にした。美術館のボリュームを地上から8メートル浮かせることで「見晴らし台」を保存すると共に、街に開かれた公共空間をつくり出した。敷地内を舗装した地域原産の石は道路の縁石まで続き、柱の根元の水盤には水生植物が植えられた。ここには日々多くの人びとが集い、美術館が街と市民をつなぎ、生活・思想・文化が往来する、真に豊かな都市空間となっている。

デザインにあたっては膨大なドローイングが描かれ、ガラスのピラミッド*3などのさまざまな造形や素材が構想されていた。現在の形態に整ってきた段階でも、映画上映や屋外展示の背景となることを想定した、粗い石のような閉じたファサードだった（p. 210）。その後、ガラスの方が軽いことや、外に開いた美術館というコンセプトにより、現在の透明なガラスファサードとなった。リナのガラスファサードによる美術館構想は早い段階からあり、1951年の「海沿いの美術館」（実現せず）の計画にその萌芽があるが、「MASP」のもつダイナミズムはまだ見られない。「ガラスの家」（p. 012）と共にミース・ファン・デル・ローエやフィリップ・ジョンソンの透明性と比較される「MASP」のガラスファサードは、リナ自身が「醜い建築」とまで発言したように、美しさではなく自由と公共性が探求されていた*4。1985年にサンパウロを訪れた現代音楽家のジョン・ケージ*5が「これこそが自由な建築だ！」と発言したことを喜んだリナが、「（MASPの）本質を掴んでいる」とコメントしたというエピソードもある*6。

ガラスファサードの向こうには、ガラスのイーゼルが並ぶメインギャラリーが広がる。壁面ではなくイーゼルに架けられて中央に並ぶ絵画は、まるで浮いているかのように見える。鑑賞者は絵画の森を歩くような感覚を得ると共に、順路から解放され、自分の足の赴くままに作品を鑑賞することができる。また、一般的に作品の横に記載される作品名や作者名はイーゼルの裏面に

建物裏側から見た建設中の様子。道路が立体的に交差する要衝に立地していることが分かる。（1965年）
State of construction as seen from behind the building. One can see that it is located in a prime location where roads intersect three-dimensionally. (1965)

記載され、知識や先入観なく作品と向き合うことができる。歩きながら答え合わせをする楽しさもある。ヒエラルキーのない空間と展示方法には、自由な気持ちで作品と向かい合ってほしいというリナの教育的観点が表れている。ガラスのイーゼルは一時撤廃されたが近年再び採用され、当時の姿に戻されている。

*1 建て替え前のサンパウロ美術館は、通りの名前から「4月7日通りのMASP」と呼ばれている。
*2 Video *Lina e Renato*, 1990, ILBPMB.
*3 I・M・ペイによるルーブル・ピラミッドは1989年竣工。
*4 Video *Arquitetura - Transformação do Espaço*, Walter Lima Jr(dir), 1972.
*5 ジョン・ミルトン・ケージ・ジュニア。1912〜92年。アメリカ合衆国出身の音楽家。
*6 Lina Bo Bardi, (1990) "An Architectural Lesson", in *Stones Against Diamonds*, p. 112.

柱の建設の様子。(1968年)
A view of the construction of the pillars. (1968)

Lina designed the São Paulo Art Museum (MASP) where her husband, Pietro Maria Bardi, served as director. The museum is a monumental construction on two separate levels: a semi-underground platform with a civic hall and an auditorium, and a glass box suspended above ground supported by massive pillars facing Paulista Avenue. Supporting the building with columns and beams allowed the ground floor area connecting to the street to be made into an open space known as a "belvedere" (viewing platform). Lina believed that a museum should not be a mausoleum of the past and should instead be an active site of knowledge, which inspired her to design this space overlooking São Paulo into a space open to all kinds of outdoor art exhibitions and civic activities. The MASP has since become an important part of São Paulo, not only as a landmark of Paulista Avenue, but also as one of the most visited museums in the world.

Founded by Brazilian media mogul Assis Chateaubriand and directed by Pietro, the MASP[*1] opened in 1947 as a small museum taking up a number of floors in the building. Around the time talks about plans for a new construction began to accommodate the museum's growing collection, São Paulo City Hall floated a plan to turn the belvedere found on the present-day grounds into a plaza with underground restrooms. Upon hearing this, Lina is said to have declared "It makes no sense."[*2] and became determined to use this land, which is a part of the city's history, as an art museum. First, Lina enlisted the help of AP correspondent Edmundo Monteiro, an influential figure in Brazilian media, to engage in discussions with then São Paulo mayor and presidential candidate,

Adhemar de Barros, thereby securing the approval of her museum plans and the withdrawal of City Hall's plan in return for media support in the presidential run. Despite numerous setbacks due to MASP's financial problems and the city government, the museum was completed in 1968, 11 years after the start of construction work. The Queen of the United Kingdom, Elizabeth II, was present at the dedication ceremony of the museum.

The structural system is supported by massive red columns and beams of prestressed concrete. The top floor ceiling is supported from the top by two lateral red beams, the slab is supported from the bottom by the ceiling beam on the 1st floor, and each beam is supported by four red pillars. Furthermore, the building features columnless spaces on all floors, including a freestanding open space on the ground floor, by having the slab of the 1st floor hang with a wire from the top beams. By keeping the volume of the museum floating 8 meters above the ground, Lina was able to preserve the "belvedere" and create a public space opened to the city. The site features pavement with locally sourced stones that continues up to the curb of the road as well as basins with aquatic plants at the base of the pillars. In this space where many gather everyday, the museum connects the city and its citizens, making it a truly rich urban space filled with life, ideas, and culture.

During the design phase, enormous study drawings were drawn, and various shapes and materials, such as a glass pyramid[*3], were conceived. A closed facade made of coarse stone was considered to serve as a background for movie screenings and outdoor exhibitions, even at the stage where it had taken its present form. Apart from glass being lighter, the transparent glass facade we know today came to be as a result of the MASP's concept as an art museum open to the exterior. Lina's concept for a museum with a glass facade was established early

工事中、ガラスのイーゼルのスタディをするリナ。
事務所をもたないリナは、いつも現場の仮設事務所で作業を進めた。
Lina studying glass easels during construction.
Having no office, Lina always worked by using a makeshift office on the spot.

on, and while the germination for this idea can be found in the "Museum on the Seashore" project (unrealized), the dynamism associated with the MASP is yet to be seen. The glass facade of the MASP, along with the "Glass House"(p. 012), has been compared with the transparency of Mies van der Rohe and Philip Johnson. However, Lina explained that she did not search for beauty, but searched for freedom and commonality, going as far as to call it "ugly architecture"[*4]. Moreover, while visiting São Paulo in 1985, avant-garde composer John Cage[*5] is said to have exclaimed "This is the architecture of freedom!", a characterization welcomed by Lina as follows. "I felt the judgment of this great artist had perhaps captured the essence of what I wanted to say when I designed MASP."[*6]

Beyond the glass facade, glass easels line the lofty main gallery. By mounting the artwork on easels in the middle of the exhibition space instead of mounting it on the walls, the paintings appear to be suspended in the air. Visitors experience a feeling akin to walking in a forest of paintings, free to walk around as they please and appreciate the works of art without having to follow predetermined routes. Information about the artworks, generally found next to the works, is provided instead on the reverse of the panels, so that the viewer can face the work free from knowledge or prejudice. There is also the pleasure associated with discovering the answers while walking at leisure. Lina's educational stance whereby artworks should be met with a feeling of freedom is reflected in this space and exhibition method without hierarchy. After being removed for a time, the glass easels were recently restored and visitors can once again enjoy the original display.

*1   Before the rebuilding of the São Paulo Museum of Art, the museum was known as "MASP 7 de Abril" from the street on which it was originally located.
*2   Video *Lina e Renato*, 1990, ILBPMB.
*3   I.M. Pei's Louvre Pyramid was completed in 1989.
*4   Video *Arquitetura – Transformação do Espaço*, Walter Lima Jr. (dir.), 1972.
*5   John Milton Cage Jr. (1912 – 1992) was an American composer.
*6   Lina Bo Bardi, (1990) "An Architectural Lesson", in *Stones Against Diamonds*, p. 112.

「海沿いの美術館」の模型。(1951年)
A model of the "Museum on the Seashore". (1951)

ガラス窓の取り付け作業中の様子。(1968年)
State of work when installing glass windows. (1968)

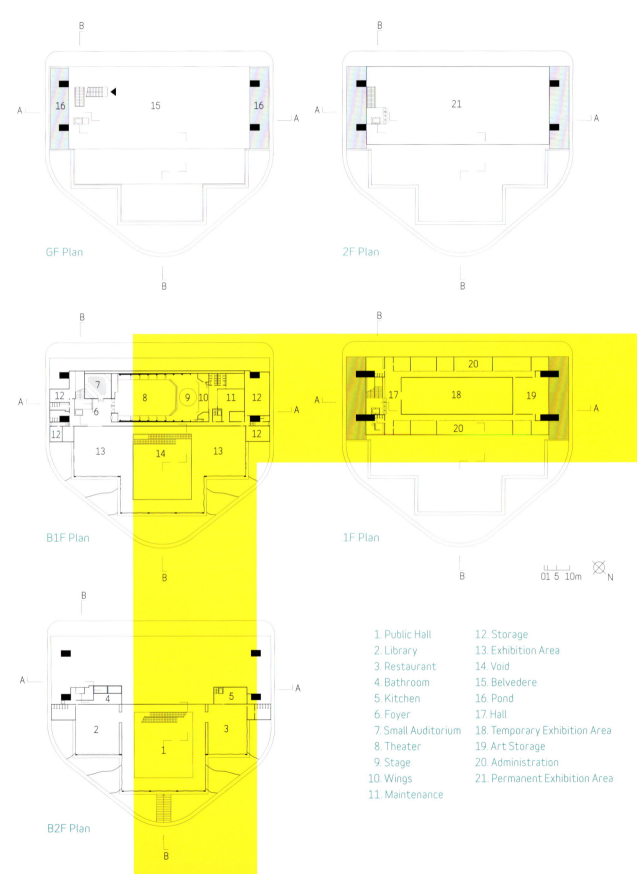

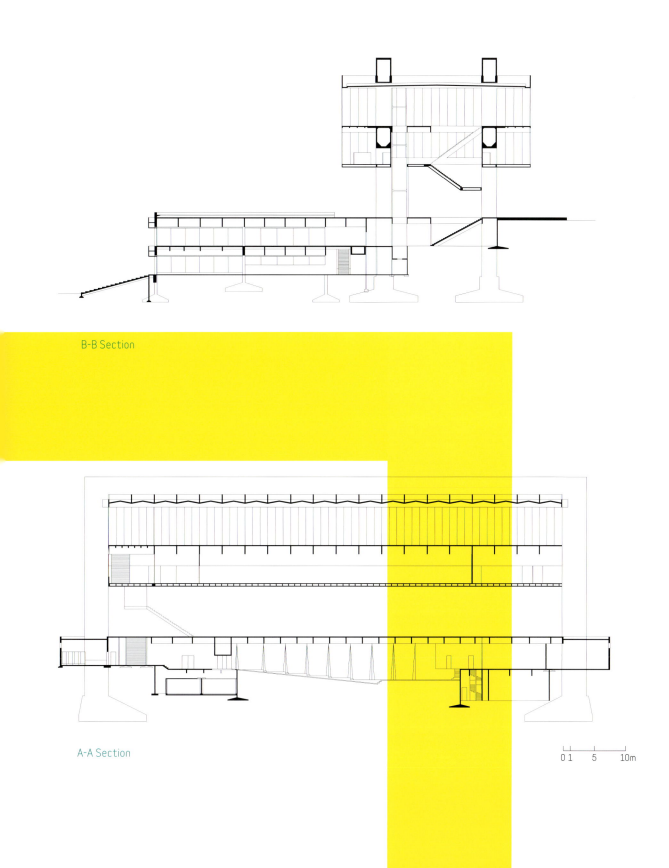

B-B Section

A-A Section

0 1 5 10m

短手側のファサード
A facade on the shorter side

São Paulo Art Museum

見晴らし側のファサード。
ガラス越しに内部空間が見える。
「ベルヴェデーレ」の向こう側には道を行き交う人びとや
車、熱帯植物であふれるパウリスタ公園が見える。
A façade on the panoramic side. The inner space
is visible through the glass. The coming and going
of people and cars, and Paulista Park, overgrown
with tropical plants, are visible on the opposite
side of the "Belvedere".

裏側。土地の傾斜に沿って「ベルヴェデーレ」の下に地下二層の基壇部がある。全体が大きな花壇のように植物であふれる。
The rear side. There is a two-layer foundation underground below the "Belvedere" that runs along the inclination of the ground. The entire thing is overflowing with flora as though it were a flower bed.

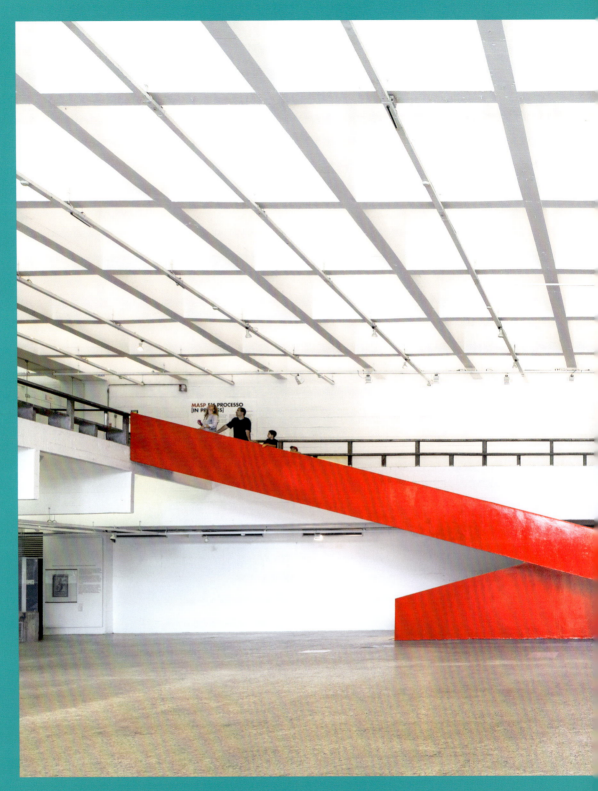

地下の市民ホール。市長の要望によりダンスホールとしてつくられたが、リナはのちに集会スペースに変更できるよう計画していた。現在は展示スペースなどに使われている。
The underground public hall. It was built as a dance hall according to the request of the mayor, but Lina planned it so that it could be changed into a gathering place later on. It currently serves as an exhibition space, among other things.

São Paulo Art Museum

地下1階の劇場。
The basement 1st floor theater.

地下2階の食堂。リナのデザインによる「キリンの椅子」に座ってブラジル料理が楽しめ、平日でも満席になる。
The basement 2nd floor restaurant. One can enjoy Brazilian cuisine while sitting on a "Giraffe Chair" designed by Lina. It becomes filled even on weekdays.

2階の階段とエレベーターホール。
The 1st floor stairs and elevator hall.

3階のメインギャラリー。ガラスファサードに面し、無柱空間が広がる。
The 2nd floor main gallery. Facing the glass façade, the pillarless space spreads outward.

São Paulo Art Museum 058

さまざまなジャンルの芸術が、ガラスのイーゼルとガラスケースに展示される。
Various genres of art are displayed on glass easels and in glass cases.

イーゼルを横から見る。ガラス板をコンクリートの台座に挟み、木片で固定している。
Looking at an easel from the side.
The glass panel is inserted between concrete pedestals and fixed by wooden wedges.

ガラスのイーゼルのスケッチ。鑑賞者が先入観なく作品と向き合えるよう、作品名や作者名は裏側に書かれる。
A sketch of a glass easel. The names of works and artists are written on the back so that guests can come face-to-face with the works without any preconceptions.

モディリアーニの絵画が架けられたガラスのイーゼル。(1970年)
A glass easel featuring a painting of Modigliani. (1970)

São Paulo Art Museum

「ベルヴェデーレ」を描いたコラージュ。植物や彫刻にあふれ、市民が集まる憩いの場がイメージされている。
街に開いた美術館というコンセプトが分かる。
A collage depicting the "Belvedere".
It is conceived of as a place that is filled with flora and sculptures, and serves as an oasis for city dwellers.

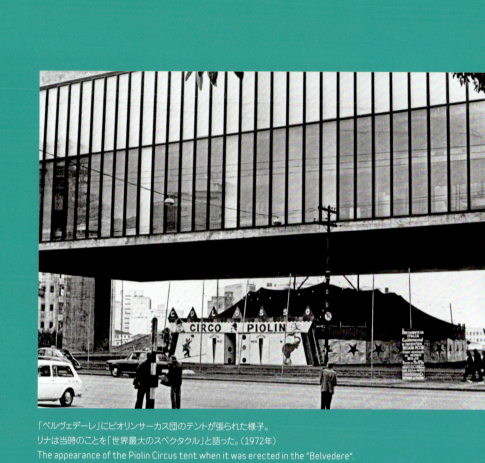

「ベルヴェデーレ」にピオリンサーカス団のテントが張られた様子。
リナは当時のことを「世界最大のスペクタクル」と語った。(1972年)
The appearance of the Piolin Circus tent when it was erected in the "Belvedere".
At the time, Lina spoke of it as "the biggest spectacle in the world". (1972)

São Paulo Art Museum

ブラジルの国民的歌手、ダニエラ・メルクリによる
「ベルヴェデーレ」でのコンサートの様子。(1992年)
The atmosphere of the concert at the "Belvedere" by popular
Brazilian singer Daniela Mercury. (1992)

「ベルヴェデーレ」に憩う人びと。舗装に用いた地域原産の石は通りの縁石まで続く。
People relaxing at the "Belvedere". The indigenous stones used as pavement extend until the roadside curb.

美術館の側には熱帯植物が茂るトリアノン公園がある。
背後は交通の結節点であると共に経済の中心地でもあり、高層建築がそびえる。
Parque Trianon, thick with tropical flora, is located opposite the museum.
In the background stand high-rise buildings in an area that serves as a transportation hub as well as an economic center.

SESC
ポンペイア文化センター
SESC-Pompéia
Factory Leisure Center

São Paulo, 1986

To eat, sit, talk, walk,
sit around in the sun...
Architecture is not just a utopia,
but a means to attain
certain collective results.
Lina Bo Bardi, 1986

食べる、座る、話す、歩く、日だまりの中でのんびりする……。
建築とは単なるユートピアではなく、
みんなに実りをもたらすひとつの手段なのです。
リナ・ボ・バルディ、1986年

かつての敷地。元はドラム缶工場だった。(1940年)
The former site. Originally a steel drum factory. (1940)

「SESCポンペイア文化センター」*¹は、サンパウロ市のポンペイア地区にある労働階級地区で、廃業したドラム缶工場を公共のスポーツ文化センターに改装するという、リナの生涯でも最大といえるプロジェクトである。リナは既存の工場を修復・改装し、図書館や展示スペース、劇場などを含む公共スペースに再生すると共に、工場の隣に2棟のコンクリート造の建物と、煙突型の貯水塔を新築した。プールと運動場が入った主屋と、更衣室と階段・エレベーターが入ったサービス棟の2棟は、向かい合いブリッジでつながっている。主屋の壁に開けられた「雲形窓」はガラスがはまっていないただの「穴」で、常時換気を可能にしている。リナはこの場所が街を守る希望の場所になるようにと願いを込めて、施設全体を、ポルトガル語で塔や砦、ゴールなどを意味する「シダデラ（Cidadela）」と名付けた。単純かつ質素でありながらも威厳をもち、人びとの生活を豊かにする建築を目指した。ブラジルの民衆へ常に関心を抱き続けた、リナならではのプロジェクトといえる。

リナがこのプロジェクトに参加する前は、1938年に建設された既存の建物を壊して11階建てのビルを新築する計画だった。しかし、工場の小屋群の視察を通してフランス人技術者のフランソワ・アンネビック*²が考案した「アンネビック式」を思わせる歴史的にも貴重な美しい構造や、壊れた屋根も気にせずに楽しく休日を過ごす近所の家族たちを見て、「この幸せをこのまま残さなければならない」*³と決意し、計画関係者たちを説得して既存の建物を生かす新たな計画をスタートさせた。隣接する数軒の小屋の壁を取り払い、ラウンジ・図書館・展示スペース棟、食堂棟、劇場棟、工房棟の4つの大空間をつくった。入り口に最も近い部分にあるラウンジ・図書館・展示スペース棟は、吹き抜けを利用して1、2階をはっきりと分けないことで、人びとが同じ空間にいながらさまざまな活動ができるようにした。ラウンジの大きな暖炉には、「ヴァレリア・P・シレル邸」(p. 148)にも見られるような、フランク・ロイド・ライトからの影響が感じられる。曲がりくねった水盤（池）は、ブラジルを流れる大河と同じ「サンフランシスコ川」*⁴と名付けられた。それぞれの棟は屋根や壁の材に変化を付けて雰囲気を異にしている。注目すべきは劇場棟だ。向かい合う客席の間に舞台が配置され、劇場の新たな形式に挑んでいる (p. 095)。

小屋群を抜けると、スポーツ棟へ向かう長いウッドデッキが続く。この部分は建設が不可能なエリアで、当初は丸ごと水路に

する計画だったが、最終的には屋外シャワーが設置されたウッドデッキとなり、都会の真ん中で水着姿の人びとが日光浴を楽しむことのできる場所となった。リナは都市に「海辺」を出現させたのだった。

このプロジェクトの驚くべき点は、商業施設がないという事実だ。空間はこの場に参加する人びと——建設中の施工者、そして訪問者——の創造性に任されている。リナは現場で施工者と直接対話をしながら共に設計し、空間ごとにつくって欲しいものを依頼したそうだ。ちょっとしたところに配された小さな彫刻やディテールの手づくり感も愛らしい。スポーツ棟のコンクリート、小屋のれんが、小屋間の歩道を覆う地域原産の小石、木材、モルタルで粗く重ねたブロックなど、テクスチャーも非常に豊かだ。ダクトは電気・水・空気の用途別に色分けされて小屋内外の壁をぐねぐねと巡り、意匠上のアクセントにもなっている。

またリナは建物だけでなく、椅子や標識、職員の制服、アイスクリームの屋台、ポスターなどあらゆるものをデザインした。リナにとって建築とは、建物だけではなく、その空間にまつわるすべての体験を含むものであった。ポスターに描かれた「SESC」のアイコンでもある煙突は、煙ではなく花を戴いている。それは、工場だったこの場所の歴史を宿しながらも、工場労働という悪しき記憶を消し去り、都市へ喜びを振りまいている。

*1 SESC(Servicio Social Comercio、ブラジル商業連盟社会サービス)とは、1964年に設立されたブラジル商業連盟に属する社団法人。社会福祉環境の整備を目的として、サンパウロ州内だけでも30の文化・スポーツセンターの運営や音楽・演劇・ダンスなどの公演、一般向けの講座や環境教育などの事業を行っている。

*2 フランスの技術者。1842〜1921年。

*3 Lina Bo Bardi, (1986) "An Architectural Project", in *Stones against Diamonds*, p.097.

*4 リオ・デ・ジャネイロ州やサンパウロ州に近い南東部から北東へ向かい、旧都サルヴァドール市を含むバイーア州を通り大西洋に流れる。リナにとっては近代都市と北東文化をつなぐ象徴だったのだろうか。

リナがデザインしたポスター。(1988 年頃)
A poster designed by Lina. (*circa* 1988)

ウッドデッキ部初期案、「川」のスケッチ。(1977年頃)
A sketch of the "River" and an early draft of the wooden deck area. (*circa* 1977).

劇場のダクト。壁を抜けて内部の音響スタッフ席に貫入する。
The theater ducts. They pass through the walls to penetrate the interior sound crew seating area.

SESC Pompéia[*1], a former steel drum factory remodeled into a public sports and cultural center in São Paulo City, in the Pompéia district where many working class people live, is considered to have been Lina's most important project during her lifetime. Lina restored and remodeled the existing factory to give it new life as a public space with a library, exhibition area, and theater, as well as two newly-constructed buildings adjacent to the factory - one a set of two concrete buildings and the other a chimney-shaped water tower. Aerial walkways connect both the main building, which houses a pool and sports arena, and the service building, which houses changing rooms and stairs/elevator. Furthermore, the "cloud window" openings on the wall of the main building are simply "holes" with no glass affixed, which allows for continuous ventilation. Lina named the entire facility a "Cidadela", a Portuguese word meaning citadel, a fortress and a field goal, to express her wish that this place should become a place of hope to protect the city. She aimed for a simple and modest yet assertive architectural design that would enrich people's lives. This project could be considered unique to Lina, who was constantly interested in the people of Brazil.

Before Lina joined this project, the plan was to demolish the existing building constructed in 1938 and build a new 11-story building. Upon inspection of the factory's group of sheds, however, Lina determined that she must "leave this place of happiness as it is"[*2] after observing local families enjoy the historically important and beautiful structure regardless of its broken roof. This was reminiscent of François Hennebique[*3] and his "Hennebique

Method". Following her decision, Lina then convinced all of the other planners, thus signaling the start of a new plan to take full advantage of the existing building. Several of the adjacent sheds had their walls removed in order to create four large spaces: a multi-use space / library/exhibition building, a cafeteria building, a theater building, and a workshop building. For the multi-use space/library/exhibition building in the area closest to the entrance, the stairwell was used to blur the line between ground and first floors so that people could engage in diverse activities while sharing the same space. The large fireplace in the multi-use space shows the influence of Frank Lloyd Wright as seen in "Valéria P. Cirell's Home" (p. 148). The winding shallow water basin (pond) was named the "São Francisco River"[*4] after Brazil's large river. Each building was given its own atmosphere by varying the materials used for the roof and walls. The most remarkable thing is the theater building. The stage is arranged between facing seats so it attempts to create a new theater format. (p. 095)

A long, continuous wooden deck faces toward the sports building once you break away from the group of sheds. This is part of the area in which building was not possible. At first, the plan was to make the whole area a waterway but, in the end, it became a wooden deck with showers installed. This made it a place where people could enjoy sunbathing in their swimsuits right in the center of the city. Lina had made a "seashore" appear in the city.

The surprising thing about this project is the fact that there was no commercial building. This space was entirely left up to the creativity of the people coming to this place – both the construction laborers and the visitors. Lina designed everything while talking directly with the construction laborers on site, apparently requesting them to build things according to each space. The small engravings and handmade touches here produce a lovely effect. A very rich diversity of textures can be seen in the concrete of the sports building, the brick of the sheds, the rough stack of blocks using mortar, the wood, and the local indigenous pebbles covering the walkways between the sheds. The ducts are color-coded by use for electricity, water, or air, and they zigzag along the interior and exterior walls of the sheds to accent the design.

Lina designed not only the buildings but also every other thing in it like the chairs, signs, employee uniforms, ice cream stands and posters. For her, architecture was not only about buildings but rather included all experiences to be found in that space. The chimney, which was the icon of "SESC" drawn on the poster, spread flowers and not smoke. This was a way of spreading happiness to the city by erasing the negative memories associated with factory labor while taking into account the history of this place which used to be a factory.

[*1]   SESC (Serviço Social do Comércio, Social Service of Commerce) is a corporation belonging to the National Confederation of Commerce established in 1964. In São Paulo alone, SESC carries out various projects that include the operation of 30 cultural and sports centers, music/drama/dance performances, classes aimed at the general public, and environmental education with their aim being the maintenance of a social welfare environment.

[*2]   Lina Bo Bardi, (1986) "An Architectural Project", in *Stones against Diamonds*, p. 097.

[*3]   A French Engineer. 1842-1921.

[*4]   This river flows from the southeast area near Rio de Janeiro and São Paulo towards the northeast, passing through Bahia State, home of the former capital Salvador, before connecting with the Atlantic Ocean. Perhaps Lina thought of it as symbolizing the connection between modern city life and the culture of the northeast.

サッカーチームのユニフォームのデザイン。(1982年)
The design of the soccer team uniform. (1982)

職員の制服デザイン。
リナがデザインした「SESCポンペイア」のロゴ付き。(1981年)
The design of the employee uniforms.
Attached is the "SESC Pompéia" logo designed by Lina. (1981)

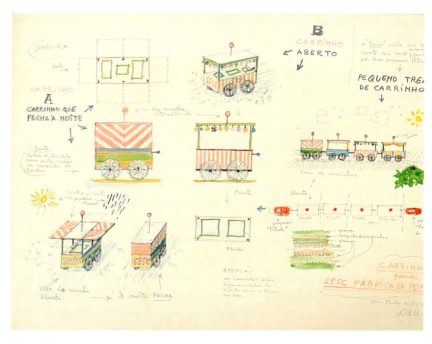

劇場に計画されたアイスクリーム屋台のスケッチ。(1985年)
A sketch of the ice cream stand planned for the theater. (1985)

SESC-Pompéia Factory Leisure Center

Newly Buildings

Existing Buildings

GF Plan

1. Swimming Pool, Gymnasium and Athletic Courts
2. Bar, Changing Rooms, Room for Gymnastics, Wrestling and Dancing
3. Water Tower
4. Solarium
5. Waterfall
6. Maintenance
7. Ceramic, Painting, Carpentry, Upholstery, Etching and Typography Workshops
8. Photo Lab
9. Theater for 1,200 Viewers
10. Covered Theater Foyer, Entertainment Hall
11. Bar and Self-Service Restaurant
12. Kitchen
13. Multi-Use Space with Ponds
14. Library and Video Rooms
15. Temporary Exhibition Area
16. Administration
17. Worker's Changing Room and Dining Area

施設全景。(1977年)
A complete view of the facilities. (1977)

Elevation

SESC-Pompéia Factory Leisure Center

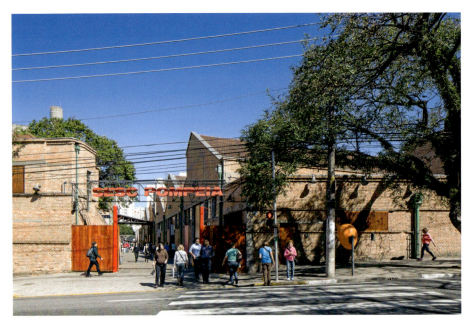

施設入り口のゲート。
The entrance gate.

小屋間を走るメインストリート。舗装には地域原産の小石を敷いている。標識もリナによるデザイン。
The main street running between the sheds. Indigenous pebbles cover the pavement. The signage was also designed by Lina.

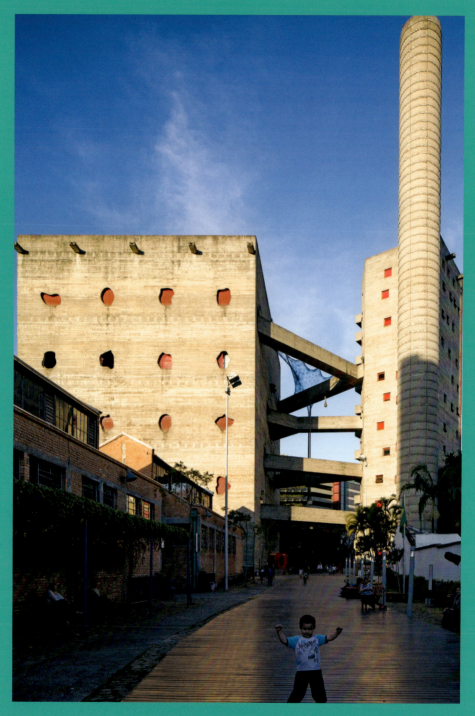

メインストリートを曲がると長いウッドデッキが延び、スポーツ棟(左:主屋／右:サービス棟)と煙突型の貯水塔が見える。
Around the corner from the main street is a long wooden deck from which the sports building (left: main building/ right: service building) and cylindrical water tower are visible.

SESC-Pompéia Factory Leisure Center

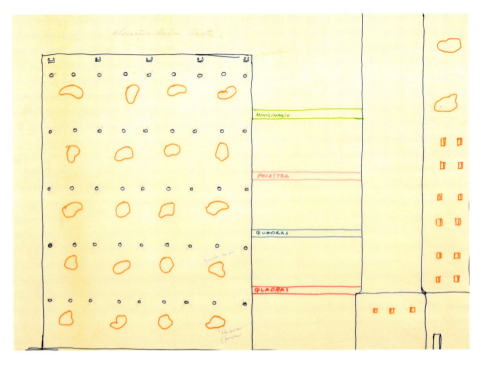

スポーツ棟の立面ドローイング。
主屋（左）には運動場とプール、サービス棟（右）にはダンスなどの練習室、更衣室、階段、エレベーターがある。
An elevation of the sports building
In the main building (left), there are gymnasiums and pool; in the service building (right), there is a rehearsal room for dancing, etc., as well as changing rooms, a stairway, and an elevator.

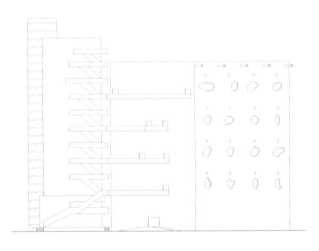

Elevation

運動場は春夏秋冬をモチーフに各階で異なる色の組合せが用いられている。
A different color combination is used on each floor as a four-season motif for the gymnasiums.

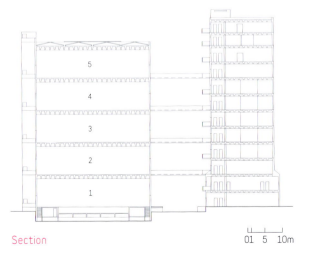

Section

1. Swimming Pool
2. Spring Court
3. Summer Court
4. Autumn Court
5. Winter Court

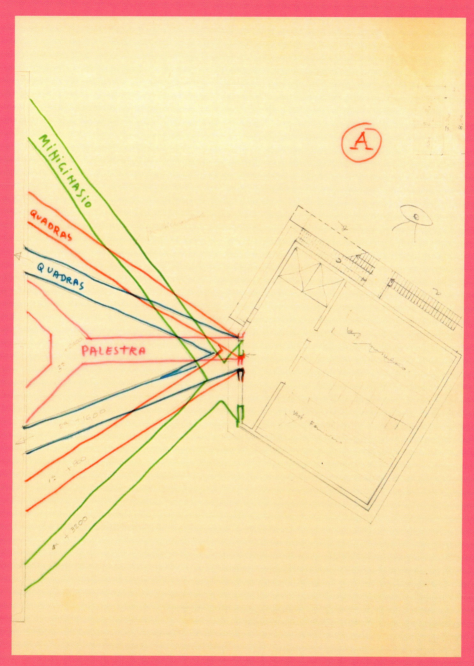

ブリッジのスタディ。フロアごとに色分けされ、接続する室の名前が記されている。(1977年)
A study of the walkways. Each one is color-coded by floor, and the name of the connected room ahead is written down. (1977)

SESC-Pompéia Factory Leisure Center

082

サービス棟裏側の外階段。
The outdoor staircase behind the service building.

サービス棟内部のドローイング。
赤色の螺旋階段が1階から最上階までの12層を貫く。(1985年)
A drawing of the service building's interior. A red spiral staircase goes through 12 layers from the ground floor to the top floor. (1985)

サービス棟正面。四角い窓がランダムに開く。
The front of the service building. Square windows open randomly.

ウッドデッキには屋外シャワーが設置されている。
Outdoor showers are installed on the wooden deck.

スポーツ棟同士をつなぐブリッジ。
A walkway connecting the service and main buildings.

ブリッジから見下ろす。入り口の位置やブリッジの角度はフロアごとに異なる。
Looking down from the walkway. The position of entrances and angle of walkways differ for each floor.

ブリッジからウッドデッキを見下ろす。
Looking down on the wooden deck from the walkway.

SESC-Pompéia Factory Leisure Center

スポーツ棟主屋1階のプール。
The pool on the ground floor of the sports building.

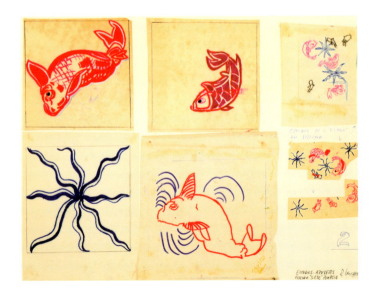

プールに使われているタイルのデザイン。(1984年)
The tile designs used for the pool. (1984)

サービス棟の軽食堂のドローイング。(1984年)
A drawing of the snack bar inside the service building. (1984)

サービス棟のダンス練習室。
A dance studio in the service building.

SESC-Pompéia Factory Leisure Center

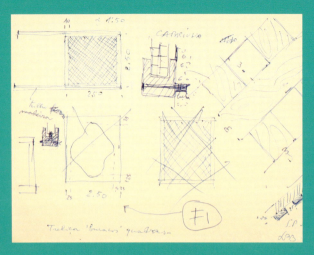

雲形窓のスタディスケッチ。(1980年)
A study sketch of the "cloud window" opening. (1980)

雲形窓、開口部のディテール。
壁は非常に厚く、粗い仕上げが施されている。
Details of the aperture for the cloud window opening. The walls are extremely thick with a rough finish.

運動場。雲形窓に付けられた格子戸により、日差しや風量を調整できる。
The gymnasium. Sunlight and airflow are mediated through the lattice doors attached to the "cloud window" openings.

雲形窓のファサード。
The cloud window opening façade.

劇場ロビー。半透明の屋根と簾のような扉から日差しが入る。
The theater lobby. Sunrays enter through the translucent roof and reed screen-like doors.

SESC-Pompéia Factory Leisure Center 094

劇場ロビーの扉。
The gate of the theater lobby.

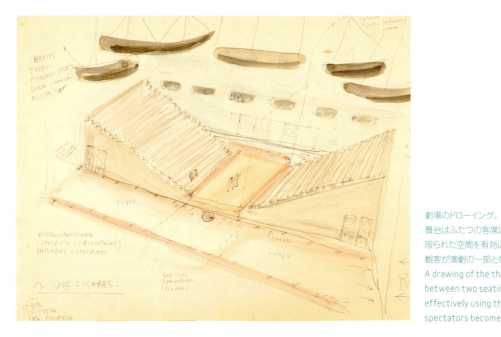

劇場のドローイング。
舞台はふたつの客席に挟まれている。
限られた空間を有効に使うと共に、
観客が演劇の一部となる。(1977年)
A drawing of the theater. The stage is squeezed between two seating areas. In addition to effectively using the limited space, it makes spectators become a part of the theater. (1977)

劇場内部。
客席の椅子もリナのデザインによるもの。
The theater interior. The seats were also designed by Lina.

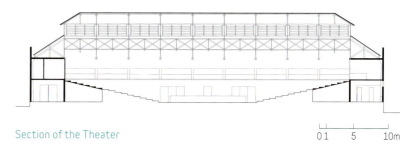

Section of the Theater   0 1   5   10m

SESC-Pompéia Factory Leisure Center

食堂。
The restaurant.

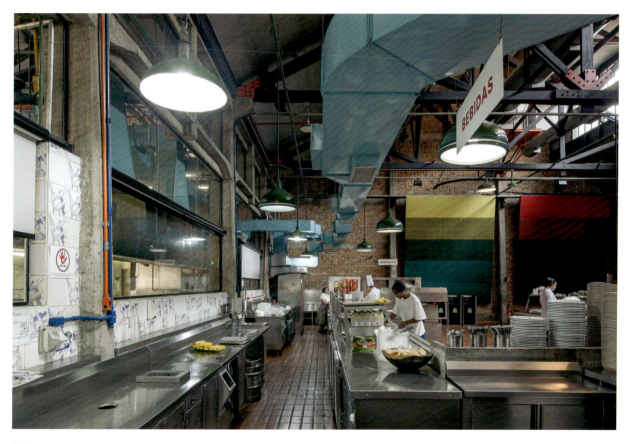

厨房。
The kitchen.

彫刻でつくられた食堂のサイン。工事中のリナの発案を受けて、職人が手作りで制作した。黒板にはメニューが記される。
A restaurant sign rendered as a sculpture. This was handcrafted by an artisan who received a proposal from Lina during construction. The menu is also written on a blackboard.

バー・カウンターのドローイング。(1981年)
A drawing of the bar counter. (1981)

施設内、各棟の入り口に架けられるサインのドローイング。
文字の読めない人でもどんな場所なのか把握できるように、
ビジュアル付きのサインを考案した。(1981年)
A drawing of the signs hanging by the entrance of each
building within the facility. These signs were devised as
a visual aid so that even people who cannot read could
understand what kind of place they were entering. (1981)

SESC-Pompéia Factory Leisure Center

工房。絵画、版画、彫刻、テキスタイル、大工などのさまざまなクラスがある。
各スペースは積み上げたブロック壁で仕切られている。
The workshop. Various classes are offered on painting, engraving, sculpture, textiles, and carpentry work. Each space is separated by walls made of stacked blocks.

図書室。椅子もリナによるデザイン。
The library. The chairs were also designed by Lina.

小屋の修復のための初期ドローイング。階段の形状は異なるが、立体的に空間をつなぐ意図がみられる。(1977年)
An early drawing for the restoration of the huts. The shape of the staircase is different, but one can see the intent to link the spaces three-dimensionally. (1977)

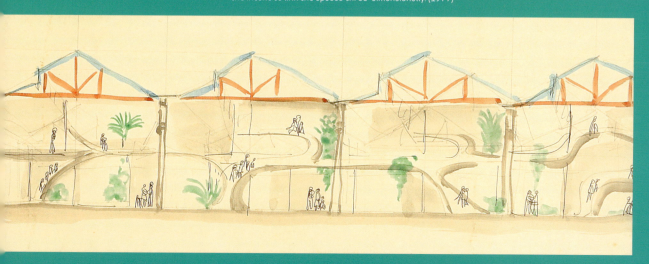

ラウンジ。広々とした空間にソファと暖炉があり、人びとは思い思いにくつろぐことができる。
ラウンジの水盤「サンフランシスコ川」には、屋外の歩道と同じく地域原産の石が用いられている。
The multi-use space. There is a sofa and a fireplace inside the lofty space, allowing people to relax however they choose. Indigenous stones were used for the multi-use space's "São Francisco River" winding shallow water basin, as well as the outdoor paths.

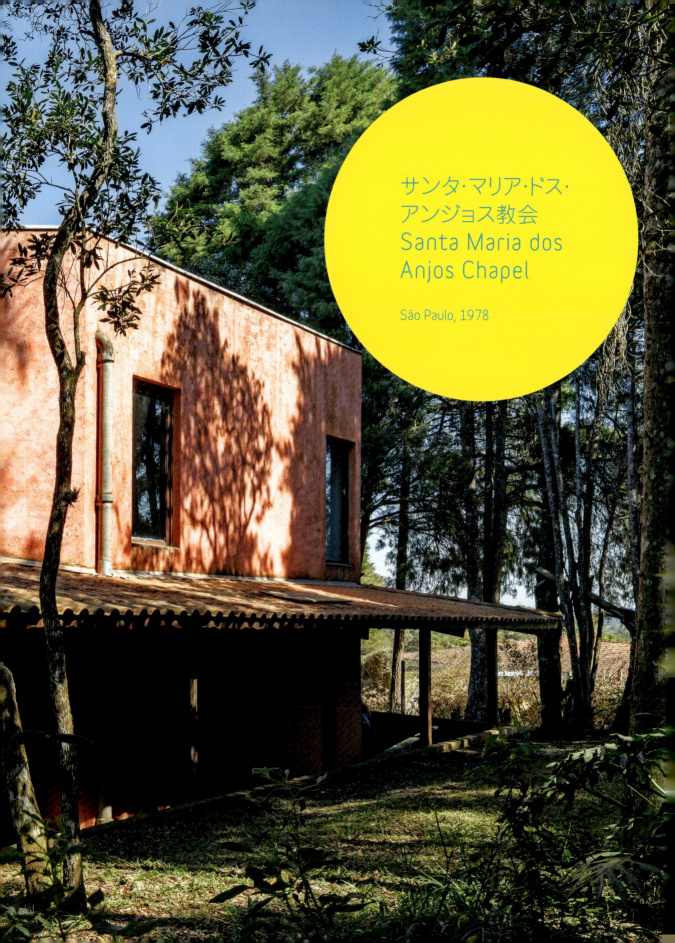

サンタ・マリア・ドス・アンジョス教会
Santa Maria dos Anjos Chapel

São Paulo, 1978

Santa Maria dos Anjos Chapel

This is another of our cheap works...
As usual, there was no money.
But the result was surprising.
In the interior there are
even reverberations and mysterious
voices during the ceremonies.
Lina Bo Bardi, 1986

これは、いつもどおり低予算のプロジェクトでした。
しかし結果は驚くべきものになりました。
セレモニーの時、教会の内部には反響が起こり、
神秘的な声が聞こえたのです。
リナ・ボ・バルディ、1986年

あるフランシスコ会員から依頼された、サンパウロ市郊外の貧困層が暮らす住宅地に建つ、聖母マリア崇拝のための聖堂である。限られた建設資金のなか、リナは「貧しい建築（arquitetura pobre）」という言葉によってシンプルな素材とミニマルなデザインの質素な建築を計画した。外壁は砂とコンクリートと地域原産の粘土を混ぜた漆喰で塗り、素朴かつ印象的な赤色とした。この作品には幾何学的なプラン、植物、屋上庭園、自然との関係性、藁屋根といったさまざまな特徴が現れ、単純な幾何学と合理主義に地域の自然や工芸が組み合わされた、リナのデザイン要素が凝縮されている。

一辺10.3メートルの正方形の対向するふたつの角を切り落とした平面形で、切り口の一方に入り口、もう一方に祭壇を据えている。このシンプルな操作が、内部に入ると祭壇を正面に、周囲の壁に包み込まれるような体感を生んでいる。窓の少ない小さな空間に、白漆喰の壁面や木を張った天井、緑色の石の床といった豊かで穏やかな色彩が空間に親密さを与えている。まるで「小さく優しいピンク色の箱」のような外観の印象は、子どもの宝箱のようだ。ダイナミックな建築が多いリナ作品のなかで、こぢんまりとしたスケール感をもち、土からそのまま立ち上がって静かに呼吸をしているかのような、独特の印象を受ける。メンテナンスの難しさから、現在では藁屋根は瓦屋根に、木の幹をそのまま用いたテラスの柱は角柱に変わっている。

「貧しい建築」について、リナはこう説明している。「貧困という意味での貧しさではなく、手づくりによる控えめな手段で表現されるみごとな気品という意味である」と[*1]。「貧しい建築」は、演出家イェジー・グロトフスキー[*2]の「貧しい演劇」（p. 203）を由来としているが、同時代のイタリアの芸術運動「アルテ・ポーヴェラ」との関係性も見出せる。「アルテ・ポーヴェラ」とは絵具と絵筆といった伝統的な道具ではなく、工業的素材や自然の木や石など身の回りのものをそのまま用い、「使われるもの

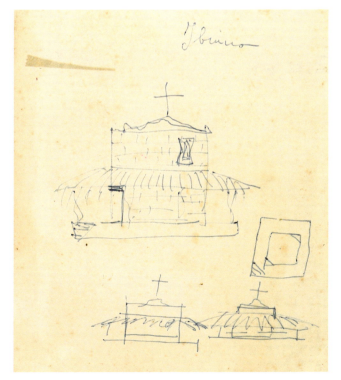

外観。右手に走る青い階段がアプローチ。
The exterior.
The blue staircase running down the right side forms the approach.

初期のスケッチ。
ボリューム・スタディに加え、藁屋根や平面形状など、
最終形の構想がすでに描かれている。（1978年）
An early sketch. In addition to a volume study, the structure of the final form, including thatched roof and surface shapes, is already depicted here. (1978)

すべてを、最小限の基本要素にまで、削り取り、還元しようとする」*3 表現方法である。直訳すれば「貧しい」となるこの言葉は「余計なものを取り去る」思想として発展した。リナはこの言葉を、建築を設計する上で重視していた要素——単純な操作、シンプルさ、工芸、その土地の自然との共生、人びとに使われるための開かれた空間——の表現として適用した。

　リナは、「ガラスの家」（p. 012）や友人の邸宅など、初期にわずかな住宅を手掛けたのみで、生涯にわたり公共建築を手掛けている。当時のブラジルは発展途上であることに加えて軍事政権の独裁下にあり、建設プロジェクトはこのアンジョス教会のように低予算であることがほとんどだった。それでもリナは、一部の富裕層だけではなく、ブラジルで暮らすあらゆる人びとが豊かに過ごせることを考え続け、低予算でも仕事を引き受け実現させた。「アンジョス教会」は、リナの美的思想と道徳的思想がみごとに示された、小さな記念碑でもある。

*1　Catherine Veikos, (2014) "The Hands of the People: SESC Pompeia", in *Lina Bo Bardi 100*, p. 119.

*2　ポーランドの演出家。1933〜99年。

*3　ルイージ・メネゲッリ「アルテ・ポーヴェラ」『アルテ・ポーヴェラ展カタログ』児玉画廊、1992年、p. 017

テラス。かつては木の幹を加工せずに柱として用い、不規則に配置されていた。現在は製材に変更されている。
The terrace. In the past, tree trunks were used as pillars without any processing, which were positioned irregularly. These have now been changed to lumber.

This church dedicated to the Virgin Mary was built in a poor residential district on the outskirts of São Paulo upon request by a member of the Franciscan Order. Having limited construction resources, Lina planned a modest type of architecture using simple materials and a minimal design in line with the idea of "poor architecture" (*arquitetura pobre*). The outer walls were painted in a simple and striking red-colored plaster made of sand, concrete and a locally produced clay. In this work appear various characteristics such as the relationship between the geometrical plan, vegetation, rooftop garden, and nature, as well as a straw-thatched roof. Lina's design elements are condensed into the local nature and handicrafts combined with a simple geometry and rationalism.

Inside the square shape with two cut off angles facing a square with 10.3 meter sides is an entrance in one section and an altar installed in the other section. This simple operation creates a natural feeling of being wrapped up in the surrounding walls as one faces the altar when entering inside. The variety of calm colors seen in the white plaster walls, wooden ceiling, and green stone floor give a sense of intimacy to this small space with a few windows. The exterior appearance resembling a "small, gently pink-colored box" gives an impression similar to that of a child's treasure chest. Among Lina's

上空より見る。
アプローチ階段の途中の折れ曲がる地点で、
訪問者は扉と祭壇に対し正面を向く。
Looking from the sky.
Visitors face the front toward the door
and altar at the bending point in the middle of the stair approach.

many dynamic architectural works, this one gives off a unique impression because of its compact scale and the way it seems to rise from the earth and be quietly breathing. Due to the difficulty of maintenance, the straw-thatched roof was changed to a tile roof and the terrace that used tree trunks for pillars now uses square pillars.

Lina explains "poor architecture" in the following manner: "poor not in the sense of poverty, but in the sense of the handmade, great dignity expressed with humble means"[*1]. "Poor architecture" is said to have originated from the "poor theater" (p. 203) of director Jerzy Grotowski[*2], but one can also see its relation to the Italian art movement "*arte povera*" from the same period. *Arte povera*, which makes use of industrial materials and other nearby objects such as natural wood and stones rather than traditional tools such as coloring materials and paintbrushes, is a form of expression used to "shave off and reduce all objects to be used to their minimum basic elements"[*3]. Translated directly, the word meaning "poor" developed into the idea of "removing all unnecessary elements". Lina adopted these words to express the elements that she considered important for designing architecture such as a simple operation, simplicity, handicrafts, symbiosis with local nature, and an open space to be used by people.

In the early days, Lina worked on a small number of residences such as the "Glass House"(p. 012) and her friends' homes, but she worked on public buildings throughout her life. In addition to being a developing country, Brazil was also under the dictatorship of a military regime at the time. Building projects were often undertaken on a low budget as in the case of the "Santa Maria dos Anjos Chapel". Nevertheless, Lina continued to think about how she could enrich the lives of everyone living in Brazil rather than just the wealthy, so she continued to accept low budget jobs and see them realized. The "Santa Maria dos Anjos Chapel" splendidly exemplifies Lina's aesthetic and ethical ideas.

*1 Catherine Veikos, (2014) "The Hands of the People: SESC Pompéia", in *Lina Bo Bardi 100*, p. 119.

*2 A Polish theater director. 1933-99.

*3 Luigi Meneghelli, (1992) "Arte Povera", in *Arte Povera Exhibition Catalog*, Kodama Gallery, p. 017.

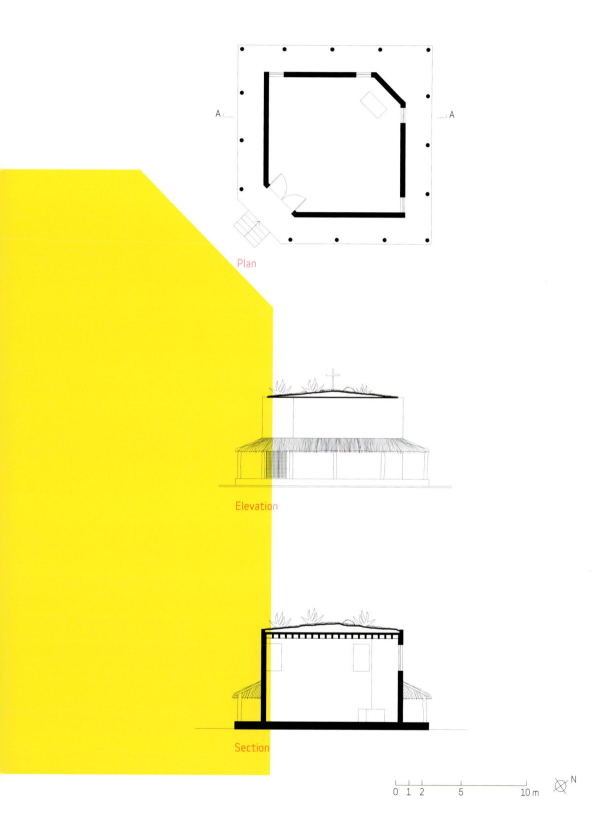

Santa Maria dos Anjos Chapel

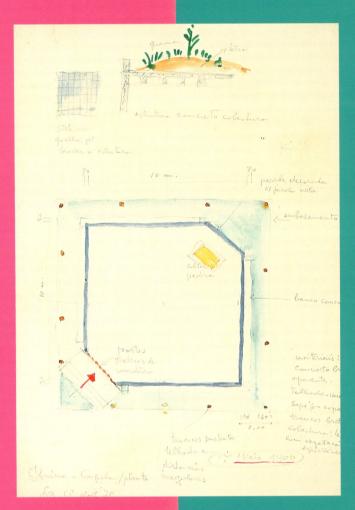

屋根の構造のディテールと屋上庭園のスタディ、平面のドローイング。(1978年)
Details of the roof structure, a study of the rooftop garden and a projection. (1978)

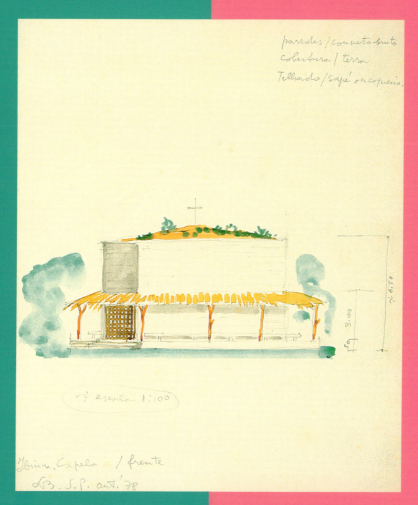

立面のドローイング。
屋上庭園、格子戸、藁屋根、木の幹を用いた柱などが見て取れる。(1978年)
An elevation.
Here can be seen the rooftop garden, lattice doors,
thatched roof and tree trunks used as pillars. (1978)

Santa Maria dos Anjos Chapel

教会内部の祭壇。壁面の高窓から差す光が、内部空間をやさしく照らす。
The altar inside the chapel. Light shining from the high window gently illuminates the interior space.

入り口の格子戸から柔らかな光が差し込む。内部空間は質素ながらもやさしい雰囲気がつくられている。
A soft light shines through the lattice doors of the entrance. The interior space is simple but warm.

Santa Maria dos Anjos Chapel

リナがデザインした教会の椅子。
「エスピリト・サント・ド・セラード教会」(p. 164) 計画時に検討されたデザインが元になっている。
幾何学図形と温かさの同居は、建物自体のコンセプトにも通じる。
The chapel chairs designed by Lina.
The design explored during the planning of "Espirito Santo do Cerrado Church" (p. 164) formed the basis.
The cohabitation of geometric shapes and warmth also come across in the concept of the building itself.

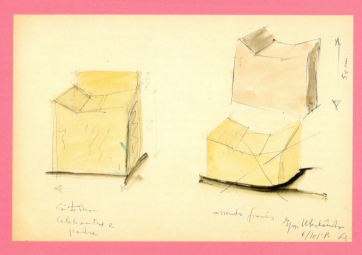

椅子のドローイング。(1980年)
A drawing of the chair. (1980)

The Historic Center of Salvador

The case for the Historical Center of Bahia is not the preservation of important architectures, but the preservation of the City's Popular Soul.
Lina Bo Bardi, 1986

バイーアの歴史的地区の場合は、
重要な建築を守ることではなく、
この街の人びとの魂を守ることでした。
リナ・ボ・バルディ、1986年

かつての「ベナンの家」。建物は火事により大きな被害を受けていた。(1973年)
The former "House of Benin". The building was severely damaged by a fire. (1973)

pp. 118-119
修復前のサルヴァドールの街を描いたドローイング。
(1986年)
A drawing depicting Salvador before it was renovated. (1986)

ブラジル最初の首都、バイーア州の州都サルヴァドール市は、丘の上の旧市街と、海岸と同じレベルにある新市街のふたつに分かれている。バロック教会をはじめとするポルトガル植民地時代の建築が残り、民衆のエネルギーにあふれ、独特の文化が形成されている。

旧市街では多くの歴史的建造物が人びとに活用されていたが、軍の支配下となった数年間ですっかり荒廃してしまった。1985年にユネスコの世界遺産に指定されたことをきっかけに、市長は街の修復をリナに依頼した。修復に際し、リナは既存の建築と都市と居住者とを一体的に考え、観光地化するのではなく、居住者の暮らしに応えることを目的に計画した。街や建築を保存すると同時に居住者の生活や伝統文化を守るため、モニュメントに限らず一般的な建物もリノベーションし、住宅や商店、地域の文化芸術センターとして機能する建物を計画した。こうして「ベナンの家」や「グレゴリオ・デ・マトス劇場」をはじめとする一連の建物が建てられた。これらの建物は市街の中心部に点在しており、現在もサルヴァドールの文化やアートを支える重要な拠点となっている。リナは、長年この地で厳しい暮らしをしてきた人びとの生活を改善し、彼らの生活と伝統文化のあり方に、新たな可能性を与えることを目指した。

各建物の修復には、建築家ジョアン・フィルゲイラス・リマ*1と共同で考案したプレキャスト・コンクリートの波板を使用し、元来のデザインを守りながら補強した。建物の状況に合わせて簡単に加工できるように板厚は可能な限り薄い16ミリとし、波板の組み合わせで生じる壁面内部の空洞は解体で出た廃棄物やセメントで埋めるという合理的な解法だ。

1988年の初め、新市長がリナの計画を受け入れなかったためにプロジェクトは停止してしまったが、状態はさまざまでありながらも一部は完成し、街に現存している。パラソル付きの椅子とテーブルが並ぶ広場「ベレヴェデーレ・ダ・セ広場」(現存せず)、「グレゴリオ・デ・マトス劇場」、「ベナンの家」、「ミゼリコーディア坂歴史的地区の修復」、音楽に特化した文化センター「オロドゥムの家」が実現した。ここでは3つのプロジェクトを取り上げる。

*1　ブラジルの建築家。通称レレ。1932〜2014年。

The Historic Center of Salvador

The city of Salvador is the capital of the Brazilian state of Bahia and is the country's first capital. The city is divided in two parts consisting of the old town on top of a hill and the new town at sea level. Brimming with the energy of its people, a unique culture has formed in Salvador, which is still home to many examples of Portuguese colonial architecture, including Baroque churches.

Many historical buildings were utilized by people in the old city, but these were totally devastated in the few years under the control of the military. Following its designation as a UNESCO World Heritage Site in 1985, the mayor of Salvador asked Lina to restore the historical center of the city. Rather than turn it into a tourist attraction, Lina's plan sought to adapt the historical center to the lives of the people and saw the existing buildings, the city and its inhabitants as a whole. In order to preserve the city and its architecture as well as to protect the way of life and traditional culture of its residents, Lina planned for the renovation of common buildings as well as monuments, buildings that function as houses, shops and local cultural art centers. Thus a series of buildings including "*House of Benin*" and "Gregório de Mattos Theater" were built. These buildings dot the center of the city and form to this day an important hub supporting Salvador's arts and culture. Lina aimed to improve the tough lives of longtime residents and to provide new possibilities to their way of life and traditional culture.

During the restoration, precast concrete corrugated boards designed jointly with architect João Filgueiras Lima[*1] were used to reinforce each building while preserving the original design. The thickness was set at 16mm to make it as thin as possible and make it easier to process according to the buildings' condition. Moreover, a rational solution presented itself whereby the cavities formed by the juxtaposition of corrugated boards were filled with waste materials from the demolition and cement.

In early 1988, renovation efforts came to a halt because the new mayor abandoned Lina's plan and the project was left in different states of completion. However, the parts what were completed can still be found in the old city, including the "Belvedere da Sé", (no longer exists) a square with tables and chairs with parasols, the "Gregório de Mattos Theater", the "House of Benin", the "Misericórdia Slope" and the "House of Olodum", cultural center specializing in music. Three such projects are presented in the following pages.

*1   Brazilian architect. Nicknamed "Lelé". 1932-2014.

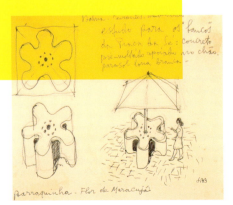

「ベルヴェデーレ・ダ・セ広場」の
コンクリート製テーブルのデザイン。(1986年頃)
The concrete table design
at "Belvedere da Sé". (*circa* 1986)

サルヴァドール旧市街修復の全体像を描いた地図。(1987年)
A map depicting an overall view of the restoration of Salvador's historic center. (1987)

リナが設計した建築／Buildings Designed by Lina

① ベルヴェデーレ・ダ・セ広場（現存せず）／ Belvedere da Sé (no longer exists)
② ミゼリコーディア坂歴史的地区の修復／ Misericórdia Slope
③ バホキーニャ・プロジェクト／ Barroquinha Project
④ ベナンの家／ House of Benin
⑤ オロドゥムの家／ House of Olodum
⑥ ピエール・ヴェルジェ記念館（実現せず）／ Pierre Verger Foundation (not realized)
⑦ キューバの家（実現せず）／ House of Cuba (not realized)
⑧ キューバの「バイーアの家」（実現せず）／ House of Bahia in Cuba (not realized)
⑨ ベナンの「バイーアの家」（実現せず）／ House of Bahia in Benin (not realized)

建築以外の構想／Non-Architectural Concepts

A サンフランシスコ教会前広場の舗装の計画／ Pavement Plan for "Largo do Cruzeiro de São Francisco"
B 滝を模した屋外シャワー／ Outdoor Shower Simulating a Waterfall
C ポップコーン、地域伝統の綿製品、飲み物、キャンディなどを積んだカート／ Carts Selling Popcorn, Regional and Traditional Cotton Goods, Drinks, Candy, etc.
D バー／ Bar
E 小さな屋台バー／ Small Stand Bar
F 街を巡るワゴンの運行経路／ Route of Wagon Traveling Around Town
G ワゴンの停車地／ Stops for Wagons

ベナンの家

House of Benin
Salvador, 1988

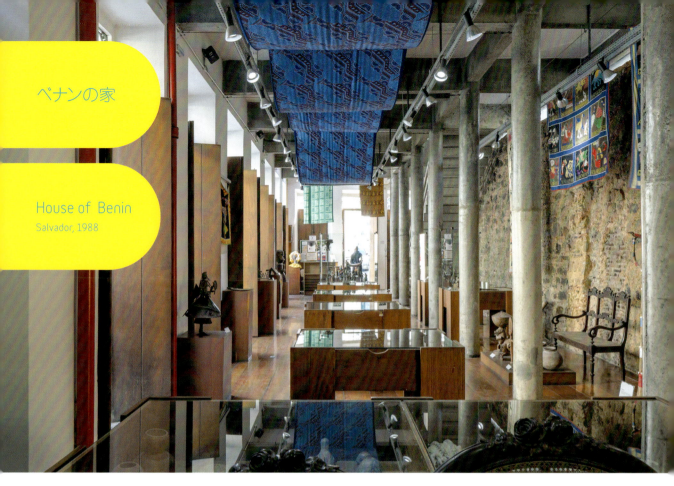

「ベナンの家」内観。1階はベナン工芸の常設展。展示品のケースもリナによるデザイン。
An interior view of "House of Benin". The ground floor has a permanent exhibit of Benin crafts. The exhibit cases were also designed by Lina.

西アフリカ、ベナン共和国の出身者が多いサルヴァドール市街中心部の重要地区、ペロウリンホ地区にあるふたつの古い住宅を一体化して修復した建物。アフリカ系ブラジル人の教育・文化センターとして、展覧会やレクチャーなどが行われる。2棟のうち広場の角地に面した住宅は、新旧の要素を織り交ぜて修復している。壁面仕上げの漆喰を取り除いて下地の美しい石と泥を表出させたり、分断されていた各階を吹き抜けでつなぎ、中央の階段を取り払って壁沿いの連続階段でつなぐことで、垂直方向に一体感をもたせた。階段や柱梁のコンクリートを薄く軽やかに仕上げることで、空間の広がりや上昇感を生み出している。コンクリートの丸柱はアフリカの工芸にならって手編みのココナッツの葉で飾り、1階の天井にはテキスタイルを天蓋のように吊り下げた。2棟の住宅は角でつながり、もう1棟の住宅には螺旋階段と波形コンクリートを挿入して修復した。1階にはレストランと商店、上階にはベナン共和国からの来客用の宿泊所がつくられた。2棟の間の中庭には、ココナッツの木と人工の滝のある小さな池や、かつてレストランとして使われていた泥れんがでできた楕円状の小さな小屋など、アフリカの土着的文化が色濃く反映されている。室内には、その形状とアフリカとにちなんで名付けられた、リナによるデザインの「キリンの椅子」(p.187)が置かれている。建物の外観は市の修復ガイドラインに従い、古いファサードを残して白い漆喰で仕上げられた。

「ベナンの家」は、「キューバの家」と、ベナン共和国とキューバ共和国それぞれに計画した「ブラジルの家」と共に国際交流プロジェクトとして計画されたが、実現したのは「ベナンの家」のみであった。旧市街のプロジェクトのなかではもっともよく保存されている。サルヴァドール市のリナの作品はサンパウロ市の建築とは異なるアプローチが用いられ、ポルトガルの植民地時代の建築の伝統と、アフリカ系ブラジル人の文化と歴史が尊重されている。

The building is the result of a comprehensive renovation of two old residences located in Pelourinho, an important district in the center of the city of Salvador where many share origins from the Republic of Benin, West Africa. Exhibitions and lectures are held in this educational/cultural center for Afro-Brazilians. While the building facing the corner of a square integrates old and new elements, a sense of unity in the vertical direction was achieved by removing the wall finish plaster, revealing the beautiful stone and mud of the foundation, joining each floor through openings, removing the stairs in the center and connecting each floor by a continuous stairway along the wall. The thin and light concrete finish on the stairs and columns give a sense of loftiness and elevation to the whole space. The round concrete pillars are decorated with hand-woven coconut tree leaves inspired by African crafts, and a textile canopy can be seen hanging from the ceiling of the ground floor. The two houses connect at the corner, and the other building was renovated by incorporating a spiral staircase and corrugated concrete. Restaurants and shops were set up on the ground floor and guest rooms for visitors from the Republic of Benin were built on the upper floors. The courtyard between the two buildings offers a dramatic representation of the indigenous culture of the African continent with coconut trees, a small pond with an artificial waterfall, and a small elliptical hut made up of mud bricks once used as a restaurant. Inside the hut is a piece of furniture designed by Lina named the "Giraffe Chair"(p. 187) for its shape and its association with Africa. Following the restoration guidelines of the city, the exterior of the building was finished with white plaster and the old façade was conserved.

The "House of Benin" was planned as an international exchange project along with the "House of Cuba" and the "House of Brazil", planned in both the Republic of Benin and the Republic of Cuba, but only the "Casa do Benin" was realized. It is also the best preserved project in the old city. In contrast with her architectural work in the city of São Paulo, the work of Lina in the city of Salvador takes a different approach where the tradition of Portuguese colonial architecture and the culture and history of Afro-Brazilians are respected.

現在のサルヴァドール旧市街中心部。中央右の白い建物が「ベナンの家」。
Presently, the heart of Salvador's historic center. The white building right of center is "House of Benin".

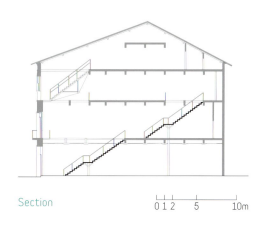

Section

The Historic Center of Salvador

中庭に面した壁は波形コンクリートで補強されている。
The walls facing the courtyard are reinforced with corrugated concrete.

小屋のドローイング。(1986年頃)
A drawing of a hut. (*circa* 1986)

平面ドローイング。中庭部分は着色され、藁屋根の形状がよく分かる。(1986年頃)
A floor plan drawing. The courtyard section is colored and the shape of the straw-thatched roof is clearly discernible. (*circa* 1986)

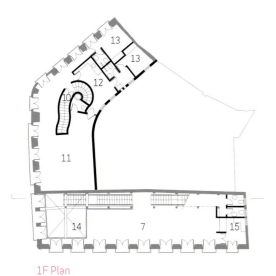

1F Plan

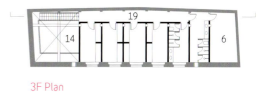

3F Plan

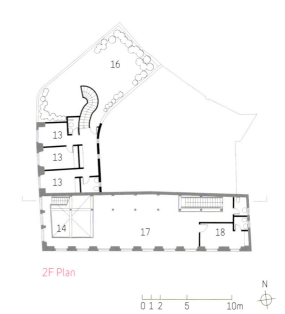

GF Plan

2F Plan

1. Square
2. Garden
3. Waterfall and Pond
4. Restaurant of Benin
5. Kitchen
6. Store Room
7. Exhibition Hall
8. Public Bathroom
9. Clay Oven
10. Entrance to the House of Benin Common Room
11. Lounge
12. Kitchen
13. Bedroom
14. Two-Story Space
15. Auxiliary Room
16. Garden Terrace
17. Library
18. Administration
19. Student's Quarters

グレゴリオ・デ・マトス劇場

Gregório de Mattos Theater
Salvador, 1987

市街地中心部のパホキーニャ地区に計画された、複合施設建設プロジェクト「パホキーニャ」は、「グレゴリオ・デ・マトス劇場」に加え、グラウベル・ローシャ映画館のファサードと内部の修復、野外映画上映所やダンススペース、屋台やバーが配されたグラウベル広場、修復して集会場やレストランとして用いられるパホキーニャ教会、ハーブの市場、トイレ、周辺地域が使用する倉庫から成る。加えて近隣に商業併用住宅も計画され、文化的施設と人びとの生活の改善とを連携しようとしていた。「パホキーニャ」は、ブラジルの映画監督グラウベル・ローシャ[*1]へのオマージュとして、映画や演劇を街の人びとへ開き、彼らの生活を豊かにすることを目的に計画された。しかし、当時完成したのは広場と劇場のみだった。

リナはこの歴史ある建物が新しい環境に適応するよう、内外に力強い要素を加えて修復した。内部に入ると、劇場空間へと導く巨大なコンクリートの螺旋階段が、飾りのないシンプルな空間に堂々と鎮座している。2階に広がる、固定した舞台も客席もない劇場空間は、演者と観客との境界をなくした。この柔軟な空間に対応するため、折りたたみ式の「エジディオ神父の椅子」（p. 187）がデザインされた。奥の増築部分に置かれたバーカウンター横の巨大な重い木戸を開くと、「SESCポンペイア文化センター」（p. 068）でも用いられた雲形窓が現れる。「SESC」よりもずっと巨大なこの窓からはサルヴァドールの街並みが広がり、劇場と街をつないでいる。

現在、劇場はリナのデザインを踏襲しながら修復されている。しかし文化的な意図が保たれる一方、本来意図されていた、文化を地域住民の住宅、商業、コミュニティ活動といった生活の改善と結びつけようとしたリナの思想は残っていない。

*1　1938〜81年。ブラジルの映画監督、俳優、脚本家。シネマ・ノーヴォの指導者。バイーア現代美術館でリナの助手を務めた。

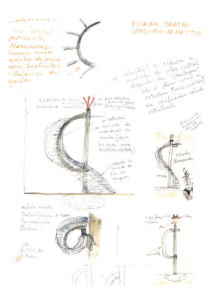

階段のドローイング。
（1986年）
A drawing of the staircase. (1986)

In addition to the "Gregório de Mattos Theater", the multi-purpose construction project "Barroquinha" planned for the Barroquinha district in the center of the city also consisted of the Glauber Rocha Cinema Club façade and its interior restoration, an outdoor movie theater and dance space, the Glauber square with its food stalls and bar, the renovated Barroquinha church which was used as a meeting space and restaurant, herb market, toilets, and warehouses used by the surrounding community. Also, neighborhood commercial businesses together with housing were planned with the aim of linking cultural facilities to the improvement of people's lives. The "Barroquinha" was planned as an homage to the Brazilian movie director Glauber Rocha[*1] for the purpose of enriching the lives of city residents and introducing them to movies and theater. But only the square and theater were completed at the time.

In order to adapt the historic building to a new environment, Lina undertook restoration by adding powerful elements to the interior and exterior. Inside, a giant concrete spiral staircase that leads to the theater space magnificently enshrines the simple and unadorned space. Having no fixed stage or seating, this theater space removes the boundary between performers and spectators as it fills the first floor. The folding "Frei Egydio chair" (p. 187) was designed to be adaptable to this flexible space. When opening the large wooden door next to the bar counter situated at the back of the additional area, a "cloud window" such as the one used at "SESC - Pompéia Factory Leisure Center" (p. 068) would appear. From this window, which was much larger than the one at "SESC", the townscape of Salvador expanded outward, connecting the theater with the city.

Presently, the theater is being restored in line with Lina's design. But while the cultural aim is being preserved, Lina's idea behind the original aim to connect the project with the improvement of life through culture in local resident housing, businesses, and community activities, does not remain.

p. 128 top
コンクリートの螺旋階段。1階は展示ホールで、2階が劇場空間。
The concrete spiral staircase.
The ground floor is an exhibition space, and the 1st floor is a theater space.

[*1] 1938 – 1981. A Brazilian film director, actor, and playwright. Leader of Cinema Novo. Worked as Lina's assistant at the "Bahia Museum of Modern Art".

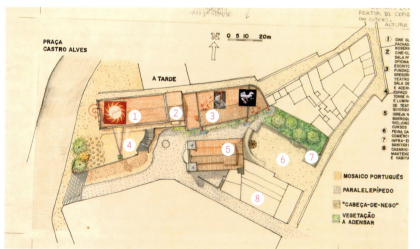

①②グラウベル・ローシャ映画館と財団 / Glauber Rocha Cinema and Foundation
③グレゴリオ・デ・マトス劇場 / Gregório de Mattos Theater
④グラウベル広場 / Glauber Plaza
⑤バホキーニャ教会 / Barroquinha Church
⑥ハーブ市場 / Herb Market
⑦トイレ・倉庫 / Toilet and Warehouse
⑧商業機能をもつ住宅 / House with Commercial Function

バホキーニャの全体計画図。(1986年頃)
The plan for the entire Barroquinha project. (circa 1986)

正面。それぞれの建物の状態に合わせた修復がなされている。左端がレストラン、右にアパートが並ぶ。
The front. Renovations were carried out according to the condition of the buildings.
On the left edge is a restaurant, and on the right are a row of apartments.

ミゼリコーディア坂
歴史的地区の修復

Misericórdia Slope
Salvador, 1988

　このプロジェクトは、かつて海と市街とをつないでいた歴史ある坂道に位置する、連続する5筆の土地の修復計画である。建物が荒廃し、土地に木々が生い茂る姿はリナの創造力を膨らませた。18世紀の住宅の遺構が残っていた4軒は壁やスラブ、階段に波形コンクリートを用いて修復し、1階を小商店や工房とし、上階を低価格のアパートにすることを提案した。荒廃のレベルに応じて異なるデザインが用いられている。石壁のみが一部残っていた空地には、新しく円筒形のレストランがつくられた。敷地に生えていたマンゴーの木が建物を貫くように設計された。波形コンクリート壁面には雲形窓が開けられ不思議な陰影が生まれている。

　その後これらの建造物は長年放置されてしまい、市街地中心部の貧困層によって占拠されていたが、政府によって追放され、現在は建物のほとんどが閉鎖されており、市の許可のみで入館できるようになっている。時おり若いアーティストがこの場所を復興しようと活動している。

　1988年の市長交替により、旧市街のプロジェクトは頓挫し、多くは放置されてしまった。利便性ではなく、その土地に眠る歴史を価値として捉え、豊かな都市空間を生み出そうとしたリナの思想は、時代に先行しすぎていたのかもしれない。しかし同時に、リナは健康状態の悪化によりかつてのように現場で作業することができず、サルヴァドールを訪れることも少なかった。そのため、このプロジェクトはリナの設計プロセスにおいて常に重要であった地域住民との対話が十分ではなかったといえる。リナは十分に住民の生活や意図を把握できず、住民はリナの描いた思想を理解していなかったと推測される。

This project was situated on a historic hill road that formerly connected the city and the sea and centered around 5 adjacent plots of land. The dilapidated buildings and trees populating the site stirred Lina's imagination. Corrugated concrete was used for the walls, slabs, and stairs to restore the remains of the four 18th century houses left standing. It was proposed that the ground floor would have small shops and a workshop while the upper floors would be used as low cost apartments. Different designs were used depending on the extent of the damage. A new restaurant with a cylindrical exterior was built on a vacant lot where only a part of the stone wall remained. The building was designed to allow the mango trees growing on the plot to go through it. The "cloud window" openings on the corrugated concrete walls created mysterious shadows.

These buildings were later abandoned for many years and then occupied by the poor from the city center. Some time later they were evicted by the authorities, and since most of the buildings are presently closed-off, it is only possible to enter with the city's permission. Young artists can sometimes be seen attempting to restore these places.

In 1988, the mayoral leadership changed and the old city projects came to a standstill, with many of them being abandoned. Lina's idea to think of the history dormant in that land as something valuable regardless of convenience and to want to create a rich city space was perhaps too forward-thinking. But at the same time, Lina's deteriorating health made it impossible for her to work on site as before, and she paid fewer visits to Salvador. Therefore, it can be said that the project suffered from insufficient dialogue with local residents, which was always important in Lina's design process. It is speculated that Lina could not grasp the life and wishes of residents sufficiently, and that they did not understand her design ideas.

立面計画図。レストランはまだないが、アパート部分は最終形に近いかたちで描かれている。
豊かな植物と元の建物を生かしつつ、白い塗装を施し、コンクリートの波板を用いて修復する構想が分かる。(1987 年)
A preliminary elevation. The restaurant is not there yet, but the apartment section depicted is close to the final form. One can grasp the idea behind the renovations from the use of corrugated concrete painted white while also taking advantage of the rich flora and the original building. (1987)

The Historic Center of Salvador

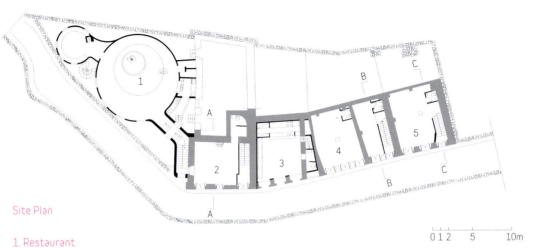

Site Plan

1. Restaurant
2. Building 1
3. Bar of Three Arches
4. Building 3
5. Building 7

A-A Section

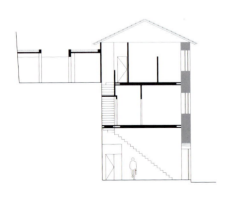

B-B Section

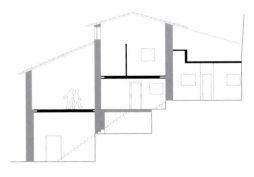

C-C Section

レストラン。テラスへ抜ける雲形の開口。
The restaurant. A cloud window opens onto the terrace.

2階のレストラン内観。ステージ中央の開口から伸びるマンゴーの木が、屋上へと抜ける。
An interior view of the 1st floor restaurant. The mango tree extending from the stage's central opening passes through onto the roof.

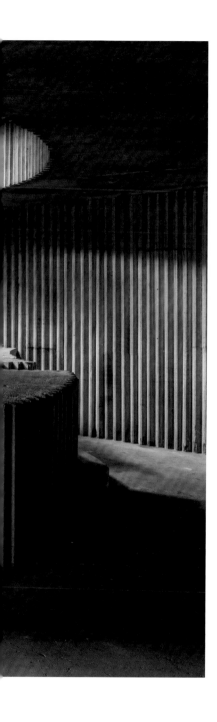

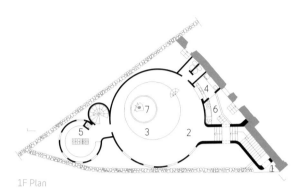

1F Plan

GF Plan

1. Entrance
2. Restaurant
3. Platform for Concerts
4. Bar
5. Kitchen
6. Storage
7. Large Mango Tree

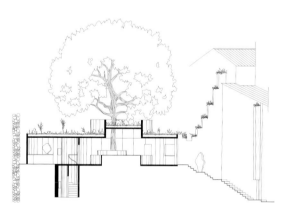

Section

テアトロ・オフィシナ
Oficina Theater

São Paulo, 1989

"The Oficina" will search
for the real meaning of the theater.
Lina Bo Bardi, 1986

「テアトロ・オフィシナ」は、
劇場というものの真の意味を探す建築です。
リナ・ボ・バルディ、1986年

軍の独裁政治へ抵抗を示した劇団テアトロ・オフィシナとリナの親交は深く、舞台美術や衣装デザインをリナが担当するなど、彼らの活動への共感が伺える。元々あった劇場が火災による被害を受け、1980年に再建プロジェクトがスタートし、9年後にはまったく新しい劇場が生まれた。

新しい劇場は、幅9メートル、奥行き50メートルの既存建物の残存部に1本の通りのようにデザインされた。入り口から奥へと3メートル下がるスロープ状の床そのものを舞台とし、壁際に組まれた3層の金属チューブを客席とした。観客はこの足場から舞台を見下ろすという、奇妙な視点で演劇を見ることになる。通りのような舞台は、観客や街の人びとを登場人物の一員とするかのような効果をも生み出した。設計プロセスには波乱があり、多くの変更が余儀なくされた。リナの初期案ではサーカスのような黄色のテントを張っており、劇場に隣接する空き地へ建物を新設する計画もあったが、資金不足で頓挫してしまう。終盤、リナはプロジェクトから距離をとり、最終的には共同設計者のエドソン・エリートが主体となり完成させた。現在も残る空き地は劇団員にとって劇場の一部であり、この地を開発から守るレジスタンスが続けられている。

自然が建築内部に堂々と入り込んでいることも、この建築の特徴だ。側面の大きなガラスファサードに加え、一部開閉式のガラス屋根は、光だけでなく外気や街の喧噪、さまざまな表情の空を劇場に採り込む。内部には井戸のような形の噴水や細長い花壇が備えられ、舞台のすぐ脇に植物が茂っている。その中の一本の大きな木は、壁を突き抜けて外部へ飛び出し、外観に強烈な印象を与えている。この一見劇場とは思えないさまざまな要素が集まる空間を、劇団員たちは巧みに使いこなし、現在も前衛的な作品を上演し続けている。ここでは自然も建築も人びとも、あるがままの姿と活力で立ち続けており、共に新たなつながりをつくり上げている。

入り口。
床面にはタイルで"TEAT(R)O OFICINA"と刻まれている。
The entrance.
The floor surface has tiles engraved with "TEAT(R)O OFICINA".

Oficina Theater

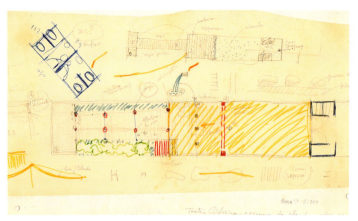

平面とディテールのドローイング。
花壇や池などに加え、
床材、トイレ、開口部の形状、防水仕様がスタディされている。(1984年)
A projection with details.
In addition to the flower bed and pond,
it provides a study of the floor materials, toilet, shape of the opening, and the waterproofing specifications. (1984)

Lina had an intimate relationship with Oficina Theater, a theater company that showed resistance to the Brazilian military dictatorship. Her sympathy towards their activities was evident in the way Lina coordinated their stage art and costume designs. After the theater was demolished in a fire, a project to rebuild it was set into motion in 1980 and, nine years later, an entirely new theater was born.

The new theater was designed like a 9-meter-wide and 50-meter-long avenue in the remains of the existing building. The stage was actually a sloped floor with an incline of 3 meters that extended from the entrance to the back of the room, and 3-layered piping built along the walls was used as seats. Spectators looked down on the stage from this scaffolding, which offered a curious perspective from which to watch a play. Moreover, the stage resembling an avenue also created an effect that made it seem as though spectators and local city dwellers were actors in the play. There were problems during the design process which forced many unwanted changes. Lina initially planned for a large yellow tent resembling that of a circus and she wanted to establish new buildings in the vacant plot adjacent to the theater, but her plan was setback due to lack of funds. Lina eventually distanced herself from the project, which resulted finally in co-designer Edson Elito taking over and completing the project. Theater company members consider the vacant plot which remains to this day as part of the theater, and they protect this land from development by continuing to show resistance.

This architecture is characterized by the bold infusion of nature into its architectural interior. In addition to the large glass façade on the side, the partially retractable glass roof takes in to the theater not only light but also the open air, the hustle and bustle of the city, and the sky with its diversity of expressions. Inside is a fountain shaped like a well, a long and narrow flower bed, and a thick growth of vegetation beside the stage. Among the vegetation is a large tree that pierces the wall and thrusts outside, creating a strong impression on the exterior of the building. At a glance, this space with its variety of elements does not appear to be a theater. The theater members are adept at making skillful use of these elements and continue to perform avant-garde works to this day. Here in this space, nature, architecture, and people continue to stand as they are with vitality, creating new relationships together.

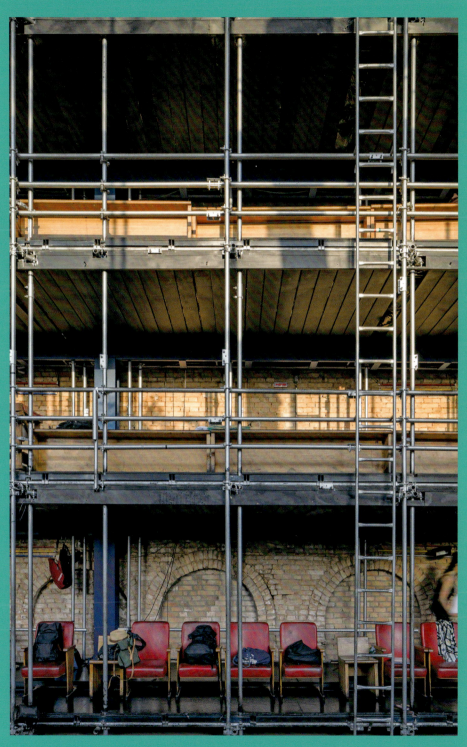
金属管で組まれた客席。
Seats put together with metal tubes.

Oficina Theater

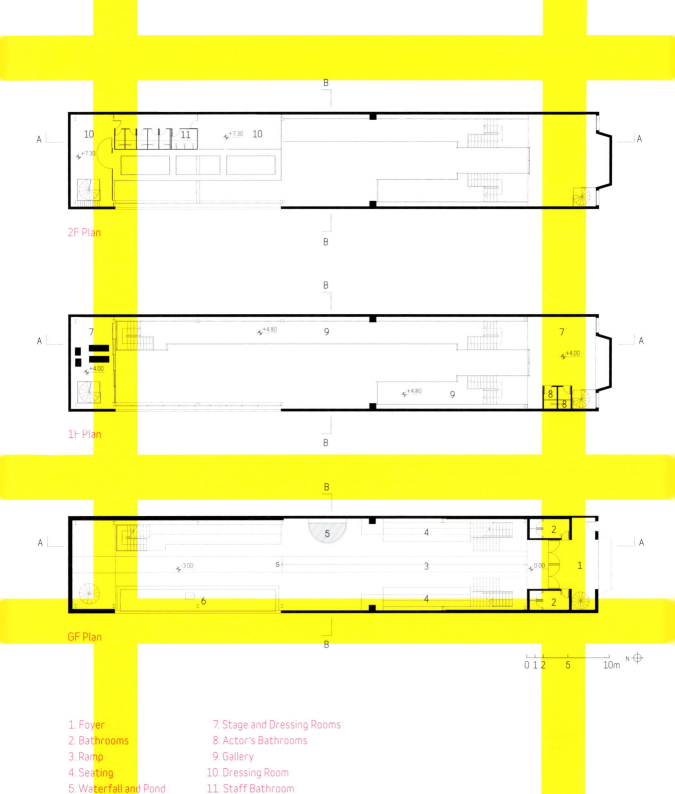

2F Plan

1F Plan

GF Plan

1. Foyer
2. Bathrooms
3. Ramp
4. Seating
5. Waterfall and Pond
6. Garden
7. Stage and Dressing Rooms
8. Actor's Bathrooms
9. Gallery
10. Dressing Room
11. Staff Bathroom

B-B Section

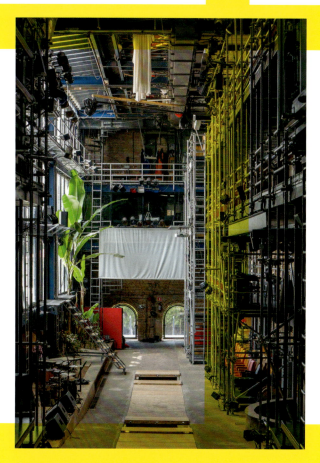

入口からの内観。中央の空間全体が舞台、右側が客席。
An interior view from the entrance.
The stage occupies the entire central space,
and the seats are on the right side.

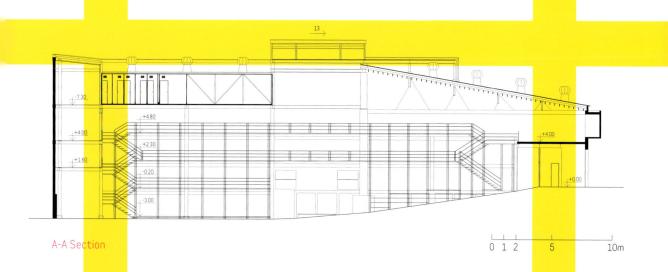

A-A Section

0 1 2   5   10m

上演中の様子。
奈落は深く掘られており、中から大勢の俳優や舞台装置が登場する。
観客は地面にも座り、俳優との距離は非常に近い。
A scene during a performance. The pit is a deep hollow from inside which many actors and stage porps appear. Spectators sit on the ground in close proximity to the actors.

2階客席。
The 1st floor gallery.

舞台脇の花壇から外部へ突き出す樹木。
れんがの基壇部とガラス板との間から、木を外へ逃がしている。
A tree that springs outside from the flower bed beside the stage. The tree escapes outside from between the brick foundation and glass pane.

入り口側から見た内観。天窓が開いた状態。
The interior as seen from the entrance side. The skylight is open.

ヴァレリア・P・シレル邸
Valéria P. Cirell's Home

São Paulo, 1958

…preserve the 'purity' of the spontaneous and primitive forms from which they derive. What they also conserve, in the irregular stone and in the carved wood, is that 'pure' and 'natural' feeling that keeps them rooted to the earth, joined with nature, immersed within the landscape.
Lina Bo Bardi, 1943

古来、自然に生まれた建物に
元来備わっている、かたちに宿る「純粋さ」を保つこと。
不揃いな石や手彫りの木材には純粋で自然な感覚があります。
地に根付き、自然とつながり、風景の一部になります。
リナ・ボ・バルディ、1943年

後年増築された離れから主屋へのアプローチを見る。小石で飾られた石壁に囲まれる。Looking at the approach to the main building from the guesthouse addition built in later years. It is enclosed by stone walls adorned with pebbles.

「ガラスの家」(p. 012)建設から7年後、友人からの依頼で同建物の近隣に建てられた住宅。両者はまったく異なった美しさをもちながら、「ヴァレリア・P・シレル邸」にはリナ作品の特徴である、自然と地域の伝統とモダニズムの融合が、より進んだかたちで現れている。「ガラスの家」のようなミニマルな美しさに豊かなテクスチャーが付加され、リナのデザインがヨーロッパ的なものから徐々にブラジルに馴染んできたことが感じられる。アントニオ・ガウディからの影響を思わせる*1小石と陶器の破片が散りばめられたファサードや、壁面に加えプールや屋上庭園など、随所に植物が生えていることから「水晶の庭の家」とも呼ばれている*2。主屋は幾何学的な立方体で、サービス空間が小さな中庭を介して連なるとともに、周囲を巡るテラスが内外を緩やかにつないでいる。木とれんがによる構造や、草屋根といった工芸的な要素が、自然と人工、モダニズムとヴァナキュラーといった対立を打ち消し、さまざまな要素が混在しながら有機的に同居している。リビングルームは螺旋階段で三角形の平面形をもつ中二階につながり、天窓からの自然光と豊かな色彩にあふれた開放的な空間となっている。中央の煙突はデザインの主軸であると同時に、構造の主軸も担っている。

この住宅には、近代建築への深い理解に加え、ガウディやフランク・ロイド・ライトの有機的な作品から得たエッセンス、土着的な住宅と工芸への愛情、そしてブラジルの自然が混ざり合い、リナのデザインに変化のきざしが表れている。ここではまだ「サンタ・マリア・ドス・アンジョス教会」(p. 104)のような「貧しい建築」のシンプルさは見られないが、この後、サルヴァドールでの民芸品との出合いを経て、よりヴァナキュラーかつシンプルなデザインへと向かう。

*1 リナは1957年にバルセロナを訪れている。
*2 Gabriella Cianciolo Cosentino, (2014) "Casa Cirell", in *Lina Bo Bardi 100*, p. 209.

主屋外観。 The exterior of the main building.

Seven years after constructing the "Glass House" (p. 012), this house was built adjacent to it as requested by her friend. While both houses possess their own distinct beauty, "Valéria P. Cirell's Home" displays a more advanced form of the fusion of nature and local traditions with modernism that characterizes Lina's works. A plethora of textures were added to the kind of minimal beauty seen in the "Glass House", giving the impression that Lina's design gradually went from European to something more adapted to Brazil. This house is called a "crystal garden house"[*1] due to the façade strewn with pebbles and fragments of pottery as well as the vegetation growing everywhere, including wall surfaces, the pool, and the rooftop garden, that suggests the influence of Antoni Gaudí[*2]. The main building is a geometrical cube, while the service space extends through a small courtyard where a surrounding terrace gently connects the interior and exterior. The handicraft elements such as the wood and brick construction along with the thatched roof negate the opposition of nature and artificiality as well as modernism and the vernacular. These various elements mingle and organically coexist. The living room connects by a spiral staircase to a mezzanine with a triangular planar shape, creating a wide-open space filled with natural light and an abundance of colors through the above skylight. The central chimney serves as both the pivot of the design and of the structure.

In addition to a deep understanding of modern architecture, this house embodies the fomenting transition of Lina's design through an essence gained from the organic works of Gaudí and Frank Lloyd Wright, her love for indigenous housing and handicraft, and her blending in of Brazilian nature. The simplicity of "poor architecture" as seen in "Santa Maria dos Anjos Chapel" (p. 104) is not yet visible here but, through her later encounter with folk craft in Salvador, she would head toward a design style that was more vernacular and simple.

*1 Gabriella Cianciolo Cosentino, (2014) "Casa Cirell", in *Lina Bo Bardi 100*, p. 209.
*2 Lina visited Barcelona in 1957.

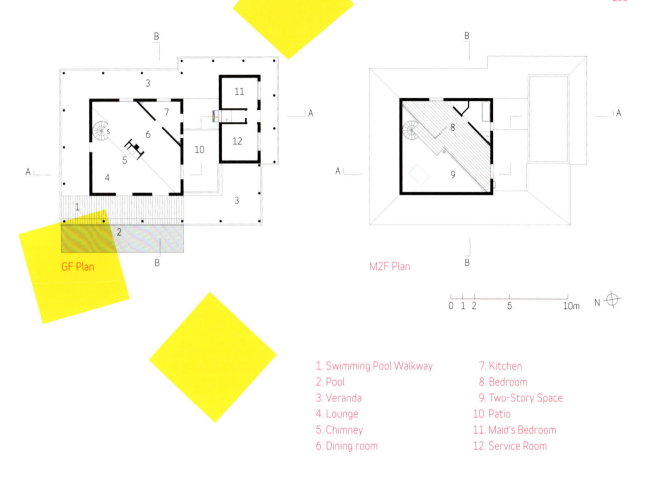

GF Plan

M2F Plan

1. Swimming Pool Walkway
2. Pool
3. Veranda
4. Lounge
5. Chimney
6. Dining room
7. Kitchen
8. Bedroom
9. Two-Story Space
10. Patio
11. Maid's Bedroom
12. Service Room

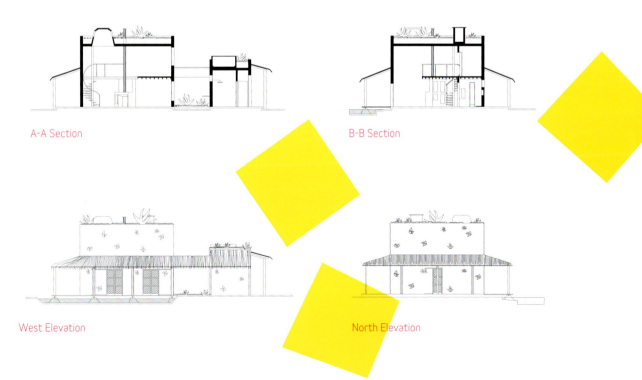

A-A Section

B-B Section

West Elevation

North Elevation

色彩豊かなリビングルーム。
棚が付属する暖炉は構造の軸でもある。
奥の螺旋階段はロフトへつながる。
The colorful living room.
The fireplace to which shelves are attached forms
the main axis of this structure.
A spiral staircase in the back connects to the loft.

彫刻が施された扉。
An engraved pillar.

傾斜のある広い敷地内には、階段や小道があちこちに走っている。
There are stairs and paths running here and there on a large inclined site.

後年増築された離れの屋上庭園。
The roof garden of the guesthouse addition built in later years.

離れの階段。陶器の破片で飾られる。
The guesthouse staircase. It is adorned with pieces of ceramic.

民衆文化伝承館
Solar do Unhão –
Popular Art Museum

Salvador, 1963

In a given country, creating a vast living museum, a Museum of Craftmanship and Industrial Art, that would illuminate the historical and popular roots of a nation's culture. This museum could be completed with a school of industrial art in order to foster contact between technicians, draughtsmen and makers.
Lina Bo Bardi, 1958

ある国に、壮大な生活のミュージアムをつくる。
その国の文化の歴史と大衆のルーツに光を当てるような、
熟練工と工芸のミュージアム。
これは、技術者・製図工・製造者の結び付きを強くするような
工芸学校を置くことで完成する。
リナ・ボ・バルディ、1958年

海側より見た施設全景。サルヴァドールの港町と古い波止場の遺構が見える。
A panoramic view of the facilities as seen from the sea side. Remnants of Salvador's port city and old wharf are visible.

リナは1958年に初めてバイーア州サルヴァドール市を訪れ、この地の人びとがつくる民芸品に魅了された。1年後にバイーア現代美術館（MAM-BA）の館長に任命され、劇場のロビーを借りた小さなスペースで数々の展覧会をキュレートした。4年後、MAM-BAはリナの設計で修復された16世紀の植民地時代の邸宅に移転し、再オープンした。これが工芸の研究施設や工房、インダストリアル・アートの学校を含んだ複合施設「民衆文化伝承館」である。この施設の目的は、芸術としての民芸品の展示だけでなく、工芸と現代の工業とをつなぐことにもあり、初回の展示は、リナのキュレーションでバイーアの民芸品をテーマとした「北東」展であった (p. 196)。

リナは、既存の美しい木構造や古い手動エレベーターを残し、内部の壁を取り払うと共に、古い石の階段に替えて地産木材による軽やかな螺旋階段を導入することで、開かれた明るい空間をつくり上げた。この階段には金具が一切使われておらず、日本の継手・仕口のように木部材を組み合わせて立ち上がっている。非常に幅の広い踏み面と蹴上げの低いこの巨大な螺旋階段は、建築家アルド・ファン・アイク[*1]が「この世で最も美しい階段のひとつだ」[*2]と語ったように、どっしりとした安心感と浮遊感とが同居して、階段そのものがひとつの建築のようだ。19世紀にブラジル初の工場として利用されていたこの建物で行われていた奴隷労働の事実が人びとの記憶から失われないよう、当時の台車の轍を地下のレストランの床にあえて残した。

リナは民芸品を「フォークロア」とノスタルジックに解釈することを嫌い、この施設を「民族」ではなく、今まさに現実と戦っている「民衆のミュージアム」と呼んだ[*3]。しかし、クーデターの勃発と軍による建物の占拠から、研究施設と学校の建設は実現することなくこの地を離れることになった。それでもリナは、民芸品の価値を世に広く伝えることに熱中し続けた。建物は、資金的な問題から民芸品ではなく現代美術の美術館として現存している。

*1 　オランダ人建築家。1918〜99年。1960年代からリナ作品を賞賛していた。
*2 　Video *Tarde da Noite depois de um Passeio - Vá pra Bahia*, Disse Lina, Thoelke Berkelbach (dir.), George Brugmans (ed.), 1996.
*3 　Lina Bo Bardi, (1963) "The Northeast", in *Stones against Diamonds*, p. 071

Lina visited Salvador, Bahia for the first time in 1958 and was struck by the handicrafts made by local people. One year later she was appointed the director of the Bahia Museum of Modern Art (MAM-BA), which was placed in a small space inside a theater lobby and where she curated a number of exhibitions. Four years later, the MAM-BA reopened in a residence from the colonial era in the 16th century that was restored according to Lina's designs. This became the "Solar do Unhão – Popular Art Museum" multipurpose facility including industrial art research facilities and a workshop as well as a school for industrial arts. The purpose of this facility was to display handicrafts as art in addition to connecting industrial art and modern industries. The first exhibition was the "Northeast (*Nordeste*)" exhibition curated by Lina on the theme of the handicrafts of Bahia. (p. 196)

Lina left the existing beautiful tree structure and old manual elevator, but she removed the interior walls and replaced the old stone staircase with a light spiral staircase made of locally produced timber to create a bright, open space. There were no metal fittings used in this staircase, which was put together by combining wooden materials similar to the coupling methods used in Japan. The very wide steps and low rise of this giant spiral staircase were said to be "really some of the most beautiful stairs in existence"[*1] by architect Aldo Van Eyck[*2]. There was a substantial sense of security together with a sense of levitation, making it appear as though the staircase itself were a piece of architecture. This building had been used as the first factory in Brazil in the 19th century, and had employed slave laborers. Lina purposely left a wagon wheel track from that period on the floor of the basement restaurant so that people would never forget this fact.

Lina disliked the nostalgic interpretation of handicrafts as being "folklore", which is why she called this a "Museum of Popular Art" struggling against reality instead of an "ethnic museum"[*3]. However, construction of the research facilities and school was never realized due to the outbreak of a coup d'état and occupation of the building by the army, leaving Lina no choice but to leave this place behind. Nevertheless, Lina continued to be enthusiastic about broadly communicating the value of handicrafts to the world. The building exists today but, due to funding issues, it is now a museum of modern art instead of industrial art.

[*1] Video *Tarde da Noite depois de um Passeio - Vá pra Bahia*, Disse Lina, Thoelke Berkelbach (dir.), George Brugmans (ed.), 1996.

[*2] A Dutch architect. 1918 – 99. He praised Lina's works since the 1960's.

[*3] Lina Bo Bardi, (1963) "The Northeast", in *Stones against Diamonds*, p. 071

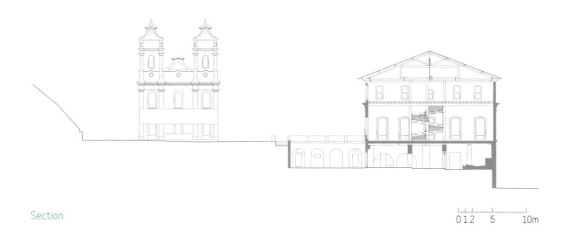

Section

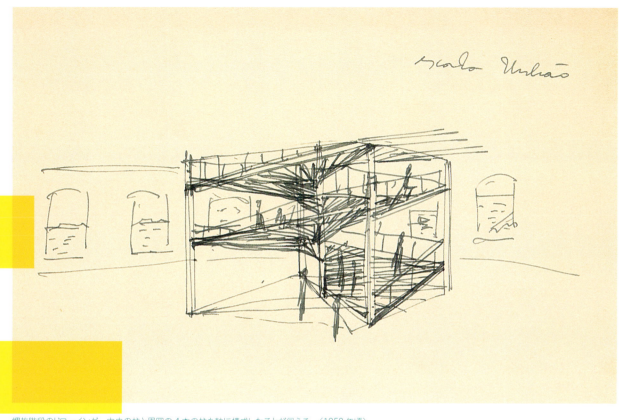

螺旋階段のドローイング。中央の柱と周囲の4本の柱を軸に構成したことが伺える。(1959年頃)
A drawing of the spiral staircase.
One can see that the central pillar and four surrounding pillars from the focal point of the structure. (*circa* 1959)

螺旋階段のディテール。
踏み板が中央の柱に寄り添う。踏み面の狭い中心部と広い周縁部では異なる体感が得られる。
Detail of the spiral staircase.
The steps come close to the central pillar. The narrow central part and the wide outer part of the step offer different sensations.

Solar do Unhão – Popular Art Museum

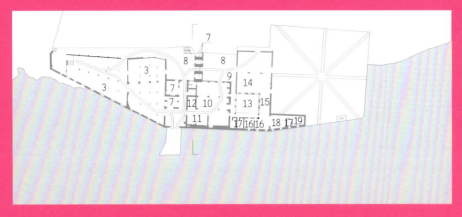

Plan of the Museum Entrance Level

1. Entrance Square
2. Before: Chapel, Now: Main Lecture Room
3. Workshops
4. Square
5. Footbridge
6. Main Exhibition Hall
7. Museum Store Rooms
8. Garden
9. Old Rail for Wagon
10. Restaurant
11. Kitchen
12. Kitchen Storage
13. Herb Garden
14. MAM-BA Archive
15. Administration
16. Secretarial Office
17. Bathrooms
18. Meeting Room
19. Managing Office

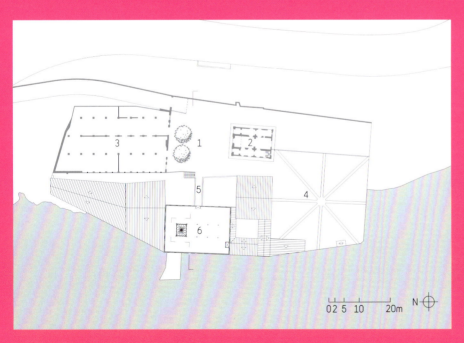

Plan of the Restaurant and Workshop Level

中庭に残る奴隷労働時代の台車の轍の遺構。
開いているドアはレストランへの入り口。
Remains of wagon wheel tracks in the courtyard left over from the era of slave labor.
The open door is the entrance to the restaurant.

レストラン入り口。
The restaurant entrance.

工房。
The workshop.

エスピリト・サント・ド・セラード教会
Espírito Santo do Cerrado Church

Minas Gerais, 1982

The most important thing during the construction of the Espírito Santo church was the possibility of a joint effort, between architect and labour.
Lina Bo Bardi, 1986

エスピリト・サント・ド・セラード教会の建設中におけるもっとも重要な課題は、
建築家と労働者とが共に努力することができるかどうか、ということでした。
リナ・ボ・バルディ、1986年

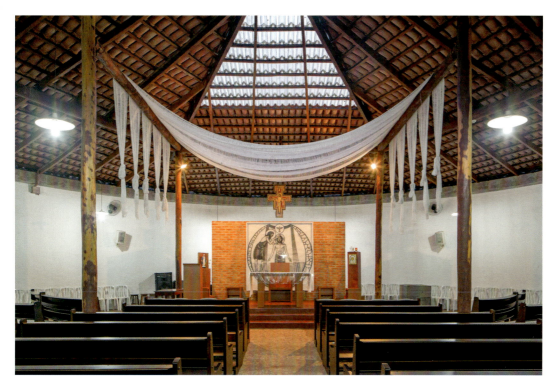

教会内部。祭壇上の三角形の天窓から光が入る。
The church interior. Light comes in from the triangular skylight above the flower bed.

　ブラジル南東部のミナスジェイラス州ウベルランディアの郊外に建つ、3人のシスターのための居住スペースとコミュニティの集会場をもつ教会である。予算の少ない中、リナは地域の材料の使用と地域住民の積極的な建設活動への参加によって、この複合建築を完成させた。段階的な建設とプライバシーの保持のため、建物を機能ごとに3つの円筒形に分け、それぞれに少しずつ異なるデザインを施しながら徐々に地面の高さを下げて配置した。一番高い位置にある教会は、円柱状の鐘楼と入口に立つ木製の十字架が特別な存在感を示している。瓦屋根は地域原産のアロニアの木製フレームに載せられており、祭壇上部ではガラスをはめて自然光を落とし、神聖な雰囲気を演出している。当初、鉄筋コンクリートの骨組みをれんがで埋めた壁には、カラーガラスの窓がランダムに設けられる予定だったが実現しなかった。中央の居住スペースは表通りから少しセットバックしており、前庭が各エリアへのアクセスの起点でもある。3人のシスターたちの部屋、居間、共有スペースがあり、キッチンは小さな噴水のある中庭を取り囲むように配置されている。個室の周囲に廊下を巡らせることで外部に面する窓を最小限に抑え、静かな内部空間をつくり出している。居室と共有スペースの床は材質を分け、木材とセメントが用いられている。一番低い位置にある小屋は、土間[*1]とし、屋根、柱、柵という極限までシンプルな構造にすることで、周囲の環境と調和した、外に開かれたホールである。垂木を支える中央の木のジョイントによって無柱空間を実現した。地域コミュニティからの要望で、小屋の隣には小さな東屋と屋外サッカー場がつくられた。3棟の屋根形状と壁の材質は、統一と変化を織り交ぜながら構成され、居住スペースから小屋へと高さを変えてつながる壁面や、鐘楼、コンクリートのテラスが、3つ並んだ円筒形のアクセントとなっている。静けさのなかにサーカス小屋のような賑やかさもあり、教会と住居、コミュニティスペースという機能と、周辺環境の雰囲気を、リナはそのまま建築として立ち上がらせている。

[*1]　現在はセメントに変更されている。

Espírito Santo do Cerrado Church

A church, including living quarters for three nuns and an assembly room, built in a suburb of Uberlândia, a municipality in the state of Minas Gerais, Southeastern Brazil. The design was requested by friars of the Franciscan Order that shared Lina's stance on social contribution. With a low budget, this multi-purpose complex was completed by using locally sourced materials and actively involving local residents in its construction. Because the construction was performed in phases and for the preservation of privacy, the building was divided into three cylindrical units according to each function, different designs were applied to each phase and the height of the ground was lowered at each step. The church occupies the first and highest position and features a cylindrical bell tower as well as a wooden cross standing at the entrance, lending it a special presence. The tile roof rests on a wooden frame of indigenous aronia, while natural light falls from a skylight above the altar, creating a sacred atmosphere. Originally, colored glass windows were to be placed randomly within the reinforced concrete framework walls filled with bricks, but this was never implemented. The residential space in the middle is slightly recessed from the main street, while the front court acts as the starting point of access to each one of its areas. These include the three nun's rooms, a living room, a common space, as well as a kitchen surrounding an inner court with a small fountain. Surrounding the private rooms with a corridor minimizes the number of windows facing the outside and creates a quiet interior space. In order to differentiate the construction materials, wood was used in the floor of the living room while cement was used in that of the common space. The tail hut at the lowest position is a foyer open to the outside in harmony with its surrounding environment with an ultra simple structure consisting of a floor made of dirt[*1], a roof, pillars and a palisade. A column-free space was obtained by supporting the rafters with a wooden joint at the center. Furthermore, a small pavilion and an outdoor soccer field were added next to the hut at the request of the local community. While the roof shapes and the materials used in the walls of the complex alternate between unity and change, the gradual change in the height of the wall connecting the living quarters to the hut, the bell tower and the concrete terrace all contribute to accentuate the design consisting of three aligned cylindrical shapes. Lina took the functions of a church, a residence and a community space as well as the atmosphere of the surrounding environment and built it into a structure that has the liveliness of a circus tent standing in stillness.

*1 Currently cement.

ホール内部。
The foyer interior.

全体外観。
右から教会、住居、ホール、サッカー場。
The overall appearance.
From the right are the church, residential building, foyer, and soccer field.

1. Entrance
2. Nave
3. Altar
4. Bell Tower
5. Meeting Room
6. Patio and Cloister
7. Nun's Bedrooms
8. Kitchen
9. Parlor
10. Water Tank Tower
11. Foyer
12. Soccer Field

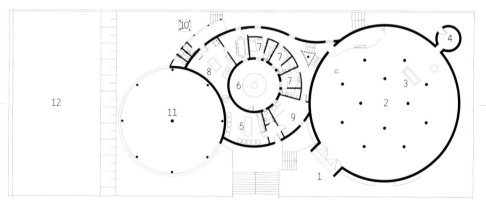

Plan

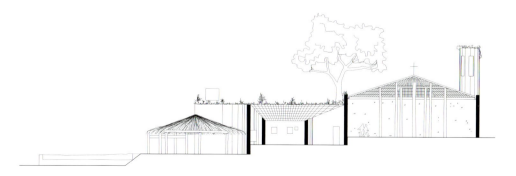

Section

Espírito Santo do Cerrado Church

教会入り口、内部から。
扉の前には木製の十字架が立つ。
The church entrance as seen from the interior.
A wooden cross stands in front of the pillar.

住居中庭の噴水。
The courtyard fountain of the residential building.

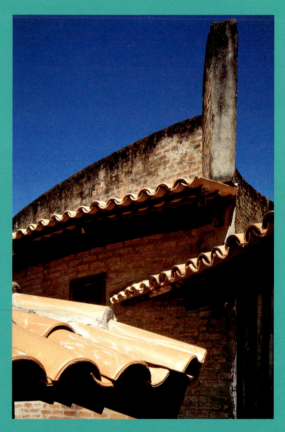

住居とホールの接続部。
住居棟から出る庇、集会場の屋根、小さな東屋の屋根が、壁の曲面に添うように架けられている。
The connecting section between the residential building and foyer. The eaves of the residential building, roof of the meeting room and small gazebo roof are suspended along the curved surface of the walls.

西面の壁。奥に見えるのは教会の鐘楼。
The western surface of the wall.
The church's bell tower is visible in the back.

サンパウロ・シティ・ホール
São Paulo City Hall

São Paulo, 1992

It is necessary to consider the past as the historical present, still living, a present that help us to avoid the various pitfalls.
Lina Bo Bardi, 1989

過去は歴史でありながら、現在も生きているものです。
私たちがあらゆる危険に陥らないように助けてくれる現在として、
過去を捉えることが必要なのです。
リナ・ボ・バルディ、1989年

pp. 172-173
計画案のドローイング。新築部分のガラスファサードと熱帯植物のファサードが描かれている。(1990年)
A preliminary drawing. The newly-built glass façade and the tropical plant façade are depicted. (1990)

地下のオフィス空間。The underground office space.

20世紀初頭の邸宅を新たなシティ・ホールに改修した、リナの最後のプロジェクトである。過去は生き続け、今の生活に続いているという考えを示した「歴史的現在」はリナのリノベーションにおけるキーワードである。古い建物をただ保存するのではなく、価値ある建物のもつ尊厳を人びとの生活と共に守ろうとした。荒廃したかつての都市の中心部を復興するため、建物が建つドン・ペドロ2世公園も含めた修復計画が立てられた。邸宅部分の広い地下には、レストランやビアガーデン、子どもの遊び場、オフィスなどのさまざまな機能が入っている。オフィスはテラコッタの柔らかい色調で統一されているのに対し、2階の「青のホール」は青一色で塗られ、神聖な美しい雰囲気がつくり上げられている。

邸宅だけでは要求された機能のすべてを収容できないため、リナは邸宅に加えて、広場の機能をもつ建物を通り沿いに新築しようと考えた。新築部分は通りに沿ってカーブし、それぞれエレベーター、階段、洗面所が収められた3つのボリュームによって地面から5メートルもち上げられ、吹き抜けを設けた開放的なプランが採用された。ホールとテラスをもつこの建物は、通り側に都市に開いたガラスファサード、旧邸宅側に熱帯植物によるファサード(p. 216)が計画され、旧邸宅と新築部分の間のパブリックスペースには、滝のように水が流れる貯水塔も計画されていた。リナはこの広場を「子どもたちのための広場」、「大衆が参加する」場所などと呼び、古代ギリシャの中庭に設けられたエクセドラに例えて人びとが集い、議論する空間として構想した[1]。

残念ながら、1992年のリナの死により計画は中断し、新築部分と広場は実現しないままに終わった。邸宅の修復には変更がありながらも、「シティ・ホール」として完成に至った。しかしうまく運用されず、2004年にシティ・ホールの機能は別の建物に移転し、2009年からは州立の科学センターとして使われている。このプロジェクトには、既存部分の活用、ピロティ、開かれたプラン、ガラスや植物のファサード、滝、貯水塔、色調の統一など、リナがこれまで用いたさまざまな手法が見受けられる。大都市サンパウロの行政の中心を、いかに豊かで開かれた場にしようとしていたのか。そのビジョンにはリナの熱意が表れ、現代にも通じるヒントが散りばめられている。

[1]　Zeuler R. M. de A. Lima, (2013) *Lina Bo Bardi*, New Heaven and London, Yale University Press, p. 207

São Paulo City Hall

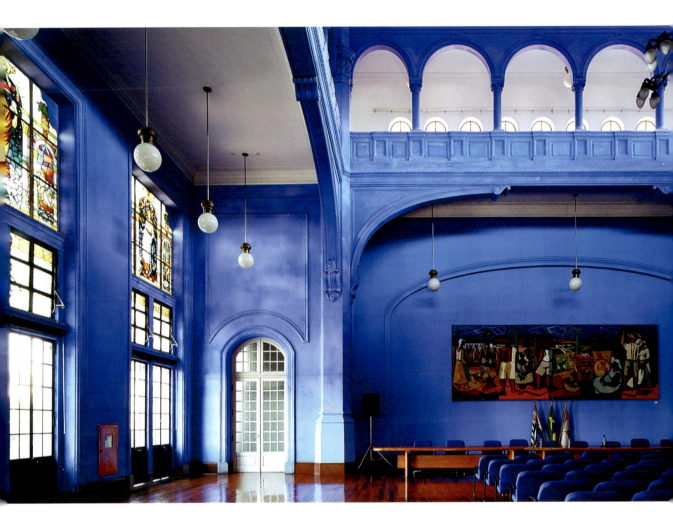

青のホール。椅子も青で統一することで、ステンドグラスやシャンデリアを強調している。(2002年)
The blue hall. The unified chairs in blue enhance the stained glass and chandelier. (2002)

The renovation of a residence from the beginning of the 20th century into a new city hall was the final project undertaken by Lina. The keyword for Lina's renovation was "historical present", which demonstrated the idea that the past continues to live on in people's present lives. Not only preserving historical buildings, but protecting the dignity of valuable buildings along with the lives of people. The purpose of this restoration project was to revitalize the run down former city center, and it included the Dom Pedro II Park on which the building stood. She planned various functions for the open basement area of the residence such as a restaurant, beer garden, children's playground, and office. In contrast with the terra cotta's unified soft color tone in the office, the "Blue Hall" on the 1st floor was painted all in blue to create a sacred, beautiful atmosphere.

Since the building was small in relation to its essential function, Lina planned to newly construct a building that would possess the function of an open plaza in addition to the restored house. Curving along the street, the newly built part would be elevated 5 meters from the ground through 3 volumes, each containing an elevator, staircase, and washroom. An open plan with an atrium was adopted. For this building with its hall and terrace, Lina planned a glass façade opening out onto the city on the street side as well as a tropical plant façade (p. 216) on the former residence side. She also planned for a water tower with running water that would resemble a waterfall in the public space between the former residence and newly-built part. Lina called this area "a plaza for children" and a place for "the participation of popular life". She compared it to the "exedra" found in the courtyards of ancient Greece as a space where people could gather and hold discussions.[*1]

Unfortunately, the project came to a halt due to Lina's death in 1992 so the newly-built part and plaza were never realized. Despite changes made during the restoration of the residence, it came to completion as "São Paulo City Hall". But due to mishandling, functions pertaining to municipal matters were relocated to another building in 2004, and the restored residence has been used as a state-run science center since 2009 This project features the full range of techniques used by Lina, such as taking advantage of existing parts, pilotis, an open plan, a façade of glass and vegetation, a waterfall, a water tower, unified color tones, and so on. Her attempt was to create a rich, open space to become the administrative center of the São Paulo metropolis. Lina's vision makes evident her sense of enthusiasm and offers hints that are pertinent for the modern era.

*1   Zeuler R. M. de A. Lima, (2013) *Lina Bo Bardi*, New Heaven and London, Yale University Press, p. 207.

São Paulo City Hall

南東部から見た全景。
道路のカーブに合わせて新築部分が計画されていた。
A panorama seen from the southeastern section.
The newly-built part was planned to align with the curve of the road.

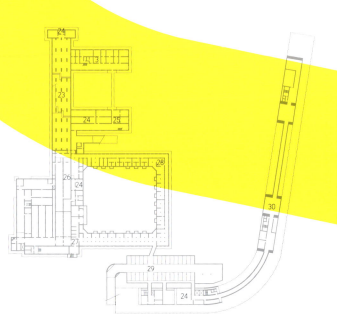

B1F Plan

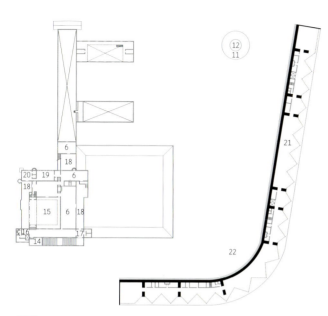

1F Plan

1. Foyer and Exhibition Rooms
2. Auditorium
3. Children's Play Area
4. Loggia
5. Garden
6. Staff Rooms
7. Main Hall
8. Veranda
9. Vice Mayor's Office
10. Hall
11. Reflecting Pool
12. Water Tower
13. Bonfire
14. Great Staircase
15. Blue Room
16. Gallery
17. Watchtower
18. Terrace
19. Mayor's Office
20. Mayor's Apartments
21. Offices
22. Vertical Garden
23. Restaurant and Beer Garden
24. Machinery
25. Changing Rooms
26. Kitchen
27. Mayor's Quarters
28. Staff Room
29. Garage
30. Support Areas

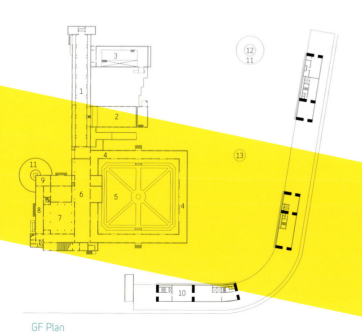

GF Plan

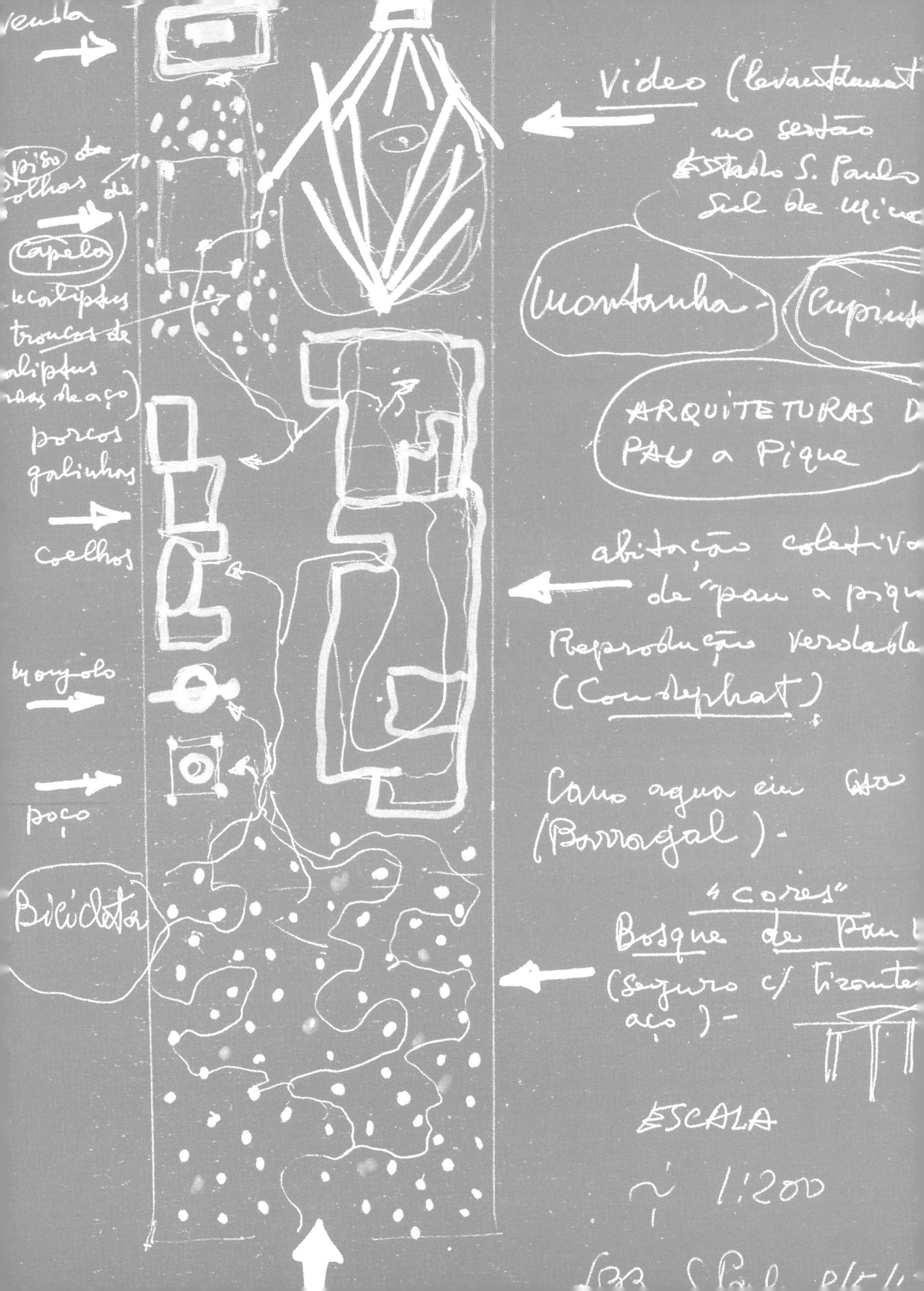

venta →

← Bico de olhos de
(Capela)
"eucaliptos troncos de eliptus nas de aço"
porcos
galinhas
→ Coelhos

→ monjolo

→ poço

Bicicleta

Vídeo (levantamento
no sertão
Estado S. Paulo
Sul de Minas ←

Montanha — Cupins

ARQUITETURAS D
PAU a Pique

← abitação coletiva
de pau a pique
Reprodução verosable
(Condephat).

Cano agua em ωσα
(Barragal).

"cores"
Bosque de Pau
← (seguro c/ horizonte
aço).

ESCALA
~ 1:200

建築周辺のデザイン
Around the Architecture

Around the Architecture

ゆりかごや収納付き2段ベッド、照明などが描かれた、雑誌掲載用の子ども部屋のドローイング。
A drawing of a children's room to be featured in a magazine that depicts a cradle, a bunk bed with storage space, lighting, and so on.

Furniture Design
家具デザイン

Furniture also has its morality and its reason for being in its own times.
Lina Bo Bardi

家具はそれ自身に、その時代に存在することへの道義と理由をもっています。
リナ・ボ・バルディ

椅子とリビングルームのドローイング。(1941年)
A drawing of a chair and living room. (1941)

鏡台のドローイング。
A drawing of a dressing table.

ブラジル初のモダン家具

リナのキャリアはインテリア・デザインの仕事からはじまった。ミラノ時代に「イタリアモダンデザインの父」ジオ・ポンティのもとで家具デザインの仕事に携わったことが、その後の基礎になったといえる。その経験を生かし、ブラジルに移住後の1949年にイタリア人建築家ジャンカルロ・パランティ[*1]と共にデザイン会社「スタジオ・ダルテ・パルマ(Studio d'Arte Palma / Oficina Paubra)」を設立し、インテリア・デザインや家具、ショーウィンドウのデザインをはじめた。主な目的はブラジル初の国産モダン家具の生産で、合板と地域原産の材料を用い、シンプルな構造で素材の魅力を引き出した家具を発表した。パランティとの活動は2年弱で終了するが、独立後もリナは継続して家具を制作した。

*1 1906-77年。ミラノ生まれの建築家。1946年にブラジルに移住して活動した。

The First Modern Furniture in Brazil

Lina's career began from interior design work. Her involvement in furniture design work during the Milan period under Gio Ponti, the father of Italian modern design, is thought to have laid the foundation for what came later. In 1949, together with the Italian architect Giancarlo Palanti[*1], Lina established a design company called «Studio d'Arte Palma / Oficina Paubra». Building on her previous experience, she then began working on interior, furniture and display design. Lina's venture with Palanti was the first company in Brazil to begin making domestically-produced modern furniture. It aimed to bring out the charm of materials through simple structures that used plywood and locally-produced materials. They worked together for just under two years, but Lina continued to produce furniture after becoming independent.

*1 1906 – 77. An architect born in Milan. Active in Brazil after immigrating there in 1946.

「スタジオ・ダルテ・パルマ」内部。(1948年)
Interior of "Studio d'Arte Palma". (1948)

Around the Architecture Furniture Design

人体寸法、アートと工業

初期のデザインはイタリアモダンの影響から、はっきりとした色彩や新しい素材を用いた、シンプルかつ洗練されたデザインが特徴的であった。木材や金属の構造体に布や革やひもなどのさまざまな素材が組み合わされたものが多く、それらは今も「ガラスの家」（P. 012）に置かれている。初期のデザインを代表する最も有名な作品は、1951年に制作された「ボウル・チェア」である。4本の金属製の脚部に、革や布でできたボウル状のシートを載せたシンプルな構造で、深い座面がゆったりとしたくつろぎをもたらす。球形で背もたれがないシートへは、どの方向からも座ることができる。脚部とシートは取り外しが可能で、シートのみを重ねて収納することもできる。シートは色や素材を変えて、さまざまなバリエーションで製作された。

　1957年にイタリアの街カントゥで開かれた家具コンペティションでは、人間の身体の動きや位置に適応する、ブーメラン形の合板ユニットによる構造システムを提案した。合板を用いる理由に「経済性、強度、加工による形の多様性、シンプルな構造システム」[*2]を挙げたように、リナのデザインは見た目の美しさのみに溺れることなく、あくまで機能性を担保している。イタリア時代にジャーナリストとして手がけたインテリアに関する記事やイラストからは、意匠、構造、材料、環境性能、そして生産体制や経済性にまでわたる広い視野が伺える。機械による大量生産の時代、ひとつの家具からいかに多様なバリエーションを生むか、アーティスティックな表現をいかに機械生産と結び付けるかが、リナの命題であった。アートと工業の境目がなかった頃の、職人による手工業的生産形態が消えてしまった時代に、デザインと生活とを結び付ける場所として、リナは住宅を挙げた[*3]。人間にとって生活の根元となる住宅のインテリアから、インダストリアル・デザインのあるべき姿を探ろうとしていた。

*2　Lina Bo Bardi, (1958) "Furniture Competition", in *Lina Bo Bardi*, p.096.

*3　Lina Bo Bardi, (1944) "The Design of Interior", in *Stones against Diamonds*, p.027.

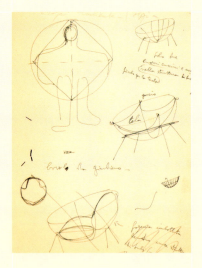

「ボウル・チェア」のスタディ・スケッチ。人体の形に適応するように、座面の角度の調整や、クッションの位置を考えている。
A study sketch of the "Bowl Chair". Thought was given to adjusting the seat of the chair and the position of the cushion to have it adapt to the shape of a human body.

「ボウル・チェア」のディテールと色のスタディ。ボウルの縁の形、金属の台座との組み合わせ方に加え、ボウルを重ねた時の色合いまで考慮している。
A study on the details and color of the "Bowl Chair". Lina carefully considered everything from the shape of the bowl's edge and its combination with the metal pedestal to the tint when the bowl was placed on it.

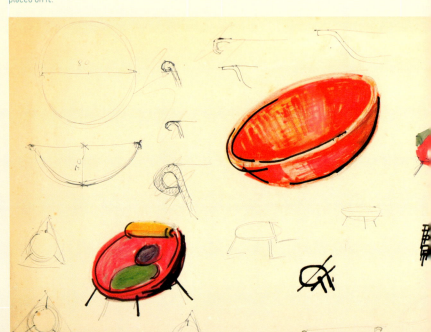

Human Scale, Art and Industry

Influenced by Italian modern design, Lina's early designs were characterized by a simple and refined design using clear colors and new materials. Many of her designs combined various materials such as cloth, leather and string inside structures of wood and metal. These can still be found today inside the "Glass House"(p. 012). The work most famous for being representative of her early designs is the "Bowl Chair" produced in 1951. A sheet made of leather or cloth takes on a bowl shape when placed on the simple construction with its four metal legs, and the deep chair seat brings about a feeling of comfort and relaxation. The sheet can be sat on from any direction because of the chair's spherical shape and lack of a backrest. The legs and sheet are removable, and the chairs can be stored by stacking only the sheets. Many variations of the sheets were produced by altering the colors and materials.

Lina proposed a structural system using boomerang-shaped plywood units that would adapt to the movement and position of the human body at a furniture competition held in the Italian town of Cantù in 1957. In the same way she gave "economy, strength, the large variety of forms obtainable and a simple, clear construction system"[*2] as reasons for using plywood, Lina's designs focused not only on indulging in visual beauty but, more importantly, on assuring functionality. At the beginning of her career in Italy, Lina worked as a journalist on a great number of articles and illustrations concerning interior design. We can infer from the content her broad outlook on design, structure, materials, environmental performance, and system of production as well as economy. In an age of mechanical mass production, the challenge for Lina was to see how many diverse variations she could create from one piece of furniture and how she could combine machine production with her own artistic expression. In an era where handicraft industry production through artisans who know no boundaries between art and manufacturing has all but vanished, Lina identified home as a new place to combine design and daily life[*3]. She was searching for an ideal form of industrial design through the interior design of houses, which serves as a foundation for peoples' daily lives.

革シートの「ボウル・チェア」。
A leather seat "Bowl Chair".

[*2] Lina Bo Bardi, (1958) "Furniture Competition", in *Lina Bo Bardi*, p. 096.

[*3] Lina Bo Bardi, (1944) "The Design of Interior", in *Stones against Diamonds*, p. 027.

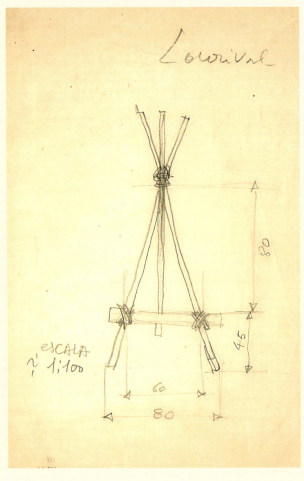

「道ばたの椅子」のドローイング。（1967年頃）
A drawing of the "Roadside Chair". (*circa* 1967)

道ばたの椅子

その後、サルヴァドールでの民芸品との出合いを経て、1967年に「道ばたの椅子」を制作する。4本の木の棒を植物のつるで結び付けただけで、リナが民芸品から受けた影響——デザインの純粋さ、シンプルさ、楽しさ、おおらかさ——を端的に示している。「道ばたの椅子」以後、リナが自らの建築作品と共に発表した椅子の多くは、木材のみから成る、無駄のないシンプルさと合理性が際立っていった。そして1枚の板のように折り畳める「エジディオ神父の椅子」*4などが誕生したのである。

*4 「エスピリト・サント・ド・セラード教会」（p. 164）を依頼したひとりの神父の名にちなんでいる。

（左）「道ばたの椅子」。その名の通り、リナが道で見付けた木の棒を組み合わせて作られた。オリジナルは「ガラスの家」にある。
(far left) "Roadside Chair". As the name suggests, Lina made it by combining sticks she found on the road. The original is inside the "Glass House".

（右）「道ばたの椅子」とリナ。ひざを掛けている部分が座面。（1967年）
(left) Lina and the "Roadside Chair". The seat is the part where the legs are dangling. (1967)

Roadside Chair

Later, she produced the "Roadside Chair" in 1967 after encountering Salvador's handicrafts. By simply binding four wooden poles with vines, Lina directly demonstrated the influence she received from handicrafts - purity of design, simplicity, fun, and serenity. Following the "Roadside Chair", most of the chairs that Lina presented together with her architectural works were only made of wood, and they were conspicuous for their simplicity without waste and their rationality. And thus was born the "Frei Egydio Chair"*4 that folds like a single plank.

*4 The name of the priests who commissioned Espírito Santo do Cerrado Church (p. 164)

1.「小さなキリンの椅子」。(木材：南洋杉、1987 年)
"Little Giraffe Chair". (Wood: Araucaria, 1987)

2.「エジディオ神父の椅子」。(木材：南洋杉、カルナウバロウ、1986 年)
"Frei Egydio Chair". (Wood: Araucaria, finishing with carnaúba wax, 1986)

3.「旧サンパウロ美術館講堂の椅子」。
(木材：パウリスタ・ローズウッド、革 1947 年)
"Chair for the MASP 7 de Abril auditorium".
(Wood: rosewood paulista, and leather, 1947)

4.「3 つ足の椅子」。(木材：カブレウーヴァ、革、1948 年)
"Tripod Chair". (Wood: Cabreúva and leather, 1948)

5.「自然布のソファ」。(鉄管、布、1951 年)
"Raw Fabric Sofa". (Iron tube structure and fabric, 1951)

6.「真鍮球の椅子」。(鉄管、真鍮、革、1950 年)
"Brass Ball Chair". (Tubular structure of iron, polished brass and leather, 1950)

1

2

3

4

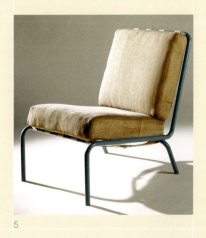

5

6

「SESC」図書室。すぐ隣に位置するラウンジの柔らかなソファと異なり、固い木の椅子が並ぶ。
The "SESC" library. Unlike the soft sofas in the multi-use space nextdoor, it is lined with hard wooden chairs.

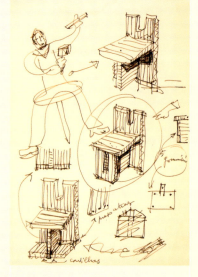

「SESC」図書室の椅子のドローイング。
厚い木の板を4枚組み合わせている。
A drawing of the chair in the "SESC" library.
It combines four thick wooden boards.

建築をつくる椅子たち

リナにとって建築とは、建物そのものだけでなく付随する体験すべてであり、多くの建築作品にはオリジナルの椅子を設計した。「ガラスの家」に現在も置かれている多様な家具をはじめ、「SESCポンペイア文化センター」（p. 068）のラウンジのソファと図書館の椅子、「サンタ・マリア・ドス・アンジョス教会」（p. 104）の幾何学的な木の椅子などがある。「サンパウロ美術館（MASP）」（p. 036）や「SESC」などの劇場の椅子では「観客と距離を取りながらも演劇に巻き込む」という古い劇場のスタイルを意図し、観客を立ち上がらせて演劇に参加させるため、あえて固い木の椅子をデザインした[*5]。サルヴァドールの「ベナンの家」（p. 124）の中庭の小屋にある「キリンの椅子」は、日本建築の継手や仕口のように、金具を用いずに組み立てられている。素材と形態は空間に応じて選択され、現在もオリジナルのまま、各建築を支えている。

*5 Lina Bo Bardi, (1986) "The Architectural Project", in *Stones against Diamonds*, p. 099.

Chairs as Architecture

For Lina, architecture was not only about the building itself but about all the experiences related to it. Beginning with the chairs in the "Glass House", she designed original chairs for most of her architectural works, which can be found in their original settings even today. For example, the lounge sofa and library chairs for "SESC Pompéia Factory Leisure Center"(p. 068), and the geometrical wooden chairs for "Santa Maria dos Anjos Chapel" (p. 104). As evidenced in the "São Paulo Museum of Art"(p. 036) and "SESC" theaters, Lina aimed for an old theater style that is "distancing and involving" the audience, so she designed purposely hard wooden chairs to force people to stand up and participate in plays[*5]., The "Giraffe Chair", found inside a hut in Salvador's "House of Benin" courtyard, is assembled without any metal fixtures in a similar way to the coupling methods of Japanese architecture. The materials and shapes of these original chairs were carefully selected according to each space in order to support the architectural work they inhabit to this day.

[*5] Lina Bo Bardi, (1986) "The Architectural Project", in *Stones against Diamonds*, p. 099.

「SESC」ラウンジのソファ。座面は広くゆったりとした座り心地で、くつろぎを提供する。
The sofas in the "SESC" multi-use space. The seats are wide and comfortable to sit on, providing ample relaxation.

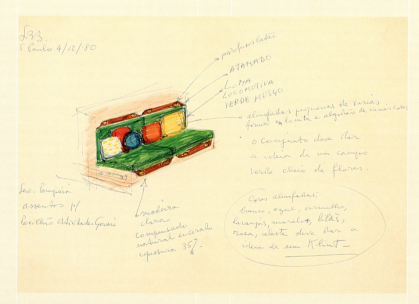

「SESC」ラウンジのソファのドローイング。
A drawing of the sofa in the "SESC" multi-use space.

Around the Architecture

「MASP」のオープンスペース、「ベルヴェデーレ」を描いたドローイング。
A drawing depicting the open space at "MASP", "Belvedere".

Curation
キュレーションと会場デザイン

The city is a public space, a great exhibition space, a museum, an open book offering all kinds of subtle readings.
Lina Bo Bardi, 1951

街というのは公共の場であり、素晴らしい展覧会場や、ミュージアムとなり、開かれた本のように多くの情報をもちます。
リナ・ボ・バルディ、1951年

独特の思想と手法

リナのキュレーターとしての仕事は、彼女の教育的・社会的価値観と行動力、そしてバイーア州をはじめとしたブラジルの北東文化への愛情をよく表している。同時に、その表現手段として用いた展示方法は革新的だった。

イタリア時代からはじまるリナの展示デザインは、イタリア未来派[*1]の手法を前提に、独特の世界を展開した。初めて展示デザインを手掛けた、1946年夏のミラノの家具市におけるロードイド[*2]製品のブースデザインでは、すでにその後の特徴となるさまざまな手法が見受けられる。リナのキュレーションのキャリアに大きく影響した経験としては以下の4つが挙げられる。夫が館長となった旧サンパウロ美術館での展覧会、バイーア現代美術館および「民衆文化伝承館」(p. 156)の館長としての経験、自ら設計した新たな「サンパウロ美術館(MASP)」(p. 036)、そして「SESCポンペイア文化センター」(p. 068)での子どもたちに向けた展覧会である。初期にすでに高いレベルに達した展示手法を徐々に発展させながら、展示内容やその思想を展開させていった。

*1 20世紀初頭にイタリアで起こった前衛芸術運動の総称。

*2 20世紀初頭に生まれた不燃で熱可塑性をもつ合成樹脂。

Unique Thoughts and Ways

Lina's work as a curator revealed her pedagogical / social sense of values and dynamism as well as her love for the culture of northeastern Brazil in places such as Bahia. At the same time, her exhibition method as a means of expression was innovative.
Lina's exhibition design beginning from the Italian period was inherited from the techniques of Italian futurism[*1] and helped develop her unique perspective. Her first exhibition design work on the booth design for Rhodoid products[*2] at the Milan furniture exhibition in the summer of 1946 already showed a number of techniques that would later become characteristic of her. There were four experiences which heavily influenced her curation career, namely her exhibition at the former São Paulo Museum of Art when her husband was director, her experience as director of the "Solar do Unhão – Popular Art Museum" (p. 156), her own newly-designed "São Paulo Museum of Art (MASP)" (p. 036), and her exhibitions aimed at children at the "SESC Pompéia Factory Leisure Center"(p. 068). Lina developed her exhibition content and ideas while gradually developing her exhibition techniques, which had reached a high level in the early stages.

*1 Generally designates an avant-garde artistic movement that originated in Italy in the early 20th century.

*2 An incombustible and thermoplastic synthetic resin created at the beginning of the 20th century.

ミラノ家具市のロードイド製品の展示ブース。(1946年)
An exhibition booth for Rhodoid products at the Milan Furniture Salon. (1946)

旧サンパウロ美術館での展示の様子。金属柱を用いて絵画とパネルを固定している。「壁から離す」展示法の最初期。
A scene from the exhibition at the former São Paulo Museum of Art. Paintings and panels were fixed in place by using metal columns. This was the initial phase of the exhibition method to "free art from walls".

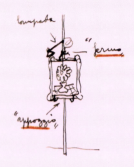

旧サンパウロ美術館にて、作品を固定する金属柱のスタディ。(1947年)
A study of the metal columns used to fix works in place at the former São Paulo Museum of Art. (1947)

展示パネルのドローイング。木製で、支柱の穴により水平部材の高さが調節できる。(1959年)
A drawing of a display panel. They were made of wood, and holes in the supporting column allowed for adjustment of the height of the connecting beams. (1959)

p.193
「MASP」ガラスイーゼルの並ぶメインギャラリー。(1970年)
The main gallery of "MASP" lined with glass easels. (1970)

作品を壁から解放する

リナの展示方法の特徴として、作品を壁から解放すること、作品同士にヒエラルキーをもたせないことが挙げられる。それは誰もが先入観なく芸術に触れてほしいという願いからであり、「MASP」のガラスのイーゼルをはじめ、さまざまなオリジナルの展示装置を考案することで実現した。旧サンパウロ美術館では主に西欧美術の普及を目的とした展覧会が開催された。ビルの数フロアという限られた展示空間で、ひと月に5回という膨大な数の展示を企画するために、さまざまな展示法が生み出された。そのひとつが、空間を最大限に利用するため、アルミ柱を天井と床で固定して、どこにでも配置することのできるパーテーション・システムである。絵画を架けるほか、ガラス板で挟んだ展示パネルを取り付け、表裏の2面を使うこともできる。のちに棒の太さを変えたり、木製にするなど、さまざまなバリエーションが生まれた。また、移動可能なパネルや、天井や床への固定が不要な、物干し竿のような装置も導入することで、さらなる柔軟性を獲得した。この装置は廃材を使用した木組みに発展し、展示空間全体に広がる迷路のような空間をつくるに至った。ガラスのディスプレイ・ケースはコンクリートの基礎や木製テーブルの上に置かれ、彫刻などの立体作品の展示に用いられた。空間的な制約に縛られず、ひとつのケースの中にさまざまな形態の作品を織り交ぜながら、高さに変化を付けて賑やかに展示した。その後、リナが設計した「MASP」で登場したガラスのイーゼルは、リナのキュレーターとして、建築家としての最高の展示装置といえるだろう。年代も作者も異なるいくつもの絵画がヒエラルキーなく同時に眺められる空間を、鑑賞者は自由に歩くことができる。新鮮な空間体験に加え、芸術と人びととの新たな関係を生み出した。

Freeing Artwork from Walls

We could say that Lina's exhibition methods were characterized by liberating artworks from walls and making no hierarchy between the works. Lina hoped that everybody would interact with her artwork without any preconceptions, and she achieved this by devising the glass easels at "MASP", and a variety of display equipment. During the former São Paulo Museum of Art, exhibitions whose main purpose was to spread Western art were held. Within the building's few floors of limited exhibition space, Lina created various exhibition methods enabling an extensive number of projects, as much as five per month. One example being a partition system devised to make the most use of the space that could be placed anywhere and fixed in place by the floor and ceiling with aluminum pillars. In addition to hanging paintings, exhibition panels inserted within glass plates were installed, which also allowed both the front and rear sides to be used. Later on, the width of the poles was adjusted or they were switched to wooden poles to create many different variations. Furthermore, Lina was able to acquire greater flexibility by introducing equipment such as mobile panels and poles which did not require a ceiling or floor to be fixed in place. This apparatus developed into a wooden framework that used scrap wood and ended up creating a maze-like space that extended throughout the entire exhibition space. The glass display cases were placed on top of concrete base blocks and wooden tables, and they were used for exhibitions of three-dimensional works such

「MASP」の「ベルヴェデーレ」で行われた「ポルチナーリ100の傑作」展。絵画の掛けられたノードとなる柱同士をコーヒーの木でつないだインスタレーション。(1970年)
The "100 Masterpieces of Portinari" exhibition held at the "Belvedere" of "MASP". This installation connected by coffee trees saw paintings hanging from columns acting as nodes. (1970)

「MASP」の地下ホールのドローイング。ガラスケースに立体作品が動的に展示されている。(1968年)
A drawing of the basement hall at "MASP". The three-dimensional works are displayed dynamically inside glass cases. (1968)

「MASP」での「モダニストの時代」展。ガラスケースと金属柱を用いた彫刻の展示。(1974年)
The "Modernist Era" exhibition at "MASP". A sculpture exhibition using glass cases and metal columns. (1974)

旧サンパウロ美術館にて「アピタ」を含む美術館発行の出版物を展示したショーケース。(1947年)
A showcase displaying publications produced by the museum that include "Habitat" at the former São Paulo Museum of Art. (1947)

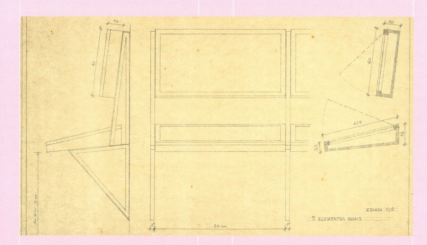

ショーケースの図面。
A layout of the showcase.

as sculptures. Unbound by spatial restrictions, Lina made exhibitions lively by changing the height of works while interweaving various forms of works inside a single case. Later, the glass easels which appeared at "MASP" designed by Lina became one of her greatest display apparatus as both a curator and architect. Visitors could freely walk around the space while simultaneously admiring several paintings from various eras and artists in a non-hierarchical way. In addition to lively space experiences, she created a new relationship between art and people.

Displaying Works Like in a Marketplace

After her fateful encounter with the folk crafts of Salvador, Lina held nearly 100 exhibitions and events over four years at the "Museum of Modern Art of Bahia" (MAMBA) where she worked as director. At the opening of the new "Northeast" exhibition (1963) in MAMBA's "Solar do Unhão – Popular Art Museum", Lina sent a strong message that "this exhibition is an accusation"[*3], and she introduced folk crafts that

[*3]   Lina Bo Bardi, (1963) "Northeast", in *Stones against Diamonds*, p. 072.

Around the Architecture Curation

市場のように展示する

サルヴァドールでの民芸品との運命的な出合いののち、自ら館長を務めた「バイーア現代美術館(MAM-BA)」では4年間で100に近い展覧会やイベントを開催した。MAM-BAの「民衆文化伝承館」としての新たなオープニングとなる「北東」展(1963年)では、「この展覧会は告発である」[*3]という力強いメッセージと共に、それまで目を向けられていなかった普通の人びとの生活から生まれた民芸品を紹介した。彫刻、人形、陶器、機織り機など多様な展示品に対応し、松の木の棚やパネル、彫刻のための木の土台や吊り糸などを用いて、むき出しのまま作品を陳列し、鑑賞者との親密な関係をつくり出した。れんがを用いたパーテーションなど豊かなテクスチャーも加わり、簡素な材料を用いながらも、建築と展示装置と展示品が一体となって空間をつくり上げた。

軍事政権により「民衆文化伝承館」での活動が不可能になって以降、リナは「MASP」でブラジルの北東地域に関する展示を続けた。民芸品を通してブラジルの人びとのエネルギーを表現した「ブラジル人の手」展(1969年)は過激化する軍事政権への抵抗を示した。「レパッソス」展(1975年)ではテキスタイル・デザイナーとコラボレーションし、伝統的な織物工房の貧しい女性たちと、彼女らを取り巻く社会構造に焦点を当てた。思想には厳しい批判精神があるが、それを表現する展示手法は遊び心にあふれ、鑑賞者を遠ざけない。リナの展示のイメージは、ブラジルの田舎の市場や、大都市のスーパーマーケットに由来していた。[*4]

[*3]　Lina Bo Bardi, (1963) "Northeast", in *Stones against Diamonds*, p. 072.

[*4]　Lina Bo Bardi, (1983) "Design in Brazil: History and Reality", in *Lina Bo Bardi*, p. 236.

「北東」展。2階には陶器や人形、テキスタイルなど小型の民芸品を大量に集めて展示した。(1963年)
The "Northeast" exhibition. A large collection of small folk art including ceramics, dolls and textiles were gathered and displayed on the 1st floor. (1963)

「北東」展。1階は空間を広々と使い、大型の民芸品が展示された。(1963年)
The "Northeast" exhibition. The wide open space on the ground floor was used to display large pieces of folk art. (1963)

「ブラジル人の手」展。さまざまな美術館や個人のコレクター、サンパウロの骨董品店などから借り受けた大量の民芸品を展示した。（1969 年）
The "Hand of the Brazilian People" exhibition. On display was a large collection of folk art on loan from various museums, private collectors, and São Paulo antique shops. (1969)

were created from the lives of regular people who had received little attention up to that point, such as sculptures, dolls, ceramics, weaving machines, etc. In order to accommodate various exhibits, display the bare works and create a feeling of intimacy with visitors, Lina used panels made from pine trees, wooden stands for holding sculptures and thread to hang paintings. Using simple materials and adding rich textures such as brick partitions, she created a space by bringing together architecture, display equipment and exhibition works. After she had to stop her activities at the "Solar do Unhão – Popular Art Museum" due to the military coup, Lina continued to hold exhibitions on Brazil's northeastern culture at "MASP". Her exhibition, "The Hand of The Brazilian People" (1969), which expressed Brazilian people's energy through folk crafts, demonstrated her opposition to the growing extremism of the military regime. Her "Repassos" (1975) exhibition, for which she collaborated with a textile designer, put the focus on the poor women working at traditional textile factories and the social structure that surrounded them.

While her approach is animated by a spirit of harsh criticism, the exhibition method used to express her ideas is filled with playfulness and stays close to its public. Lina's exhibition borrowed its visual facture from the market found in Brazil's countryside and the supermarket found in its big cities.*4

*4   Lina Bo Bardi, (1983) "Design in Brazil: History and Reality", in *Lina Bo Bardi*, p. 236.

「ブラジル人の手」展の展示の様子。（1969 年）
A scene from the display at the "Hand of the Brazilian People" exhibition. (1969)

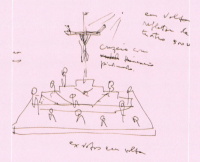

「ブラジル人の手」展、展示計画ドローイング。（1969 年）
An exhibition plan drawing of the "Hand of the Brazilian People" exhibition. (1969)

舞台のような展覧会

演劇的なインスタレーションも特徴的だ。「バイーア・イン・イピラブエラ」展（1959年）では地面に葉を敷き詰めたり、「北東」展では植民地時代の教会に芳香を焚くなど、音響や香りといった五感へ訴えかける演出を先駆的に行った。「SESC」で1981年から1985年の間に「美、そして醜いものがもつ権利」（1981年）「ブラジルのデザイン：歴史と現実」（1982年）「ブラジルの子どもたちに1000のおもちゃを」（1983年）「カイピラス、カピアウス：パウ・ア・ピケ」（1984年）「子どものための幕間」（1985年）の5つの展覧会をキュレートした。子どものおもちゃを視点に近代の工業製品とブラジルやアフリカの民芸品を比較したり、ブラジルの土着の文化や自然を紹介した。賑やかなサーカスのような演劇性を強めることで、老若男女を展示の世界に引き込み、楽しく学べる環境をつくり上げた。ブラジルの伝統的な農業を扱った「カイピラス、カピアウス：パウ・ア・ピケ*5」展では、手塗りのカラフルなメイポール*6に迎えられて進んだ奥に、建物の模型に囲まれたステージのような農場を設けた。さらに蒸留酒の製造過程を香りと共に展示し、オープニング・イベントでは生きた動物も姿を見せた。

*5 パウ・ア・ピケとは、ブラジル内陸部にある竹や土壁による伝統的民家のこと。

*6 元はヨーロッパ各地の五月祭に登場するもので、豊穣を祝って人びとが柱の下に集い踊る。

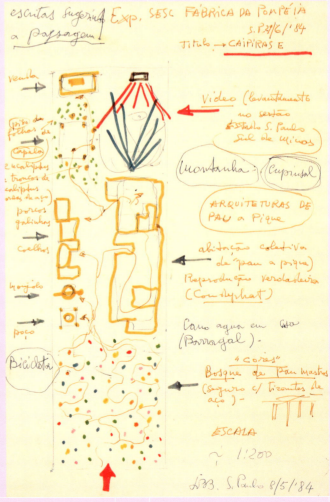

「子どものための幕間」展のためのドローイング。
遊具に加え、たくさんの巨大な動物や昆虫が壁・床・天井にまで描かれている。(1984年)
A drawing for the "Intermission for Children" exhibition. In addition to playground equipment, many giant animals and insects were drawn on the walls, floor and ceiling. (1984)

(p.198 左)「カイピラス、カピアウス：パウ・ア・ピケ」展の展示の様子。入り口に立つカラフルなメイポール。(1984年)
(p. 198 left) A scene from the "Caipiras, Capiaus: Pau-a-Pique" exhibition. Colorful maypoles stand at the entrance. (1984)

(p.198 右)「カイピラス、カピアウス：パウ・ア・ピケ」展計画平面図。入り口（下）から、メイポールの林、実寸の小屋の模型、農場を模したステージへと進む。ブラジルの田舎にある文化を「アート」として紹介した。(1984年)
(p. 198 right) A floor plan of the "Caipiras, Capiaus: Pau-a-Pique" exhibition. From the entrance (bottom) is a maypole forest, a full-scale replica of a hut, and a stage resembling a farm. The culture of Brazil's countryside was introduced as "art". (1984)

「子どものための幕間」展。巨大な動物や昆虫の模型（剥製、標本、張り子など）、手づくりのすべり台とメリーゴーランドで、おとぎ話のような空間をつくり上げた。(1985年)
The "Intermission for Children" exhibition. A fairy-tale like space was created with giant replicas of animals and insects (stuffed specimens, specimens, papier mâché, etc.) as well as a handmade slide and merry-go-round. (1985)

「MASP」の「ベルヴェデーレ」を描いたドローイング。植物や彫刻にあふれ、都市に開かれたパブリックスペースとして構想された。
A drawing depicting the "Belvedere" at "MASP". It was designed to be a public space full of flora and sculptures.

「ベルヴェデーレ」での「遊び場」展。(1969年)
The "Playground" exhibition at the "Belvedere". (1969)

アートをみんなの手に

そして、リナの展示思想は晩年の「セビーリャ万博ブラジル館」のプロポーザル(1991年)に結実する。リナは新大陸を発見したヨーロッパ人ではなく、以前からアメリカに暮らしていた先住民にフォーカスし、彼らが育てたブラジル文化のルーツを讃える展示を構想した。リナが設計したシンプルなホワイトボックスに詰め込まれた民俗的世界は非常に豊かで、資料の展示に加えて民族の祭りのパフォーマンスや伝統的な食事の提供が構想されるなど、総合的な文化の上演ともいうべきものであった。

リナにとってアートに関する教育は重要な意味をもち、常に若者に対して行動を促すメッセージが込められていた。アートを万人に開き、高尚なものとしてではなく「誰もが手の届く予言」*7として見せたいと願ったリナは、人びとがもつ先入観を取り除き、自ら疑問をもつように促した。「MASP」の「ベルヴェデーレ」はその象徴だ。同時に、リナが手掛けた展覧会の多くは、ブラジル文化を記録すると共にその可能性を示していたことから、リナはひとりの文化人類学者であったといえるかもしれない。展示品は特別な人がつくる「作品」ではなく、何でもない人びとがつくるものであり、展覧会はその創造性を讃えるものだった。

*7 Zeuler Rocha M. de Almeida Lima, (2015) "Lina Bo Bardi, Curator: a Life in Assemblage", in Giancarlo Latorraca, *Maneiras de Expor: Arquitetura Expositiva de Lina Bo Bardi*, p. 093.

Realizing Exhibitions with a Theatrical Flair

Installations featuring a theatrical flair were also characteristic of Lina's work. She pioneered productions that appealed to the senses of sound and smell by covering the ground in leaves at the "*Bahia in Ibirapuera*" exhibition (1959), burning incense inside the colonial period church at the "Northeast" exhibition, and so on. Lina curated five exhibitions held between 1981 and 1985 at "SESC"; "Beauty and the Right to the Ugly", "Brazilian Design: History and Reality", "A Thousand Toys for Brazilian Kids", "*Caipiras, Capiaus :Pau-a-pique*" and "Intermission for Children", where she compared the modern industrial products with Brazilian and African folk crafts from the viewpoint of children's toys, and introduced Brazilian indigenous culture and nature. By emphasizing the busy circus-like sense of drama, Lina drew men and women of all ages into the world of exhibitions and created an environment that made learning fun. For the "*Caipiras, Capiaus :Pau-a-pique*" exhibition[5] dealing with Brazil's traditional agriculture, visitors were greeted by colorful maypoles[6] and, moving further inside, Lina had set up a stage-like farm surrounded by dummy buildings. Furthermore, she exhibited the manufacturing process of distilled liquor along with the aroma, and she showed live animals at the opening event.

Bringing Art within Everyone's Reach

Finally, Lina's exhibition ideas came to fruition in her proposal for the "Brazil Pavilion at the Seville Expo" (1991) during her last years. Rather than the Europeans who had discovered a new continent, Lina chose to focus on the natives who had been living in America since long before by planning an exhibition that praised the cultural roots of Brazil in which they had been raised. The world of folk customs crammed into the simple white box designed by Lina was extremely rich and, in addition to displaying materials, her idea was to provide folk festival performances and traditional meals. One might say this was more of a comprehensive cultural performance.

For Lina, art education had significant meaning. Her work always included a message directed at young people to urge them to action. Opening art to everybody and wanting to show it as "a prophecy within everyone's reach"[7] rather than something lofty, Lina urged people to get rid of their preconceptions and question things for themselves. At the same time, perhaps Lina should be thought of as a cultural anthropologist because she recorded Brazilian culture and demonstrated its potential through many of the exhibitions that she managed. Items on exhibition were not "works" created by special people; they were created by ordinary people. Lina's exhibitions gave praise to their creativity.

[5] *Pau-a-pique* are traditional houses made of bamboo and mud walls in Brazil's inland areas.

[6] Erected as a part of various European folk festivals, around which people gather and dance to celebrate fertility.

[7] Zeuler Rocha M. de Almeida Lima, (2015) "Lina Bo Bardi, Curator: a Life in Assemblage", in Giancarlo Latorraca, *Maneiras de Expor: Arquitetura Expositiva de Lina Bo Bardi*, p. 093.

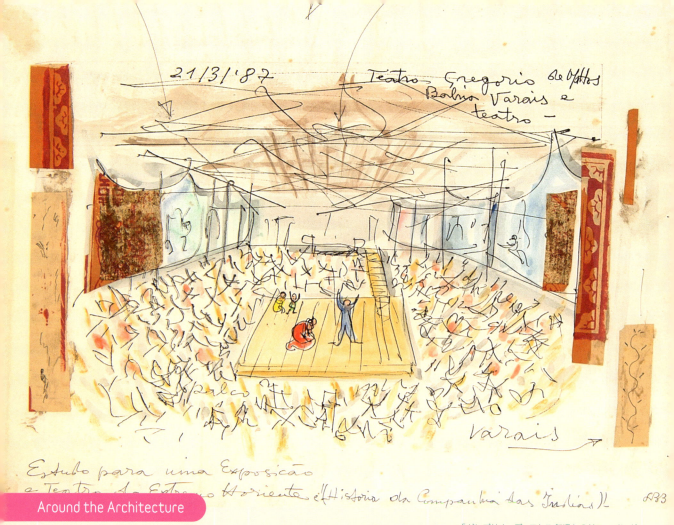

「グレゴリオ・デ・マトス劇場」のドローイング。
花道のある舞台の周りに観客が集う。(1986年)
A drawing of the "Gregório de Mattos Theater".
Spectators gather around the stage with a
passageway. (1986)

Around the Architecture

Stage Design
舞台と劇場デザイン

And where's the "Theater"? Where are all the seats, the "aisles" and the "stage", the knickknacks and bunches of spotlights? All we see here is a space, as free and open as a city as a city square. It is necessary to make the most of all the spaces in a city, finding also along with a strict respect for the past, a modern Liberty Theater.
Lina Bo Bardi, 1989

さて「劇場」はどこにあるでしょう?
客席は、「通路」は、「ステージ」は、「小道具」は、「照明」はどこでしょう?
私たちがここで目にしているのは、都市の広場のように自由でオープンな空間です。
私はみなさんが都市におけるすべての空間を最大限に活用し、
現代の自由な劇場に表れる過去への確かな敬意を発見してほしいと思います。
リナ・ボ・バルディ 1989年

貧しい演劇

リナの演劇との関わりは、1959年バイーア州サルヴァドール市の演劇学校のディレクター、マルティム・ゴンサルヴィスとの出会いからはじまった。サルヴァドールではそのほか当時のブラジルを代表する多くの前衛芸術家たちと出会っている。ブラジルの実験映画運動シネマ・ノーヴォ[*1]の創始者であるグラウベル・ローシャ[*2]、芸術運動トロピカリア[*3]のミュージシャン、カエターノ・ヴェローゾ[*4]やジルベルト・ジル[*5]、写真家で人類学者のピエール・ヴェルジェ[*6]などから影響を受け、リナの活動の幅を広げた。リナはポーランド人演出家イェジー・グロトフスキが提唱した、余計な要素を省いて俳優と観客との新たな関係を見出す「貧しい演劇」[*7]という概念に刺激され、舞台美術や劇場の設計を行った。

グラウベル・ローシャ監督『黒い神と白い悪魔』の撮影現場にて、映画監督のパウロ・ギル・スワレス、ウォルター・リマ・ジュニア、ローシャ、撮影監督のヴァルダマー・リマ、俳優のサンテ・スカルダフェーリらと。(1963 年 6 月 19 日)
Film directors Paulo Gil Soares, Walter Lima Jr., and Rocha, as well as cinematographer Waldemar Lima and actor Sante Scaldaferri on the set of Director Glauber Rocha's "Black God, White Devil". (June 19, 1963)

[*1] 1950年代後半から1960年代前半にかけてブラジルで起こった映画運動。

[*2] 1938〜81年。ブラジルの映画監督、俳優、脚本家。シネマ・ノーヴォの指導者。バイーア現代美術館でリナの助手を務めた。

[*3] 1960年代後半のブラジルで起こった音楽ムーブメント。音楽を中心に美術や映画などを巻き込んだカウンター・カルチャーとして発展した。

[*4] 1942年〜。ブラジル、バイーア州出身の作曲家、歌手。

[*5] 1942年〜。ブラジル、サルヴァドール市出身のミュージシャン、政治家。

[*6] 1902〜96年。フランスの写真家、文化人類学者。サルヴァドールに魅せられて移住し、地域の歴史と文化の研究を続けた。リナとのコラボレーションは「ピエール・ヴェルジェ財団」(サルヴァドール市、1989年、実現せず)、「アフリカ・ネグラ」展(サンパウロ美術館、1988年)。

[*7] ポーランド人劇作家イェジー・グロトフスキが1965年に『実験演劇論─持たざる演劇をめざして』のなかで発表した概念。衣装や照明や音響といった、演劇に必ずしも必要でない要素を省くことで、俳優と観客との関係という本質を浮かび上がらせた。舞台と観客との境界を取り払うなど、両者の新たな関係性を模索した。

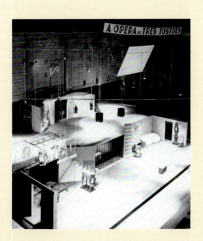

「三文オペラ」舞台セット。(1960 年)
The stage set for "The Threepenny Opera". (1960)

Poor Theater

Lina's specific involvement with theater began from her encounter with Martim Gonçalves, director of the school of theater in Salvador City, Bahia State, in 1959. Lina and Martim explored new theater experiences. Lina met many other representative Brazilian avant-garde artists at the time in Salvador. Glauber Rocha[*1], founder of Brazil's experimental film movement Cinema Novo[*2],

1964年のクーデターではじまる軍事政権下で建設活動が困難ななか、実験的な演劇作品の制作に参加することで、リナは先鋭的なデザインの実践を続けていた。その経験はきわめて豊富でかなり挑戦的なものだった。舞台美術も建築と同様、次第にシンプルに洗練されていく。1960年のベルトルト・ブレヒト作の戯曲「三文オペラ」（美術担当）では、大掛かりな舞台セットをデザインしたが、ゴンサルヴィスが監督を務めた1961年の演劇「カリギュラ」（美術・衣装デザイン担当）では、いくつかの開口部をもつ土壁を背景に、限られた小道具だけで物語が展開できるようにデザインしていた。1970年の映画「プラタ・パロモレス」（アートディレクション担当）ではレフ板を用いない照明演出でブラジル映画祭カンダンゴ賞を受賞している。

舞台と客席の境界をなくす

リナが手掛けた演劇制作の経験すべてが、建築家としての劇場設計に生かされている。リナの舞台美術や劇場設計における原則は、舞台と観客、演劇と現実、劇場と都市との境界をなくすことだった。ブレヒト作の「都市のジャングル」の舞台美術では、向かい合うふたつの客席の間に舞台としてボクシングのリングを設置した。これは、のちに「SESCポンペイア文化センター」（p. 068）の劇場の設計に発展していく。舞台と観客を対立させず、向かい合うふたつの観客席の間に舞台を置くことで、舞台を見る観客の視界には必ず反対側の客席が入り、演劇に介入する。リナの頭にあったのは、故郷ローマの古代野外劇場であり、舞台が客席に張り出した日本の能舞台だった。芸術家たちとの交流に加え、幼い記憶と歴史へのまなざしが、徐々にリナの劇場をつくり上げていったのである。

「SESC」劇場内部。階段状の客席に挟まれた中央に舞台が位置する。
The theater interior at "SESC". The stage was positioned in the center between the stair-shaped seats.

舞台「都市のジャングル」上演中の様子。ボクシングのリングを模した舞台で上演され、観客はリングを囲んで鑑賞した。
（1969年）
A scene from the stage showing of "In the Jungle of Cities". It was shown on a stage resembling a boxing ring; spectators surrounded the ring to watch. (1969)

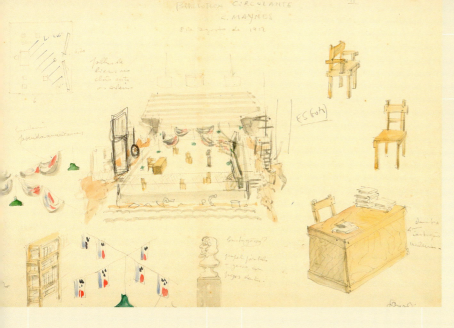

舞台「都市のジャングル」美術のためのドローイング。小道具まで詳細に構想されていた。(1969年)

A drawing for the art of "In the Jungle of Cities". Every detail was considered even down to the small props. (1969)

Caetano Veloso[*3] and Gilberto Gil[*4], musicians for the Tropicália[*5] art movement, and Pierre Bergé[*6], a photographer and anthropologist, all influenced Lina and widened the scope of her work. Lina designed sets and theaters inspired by "poor theater"[*7], which was advocated by the Polish director Jerzy Grotowski and tried to discover new relationships between actors and spectators by eliminating any unnecessary elements.

Even when her architectural work became difficult under the military regime that began with the coup d'état of 1964, Lina continued her practice of radical design work by participating in the production of experimental theatrical works. She had a wealth of experience and very provocative ideas. Her stage art gradually became simpler and more refined, just as her architecture had become. Although she designed a large-scale set for the 1960 Bertolt Brecht-produced play "The Threepenny Opera" (art), Lina's designs for the 1961 Gonçalves-directed play "Caligula" (art and costumes) allowed her to develop the narrative ark with only limited props against a backdrop consisting of a mud wall with several openings. In 1970, she was awarded the Candango award at the Brasilia Festival of Brazilian Cinema for producing lighting without reflector boards as part of art direction on the film "*Prata Palomares*".

*1   1938 – 81. A Brazilian film director, actor, and playwright. Leader of Cinema Novo. Worked as Lina's assistant at the "Bahia Museum of Modern Art".

*2   A film movement that occurred in Brazil between the late 1950's and the first half of the 1960's.

*3   1942 – . A composer and singer born in Bahia State, Brazil.

*4   1942 – . A musician and politician born in Salvador, Brazil.

*5   A music movement that took place in Brazil in the late 1960's. It developed as a counter culture focused mainly on music and also involved art and film.

*6   1902 – 96. A French photographer and anthropologist. Fascinated by Salvador, he emigrated there, where he continued to research the local history and culture. His collaborations with Lina were the "Pierre Bergé Foundation" (Salvador, 1989, unrealized) and the "Africa Negura Exhibition" (São Paulo Museum of Art, 1988).

*7   Polish playwright Jerzy Grotowski presented the concept during his "Towards a Poor Theater" in 1965. By eliminating all unnecessary elements of theater in terms of costumes, lighting and sound, the true nature of the relationship between actor and spectator emerged. He sought a new relationship for both sides by removing the boundary between stage and spectator.

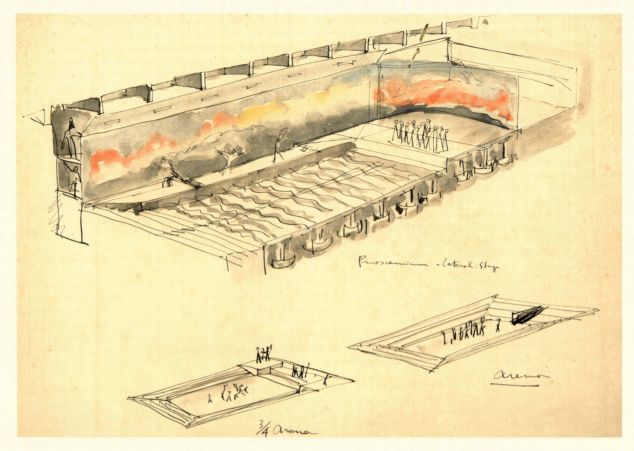

「MASP」劇場のスタディ。
花道のように舞台の端が延びたパターン、階段状の客席に四方を囲まれたパターンなど、さまざまな形の劇場が構想された。(1968年頃)
A study of the "MASP" theater. Various forms were conceived for the theater space, including a pattern where the stage edge extended like a passageway and a pattern where the stage was surrounded on four sides by stair-shaped seats. (circa 1968)

劇場を都市へ開く

さらにリナは劇場を都市へと開いていく。1986年の「ポリテアマ劇場」は19世紀の建物を修復し劇場にするプロジェクトで、バーや展示ホールも併設した、人びとの集まる場所として構想された[*8]。舞台の後ろは大きなガラス窓になっていて、街の風景が演劇の背景となる。劇場へのアクセスとなるすべり台のようなチューブとスロープ、地下の「洞窟のバー」、遊具と豊かな植栽にあふれる庭が、既存の建物に挿入された。同年の「グレゴリオ・デ・マトス劇場」(p. 128)でもサルヴァドールの風景は巨大な雲形窓に切り取られている。これは集会場や広場などと一体となった複合施設「バホキーニャ」の提案の一部であり、街を舞台にした観劇体験を意図した。

こうした思想は「テアトロ・オフィシナ」(p. 136)に結実した。舞台の不在、俳優と観客との関係性の模索は1971年の演劇「グラシアス、セニョール」(美術担当)にイメージの萌芽が見られる。そこにはステージはなく、客席は足場で設えられ、控え室も客席のすぐ隣にあり、内部には壁がない。舞台沿いの植物はファサードの壁面を突き抜けて外へと飛び出す。観客や劇団員の生活すら劇場と一体化し、同時に劇場も演劇も、まるで寺山修司の演劇のように[*9]、街や日常へと溶解していくかのようだ。

*8 実現したのはリナの死後で、既存の建物の改修にとどまった。

*9 「天井桟敷」を主宰した寺山修司(1935～68年)は観客を演劇に巻き込むような演出で知られ、「ノック」(1975年)では実際の街を舞台に、観客だけでなく何も知らない住民までもが演劇の一部となった。

Eliminating the Boundaries between Stage and Seats

All of Lina's hands-on theater production experience was put to good use when designing theaters as an architect. Lina's general rule when it came to designing stage art and theaters was to eliminate the boundaries between stage and seats, play and reality, and theater and city. For the stage art in the Brecht-produced play "In the Jungle of Cities", Lina installed a boxing ring as a stage between the two facing sections of seats. The design for the theater at "SESC Pompéia Factory Leisure Center" (p. 068) could be seen as an ulterior expansion from this.

Rather than having the stage and spectators oppose each other, Lina placed the stage between the facing spectator seats so that the opposing seats would definitely enter the field of vision of spectators watching the stage and thus intervene in the play. Lina had in mind the ancient outdoor theaters of her hometown Rome, and the stage was a Japanese Noh stage that projected into the spectator seats. In addition to exchanging ideas with artists, her childhood memories and gaze on history gradually gave form to her theaters.

Opening the Theater to the City

Moreover, Lina opened her theaters to the city. The "Politeama Theater" of 1986 was a project to restore a 19th century building and turn it into a theater. She conceived of it as a place with a side-by-side bar and exhibition hall where people could gather[*8]. The back of the stage was a large glass window so the city's scenery became the background

[*8] Realized after the death of Lina, and limited to repairs on the existing building.

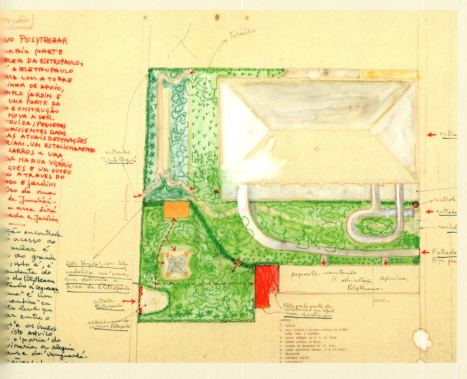

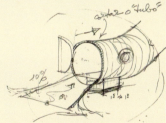

チューブ出口のドローイング。
A drawing of the tube exit.

「ポリテアマ劇場」配置図。歴史ある劇場の周囲に公園を計画し都市に開いた。正面入リ口とは別に、劇場と公園はすべり台のようなチューブでつながり、舞台から直接外に出られるスロープも計画された。
The layout of "Teatro Politeama". They planned to have a park in the area around this historic theater that was open to the city. Besides the front entrance, there was even a plan to connect the theater and park by a tube not unlike a slide, and a slope that led directly outside from the stage.

「テアトロ・オフィシナ」での上演中の様子。
A scene during a showing at "Teatro Oficina".

建築の演劇化

建築作品全体にも演劇活動による影響が見られる。「サルヴァドール旧市街地修復プロジェクト」(p. 118)以後に設計した「サンパウロ美術館(MASP)」(p. 036)や「SESC」などの巨大な公共施設で、人びとの参加が活気ある場を生み出す姿は、「建築の演劇化」とでもいうべきものだ。リナが見出したのは、"時間と、街と、今日の社会のシンボルとして"の劇場だった[10]。リナはヴァルター・グロピウスの「建築家は劇場を観察しなければならない」という言葉をよく引用し、「劇場は人生です。ある意味伝統的なセットのデザインは建築とは真逆のもので、ステージセットのない劇場が、グロピウスの言うように、純粋な建築なのです」[11]と語っている。リナは演劇という芸術に対し尊敬と愛情を抱いていただけでなく、劇場という空間に対して、建築家としての飽くなき興味をもっていた。リナの演劇体験は、建築家としての活動と表現の幅を拡げた一大要素だったのである。

[10] Lina Bo Bardi, "Politeama Theater", in *Lina Bo Bardi*, p. 264.

[11] Lina Bo Bardi, "Ubu", in *Lina Bo Bardi*, p. 260.

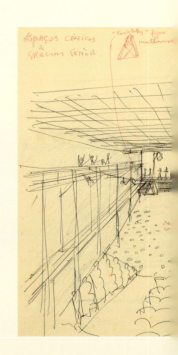

for plays. Lina incorporated into the existing building a slide-like tube and slope to give access to the theater, an underground "Cave Bar", playground equipment and a garden overflowing with plenty of trees and plants. The "Gregório de Mattos Theater" (p. 128) from the same year also features the scenery of Salvador, cut out here by a giant "cloud window" opening. Proposed as one part of the "Barroquinha" complex that combined a gathering place and plaza, it aimed to provide a theater-going experience with the city as a stage. The "Teatro Officina" was the embodiment of this concept. The absence of a stage and exploration of the relationship between actors and spectators is seen as the germination of an image for the 1971 play "Gracias, Señor" (art). Here, there is no stage, scaffolding stands for seating, the green room is right next to the audience seats, and there are no walls inside the theater. The vegetation along the stage breaks through the façade's wall surface and thrusts outside. Even the lives of audience and theater members become one with the theater, while at the same time, the theater and play go on to seemingly dissolve into the city and everyday life just like in the plays of Shuji Terayama[*9].

The Theatricalization of Architecture

The influence of Lina's theatrical activities is visible in all of her architectural works. We can find in large public facilities, such as the "São Paulo Museum of Art (MASP)" (p. 036) and "SESC" that Lina designed after "The Historic Center of Salvador" (p. 118), that the participation of people creates liveliness in a place. Perhaps it should be called it the "theatricalization of architecture".

What Lina discovered was the theater "as time, as a city, and as a symbol of today's society"[*10]. She often quoted the words of Walter Gropius, "Architects need to observe theater", and said that "Theater is life. In a sense, designing a traditional set is the exact opposite of architecture but, a theater without a stage set is, in Gropius' words, true architecture."[*11] As an architect, Lina held not only love and respect for the art of theater but also a persistent interest in the theater space. Her theater experience was a major element in expanding her activities and range of expression as an architect.

[*9] Shuji Terayama (1935-1968), supervisor of the "Tenjo Sajiki" theatrical company, was known for productions which involved spectators in the play. In "Knock" (1975), the actual city was the stage and not only spectators but also unaware residents became a part of the play.

[*10] Lina Bo Bardi, "Politeama Theater", in *Lina Bo Bardi*, p. 264.

[*11] Lina Bo Bardi, "Ubu", in *Lina Bo Bardi*, p. 260.

「グラシアス、セニョール」のためのドローイング。ステージのない舞台、階段状の客席、足場などが描かれている。(1971年)
A drawing for "Gracias, Señor". It depicts a performing area with no stage, stair-shaped seats, and scaffolding. (1971)

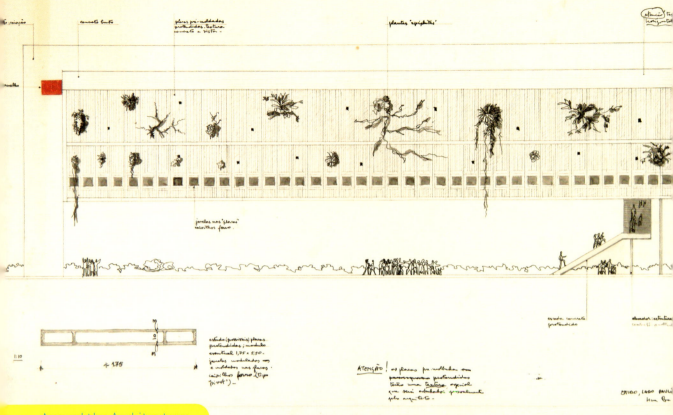

「MASP」ファサード初期の計画ドローイング。
植物の生えた石壁が構想されていた。
A drawing of an early plan for the façade at the "MASP". The idea was to have stone walls with plants growing on them.

Around the Architecture

Botanical Design
植栽デザイン

(What organic, natural architecture means)
... an 'open' architecture that accepts nature, that makes itself comfortable,
and that seeks to camouflage itself into it,
like a lizard lying on rocks in the sun.
Lina Bo Bardi, 1958

(有機的な建築、自然な建築とは）自然を受け入れ、自らを快適な空間にする「開かれた」建築です。
太陽の下で岩に寝そべるワニのように、自然の中に自分自身を溶け込ませようとするような。
リナ・ボ・バルディ、1958 年

植物の研究

ブラジル原産の熱帯植物を用いて建築をデザインすることはリナの特徴のひとつである。リナはイタリア時代から植物が単に好きだっただけではなく造詣も深く、植物の種類を見分け、その特徴について語ることができた。植物への興味は生涯尽きることがなく、自然が環境のバランスを保ち、人類により良い生き方を教えてくれるという信条が、インテリかつ現場主義者というリナの特質の根底にあった。

ふたつの世界大戦により「廃墟」となったヨーロッパからブラジルに移住したのは熱帯植物への興味もあったためだろう。ブラジルに着いてまもなくブーレ・マルクス*1とコンタクトを取り、彼の作品を見るためにリオ・デ・ジャネイロを訪れている。ブーレはブラジル原産の植物を用い、数々のブラジル現代建築の名作のランドスケープを手掛けている。彼との出会いはリナに大きな影響を与えただろう。リナはノートにスケッチした植物の絵に学術名称と一般名称を併記してブラジルの植物の知識を蓄えていった。「ガラスの家」(p. 012) の書斎にあった膨大な量の専門書がそれを物語っている。サルヴァドール市やミナスジェライス州といったブラジルの地方を旅する時や、設計前の敷地調査でも、植物をスケッチし、押し花をノートに挟んで持ち帰っていた。

*1 1909〜94年。ブラジルのランドスケープ・アーキテクト、アーティスト。

The Study of Plants

Designing architecture with tropical plants native to Brazil is one of the characteristics of Lina's work. She not only appreciated plants ever since the Italy period but also had a deep knowledge of them, being able to distinguish plant varieties and explain their features. She maintained this interest in plants throughout her life, and her belief that nature is what preserves environmental balance and teaches people a better way of life formed the foundation of Lina's distinctive characteristics as an intellectual and hands-on person.

Lina's fascination with tropical plants probably led to her moving to Brazil from Europe, which was "in ruins" due to two world wars. Shortly after arriving in Brazil, she contacted Roberto Burle Marx*1 and visited Rio de Janeiro to see his works. Burle Marx worked on the landscaping of numerous Brazilian contemporary architecture masterpieces using tropical plants native to Brazil. Lina's encounter with him would have had a great influence on her. Lina expanded her knowledge of Brazil's flora by writing both the academic and popular names of plants that she sketched in her notebook. The

*1 1909-94. A Brazilian landscape architect and artist.

「カミュリュピン」で敷地の調査中に見つけた植物のスケッチ。(1975年頃)
A sketch of flora found while surveying the site at "Camurupim". (circa 1975)

住宅を自然にさらす

リナはプロジェクトごとに場所に応じて細かく植物の種類を指定していた。植物の生えた石壁、屋上庭園、建物を突き抜ける樹木、有機的形態の応用など、いくつかの植物のモチーフが作品に登場する。植物に早くから興味をもっていたことは、これらのモチーフの多くが処女作「ガラスの家」に登場していることからも明らかに見て取れる。ここでテーマとなっていたのは「住宅を自然にさらすこと」で、建物周囲の植栽計画もリナが行い、建設当時は植生のなかった土地に、木や花や果樹をひとつひとつ植えていった。これらはすべてブラジル原産の植物だった。

「今日は早く帰るつもり、庭に植える小さい植物を買いたいから。大きいのはだめ、今は節約しなくちゃ。追々買えるといいな。庭はとてもきれい、きれいよ。」*2

とガーデニングを楽しむように、植栽計画を練っていた様子が伺える。「ガラスの家」の植物の生えた石壁は、壁に開いた排水用の穴に偶然飛び込んだ種子から草が生えたことが発想の元となっており、のちの作品にもたびたび登場している。「ヴァレリア・P・シレル邸」(p. 148)ではこの石壁を住宅全体に展開した。「シレル邸」と同時期に設計した「シャメシャメ邸」(現存せず)は、サルヴァドール市の環境を映すかのように植物で覆われていた。

「ガラスの家」外部。多様な種類の木々はすべてブラジル原産。背の高いものから低いものまで幅広い。
Exterior of the "Glass House". The diverse species of trees are all indigenous to Brazil. There is a wide range of trees, from tall ones to short ones.

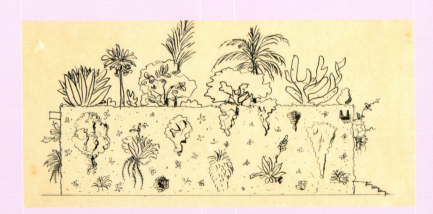

「シレル邸」の植物の生えた石壁の計画ドローイング。「ガラスの家」で偶然生まれたアイデアはさまざまな作品で構想・実践されている。(1958年頃)
A drawing plan of the stone walls on which plants grow at "Valéria P. Cirell's Home". The ideas that came about by accident at the "Glass House" were planned and used by Lina for various other projects. (circa 1958)

large volume of technical books in the study of the "Glass House" (p. 12) gives ample indication of this. Whenever she conducted a preliminary site survey or traveled to countryside areas of Brazil such as Salvador City and Minas Gerais State, she would sketch plants and bring home pressed flowers in her notebook.

Exposing a House to Nature

Lina specifically designated varieties of plants according to location for each project. Several plant motifs appear in her works, including stone walls on which plants are growing, rooftop gardens, trees that cut through buildings, and the application of organic structures. Lina's longstanding interest in plants is plainly evident from the way that many of these motifs appear in her maiden work; the "Glass House". The theme here was "exposing a house to nature", and for this purpose Lina planned to grow plants and trees around the building by planting each tree, flower, and fruit tree on land that had no vegetation at the time of building.

"Today I will return home sooner because I want to buy some small plants that I will plant in the garden; No big plants, because, for the moment, I am in a phase of

「シャメシャメ邸」断面図、立面図。斜面地に計画されたシンプルなプランに豊かな植物が付加された本作品の構成が分かる。屋上庭園や石壁の植物が描かれている。
A cross section and elevation of *"Casa do Chame-Chame"*. One can see organization of this project, adding rich flora to the simple plan designed for the sloped site. There is a depiction of the rooftop garden and plants on the stone walls.

「シャメシャメ邸」建設当時。石や陶器や貝殻で覆われたファサード、ジャックフルーツの木と調和した貝殻状の曲線プラン、住宅を侵食する植物など、有機的な造形がさらに展開した重要な作品。
At the time of construction of *"Casa do Chame-Chame"*. This was an important project that further developed organic forms, including a façade covered in stones, ceramics and seashells, a shell-shaped curve plan that harmonized with jackfruit trees, and flora encroaching on the house.

Around the Architecture Botanical Design

公共空間の植栽デザイン

「サンパウロ美術館(MASP)」(p. 036)の「ベルヴェデーレ」の初期案も、水や植物にあふれた計画が練られ、巨大なファサードも当初は植物付きの石壁が構想されていた。最終的にガラスファサードになった結果、植物は「ベルヴェデーレ」の水盤と裏の基壇部に移されている。「SESCポンペイア文化センター」(p. 068)の設計中のドローイングには、花や薬用植物の花壇、壁や屋根に植える植物について詳細に記載されており、何をどこに植えるかが指示されていた。建築でも多用されている赤を中心に、土着の花を風景、育つ時間と季節や用途も考慮しながら選んでいる。さらに小石や砂利の場所と範囲に加え、石に生える苔のことまで言及していたという(多くは建設中に変更され実現していない)[*3]。植栽を新たに計画するだけでなく、「ミゼリコーディア坂歴史的地区の修復」(p. 130)や「テアトロ・オフィシナ」(p. 136)では、敷地に立つ樹木をそのまま生かすために建物に穴まで開けてしまっている。

[*2] ピエトロへの手紙、サンパウロにて。1956年4月2日、ILBPMB所蔵。

[*3] Cathrine Veikos, (2014) "The Hands of the People: SESC Pompéia", in *Lina Bo Bardi 100*, p. 128.

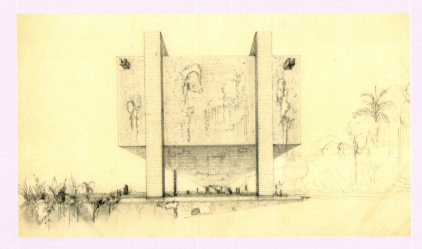

「MASP」ファサード初期の計画ドローイング、短手側。
石壁の植物が「トリアノン公園」の植物や、「ベルヴェデーレ」の水生植物と呼応している。
A preliminary plan of the façade at the "MASP", on the short side. The stone wall plants echo the plants at "Parque Trianon" and the aquatic plants at the "Belvedere".

「SESC」に計画された石壁のドローイング。石の隙間から植物と水が顔を出している。(1980年)
A drawing of the stone walls planned for "SESC". Plants and water can be seen coming out from gaps in the stone. (1980)

An arrangement plan for "Misericórdia Slope". A rooftop garden (dark green) and backyard (yellow green) are indicated with a color coding. The restaurant in the western side is home to African tuliptrees and mango trees. The area at the back (yellow) of the "bar with three arches" at the center is designated as "wild plants". (1987)

savings; It will be for later, I hope. The garden is really beautiful, beautiful."*2

This is a testament as to how she mused over planting plants to enjoy gardening. The origin of her idea for the "Glass House", with its stone walls on which plants were growing, came from the grass that grew from seeds which coincidentally sprung into the water drainage hole in the wall. This idea also appeared often in her later works. In her "Valéria P. Cirell's Home" (p.148), this kind of stone wall installed all arround the house. Designed during the same period as the "Casa Cirell", the "Casa do Chame-Chame" (currently non-existent) was covered in vegetation as though it reflected the environment of Salvador City.

Botanical Design for Public Spaces

At first, both the early draft of the "Belvedere" and the giant façade from the "São Paulo Art Museum" (p.036), both of which were deliberately planned to overflow with water and vegetation, were conceived to have stone walls with vegetation attached. But, since a glass façade was retained in the end, the plants were moved to the basin and rear foundation section of the "Belvedere". The drawings during the design of the "SESC - Pompéia Factory Leisure Center" (p.068) went into detail about the plants planted on the flowerbed for flowers and medicinal plants, as well as the walls and roof, and there were instructions on where to plant what. Mainly applying the color red, which is extensively used in architecture, Lina carefully considered and chose the landscape, tending period and season, and purpose of the indigenous flowers.

*2 A letter to Pietro, in São Paulo, April 2, 1956, ILBPMB collection.

「シティ・ホール」のファサードの計画ドローイング。
描かれているのはブロメリア、サボテン、ヤシの木、黄色のイペ、ローズウッドなど、どれもブラジル原産の植物。(1991年)
A drawing plan of the "City Hall" façade. Depicted here are bromeliads, cacti, palm trees, yellow ipês, and rosewoods. All of them are indigenous Brazilian flora. (1991)

最後のドローイング

イタリア時代に執筆したテキスト*4からは、建築を自然と関係づけたモダニズムと、建築と環境とが完璧なバランスで息付く農村住宅への興味が読み取れる。リナにとって植物はモダニズムとヴァナキュラーをつなぐ要素でもあった。自然は人間の源であり、生活の源であり、材料として、建築の源でもあると考えていた。自然の調査・研究を建築教育の必須科目にすべきだと主張していたほどだ。*5 住宅や都市における緑地の減少や森林破壊も問題視していた。建築作品の敷地内にハーブの市場を構想したこともあり、植物を実用的に、生活と一体化したものとして捉えていたことが窺える。採用する植物にはそれぞれ意味があり、敷地の植物をそのまま生かす構想は、その場にあるもの、いる人すべてを受け入れるリナの寛容さを示している。植物は建築とその土地をつなぎ、人びととその暮らしを地に根付かせるものとして、リナの建築に不可欠だった。

1990年、76歳の時に「サンパウロ・シティ・ホール」(p. 172)の設計を依頼されたリナは、20世紀初頭に建てられた邸宅を修復するのに加え、通りとの間に新たな建物を設計した。通り側はガラスファサードによって都市に開く一方、旧邸宅側のファサードを熱帯植物で覆い、邸宅との間の空間を都市の喧噪から離れたパブリック・スペースとして計画した。ファサードを描いた長さ2mを超える巨大なドローイングには、植物のディテール、その名称が細かに描き込まれている。1992年にリナが亡くなったことで「シティ・ホール」は修復の一部が実現するに留まり、このファサードがつくられることはなかった。しかしこのドローイングからは、人びとと社会への献身的な姿勢、ブラジルの自然への愛情、伝統とモダニズムの融合、都市に開いた建築といったメッセージが伝わってくる。リナの思想の集大成ともいえるドローイングだ。

*4 Lina Bo Bardi, (1943) "Architecture and Nature", in *Stones against Diamonds*, pp. 021-026.

*5 Cathrine Veikos, *Lina Bo Bardi: The Theory of Architectural Practice*, p.067.

In 1990, at the age of 76, Lina was asked to design "São Paulo City Hall" (p. 172). In addition to restoring a residence built at the start of the 20th century, she also designed a new building between it and the street. While the street side was open to the city through a glass façade, the façade on the side of the former residence was covered in tropical plants. She planned the space between the residence and the building as a public space separated from the hustle and bustle of the city. In a large drawing exceeding a length of 2m that depicted the façade, the names and properties of plants were written in detail. Due to Lina's death in 1992, only a part of the restoration of "São Paulo City Hall" was accomplished and this façade was never built. But from this drawing, we distinguish a message about devotion to people and society, love for the nature of Brazil, the fusion of tradition and modernism, and architecture that is open to the city. This drawing could be said to represent the culmination of Lina's ideas.

Furthermore, in addition to the location and range of small stones and gravel, Lina even made reference to the moss growing on stones (many ideas underwent change during construction and were not realized).[*3] She did not only plan for new vegetation but, in the case of "Misericórdia Slope" (p. 130) and "Teatro Oficina" (p. 136), she even went so far as to create holes in buildings to take advantage of trees already standing on the site.

The Last Drawing

Based on the texts[*4] she wrote during the Italy period, one can read into Lina's interest in modernism, which links architecture with nature, and her interest in farming towns, which live in a perfect balance between nature and architecture. For Lina, vegetation was an element that connected modernism and vernacular architecture. She believed that nature is the source of people, life, and architecture, as a material. Lina even claimed that the study/research of nature ought to be a required topic in architecture studies.[*5] The disappearance of green spaces and deforestation in homes and cities were also a matter of concern to her. She also conceived of an herb market on the grounds of her architectural works, which proves that she positioned plants as practical things that are integrated in daily life. Each type of plant used had its own meaning, and the idea of making use of plants on site reflects Lina's acceptance of all the things and all those who inhabit the site. Plants were essential for Lina's architecture as things that connected architecture to the land and rooted people and their lives to the land.

[*3] Cathrine Veikos, (2014) "The Hands of the People: SESC Pompeia", in *Lina Bo Bardi 100*, p. 218.

[*4] Lina Bo Bardi, (1943) "Architecture and Nature", in *Stones against Diamonds*, pp. 021–026.

[*5] Cathrine Veikos, Lina Bo Bardi: *The Theory of Architectural Practice*, p. 067.

Around the Architecture

Urban Planning
都市計画

「アニャンガバウ高架プロジェクト」のためのドローイング。高架下の公園のイメージと詳細な植栽計画、高架の勾配なども描かれている。
A drawing for the "Anhangabaú Tobogã Project". It depicts an image of the park under the elevated road and detailed flora plan, and the slope of the elevated road.

Dreams are always the true reality:
Central Park, Buon Retiro, Hyde Park, Villa Borghese, the Eiffel Tower, Braubourg...
Lina Bo Bardi, 1981

夢とはいつも、真の現実です。セントラルパーク、レティーロ公園、
ハイドパーク、ボルゲーゼ公園、
エッフェル塔、ポンピドゥセンターが証明しているように。
リナ・ボ・バルディ、1981年

街はだれの場所?

ブラジルの人びとのための場所をつくりたいと願ったリナは、都市へのビジョンをもち続けていた。それは、都市に人びとの場所をつくるということであり、人びとのための都市をつくる、ということでもあった。大勢が住み、集まる場をつくるだけでなく、その場所で人びとが楽しみ、生き生きと活動できるようにする。リナの考えた都市計画は、スケールの大きな計画に、生活への細やかな想像力が編み込まれ、視野の広さと力量、そして先鋭性が表れている。

「暮らしを知る」―集落の移転

1975年（当時61歳）、ブラジル北東部のセルジッペ州での「カミュリュピン・コミュニティ・プロジェクト」は、初めて参加したコミュニティに関わるプロジェクトであった。300人の農民と100人の労働者、その家族から成る小さな集落を、まったく新しい場所に移転させるものである。敷地は約2.5平方キロメートルの傾斜地で、中央の丘の頂上に公共施設を配置し、周囲の斜面地に3,000平方メートルの円を1単位とした400世帯の住宅ユニットを配置した。この微生物のようなプランは、イタマンブカ海岸のリゾート計画（1965年）でも登場している。円形にすることでユニット間に曲がりくねった道を通し、有機的なランドスケープを生み出そうとした。

A City for the People

Hoping to build a place for the people of Brazil, Lina continued to embrace a vision for the city. This meant building a place for people in the city, and building a city for the people. Not only building a place for the masses to live and gather, but making a place where people could enjoy themselves and be active. The breadth, capacity and edginess of Lina's perspective to incorporate fine creativity for everyday life into large scale plans appear in her city project.

"Knowing How the Population Lives" – The Relocation of a Village

The first community-involved project that Lina ever participated in was the "Camurupim Community Project" in the State of Sergipe, Northeastern Brazil, in 1975 (at the age of 61). Some 300 farmers and 100 laborers, along with a small settlement composed of their families, were transferred to a completely new place. The site was a sloping plot of land measuring approx. 2.5 km^2 with a public facility positioned on the top of a centrally-located hill, while a 400-household residential unit was arranged on the surrounding 3,000 m^2 circular sloping land.

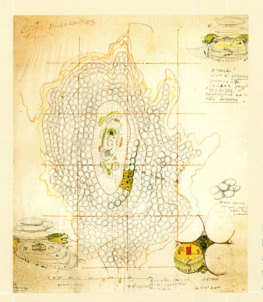

「カミュリュピン」の計画図。全体配置図と各住宅ユニットの詳細。（1975年）
A blueprint of "Camurupim". It shows details of the overall layout and each residential unit. (1975)

Around the Architecture Urban Planning

　住宅のプランは「ヴァレリア・P・シレル邸」(P. 148) の発展形で、正方形平面の中央に共有スペースを設け、各辺に配置した4つの機能をつなげるという、挑戦的な計画であった。四隅はテラスとして開放され、分節的な空間を包み込むように建物全体に藁屋根が架けられている。中央の丘の公共エリアは、屋根の架かった1本の長い歩道を軸として、コミュニティセンター、広場、スポーツ・健康センター、市場、教会、学校、レジャー施設や商業施設、シティ・ホール、刑務所などを計画していた。

　この計画において、リナは「建築家にとってもっとも大事なことは、(中略)大多数の人びとがどんな暮らしをしているのかを知ること」*1 という言葉を残しており、人びとの暮らしを事細かに調査、スケッチして設計にあたったといわれている。幾何学的で実験的なデザインのなかに温もりが感じられるのは、そのためかもしれない。リナは住民とその生活を尊重し、敷地の全体配置をはじめ、学校などの公共施設や住宅まで、あらゆるスケールのものをデザインした。文化人類学的な視点からブラジル北東部の暮らしへ高い関心をもち続けたリナだからこそ、地域特有の詩的感覚が失われずに具体的なかたちとして表現されたが、残念ながらこの計画をプロジェクトの親会社が受け入れず、実現には至らなかった。

*1　Lina Bo Bardi, (1952) "Camurupim", in *Lina Bo Bardi*, p. 203.

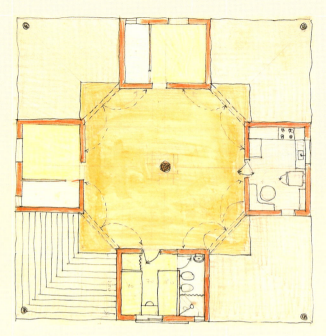

「カミュリュピン」小型住宅平面図。台所、水回り、ふたつの室が独立して配置され、中央のスペースでつながる。室の間はテラスで外に開く。(1975 年)
A small-scale residential floor plan of "Camurupim". The kitchen, water circulation and two rooms are arranged independently and connected by a central space. The area between the rooms is an open-air terrace. (1975)

「カミュリュピン」小型住宅のドローイング。
空間全体が藁屋根で覆われる。(1975 年)
A drawing of the small-scale residence "Camurupim". The entire space is covered by a thatched roof. (1975)

This kind of microscopic plan also appeared in the Itamambuca Coast Resort Project (1965). By making it circular-shaped, Lina attempted to create an organic landscape through the winding roads between units.
The house plan was a successor to "Valeria P. Cirell's Home"(p. 148), and it was an ambitious project to provide a shared space within a square plane and connect four functions laid out on each side. The four corners were opened out as a terrace and a straw-thatched roof covered the entire building as though it were wrapping the segmented space. The public area on the central hill was planned to serve as a community center, plaza, sports/health center, market, church, school, leisure and commercial facility, city hall, and jail with a long, roof-covered walkway as the focal point. With regard to this project, Lina left behind the following words: "For an architect, the most important thing is (...) to know how the majority of the population lives"[*1]. She is said to have examined people's lives in great detail, made sketches, and then applied it to her designs. This may explain why we can feel a kind of warmth in her geometrical and experimental designs. Lina placed high importance on the residents and their lives, and she went on to design the entire layout of sites of every scale, from public facilities like schools to residential houses. It was precisely because Lina continued to hold a deep interest in life in northeastern Brazil from the perspective of cultural anthropology that she

*1 Lina Bo Bardi, (1952) "Camurupim", in *Lina Bo Bardi*, p. 203.

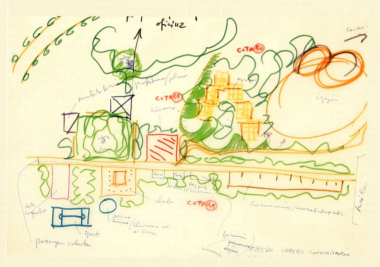

「カミュリュピン」、丘の上の公共建築群の計画図。一本の通り沿いにシティ・ホールや学校、教会、商業施設などが並ぶ。(1975 年)
"Camurupim", a blueprint of the public facilities on top of the hill. There is a city hall, a school, a church and commercial facilities standing alongside the street. (1975)

「カミュリュピン」、2タイプあるうち、大型の住宅の内部ドローイング。(1975 年)
Among the two types of "Camurupim", this is an interior drawing of the large-scale residence. (1975)

Around the Architecture Urban Planning

大都市の交通改革

都市規模のプロジェクトとしては、1981年のサンパウロ市中心部における「アニャンガバウ渓谷高架プロジェクト」の都市計画案が最も注目すべきものだろう。アニャンガバウ地区は、サンパウロ市を通り抜ける小さな川周辺の地域名であり、かつてはサンパウロ市の中心部だった。しかし1950年代の人口爆発によって街の構造が急激に変化したことで、中心部は「サンパウロ美術館(MASP)」(p. 036)のあるパウリスタ通りへと移った。このプロジェクトは、次第に荒廃していったアニャンガバウ地区の再開発のために開かれた、大々的な公開コンペティションの提出案である。勝利したチームは交通を地下化する計画を提出したが、リナはそれと真逆の方法で都市に動的な興奮を生み出そうとした。

リナが率いるチームは、歩車分離のために車道として高架道路をつくり、その下をまるごと歩行者専用の公園とする計画を提出した。上下に重なった9メートル幅の高架道路は、熱帯植物のような形をしたチューブ状の金属製の柱で支えられ、その植物が絡まるかのように、水平方向には金属製の格子状の構造が用いられた。道路には自然の道のような勾配を付け、丘のようなランドスケープを築いた。リナは、ここでは自然素材をそのまま用いるのではなく、人工的なものに有機的な性格を帯びさせることを目指した。

プロジェクト案では、道路下の緑あふれる公園は歩行者のみに開かれ、かつて川であったこの場所の歴史を示唆するような池と共に、ゴムの木やヤシの木などの熱帯植物の下には石のベンチが置かれ、アイスクリームやケバブの屋台、古本や雑誌、おもちゃを売る屋台などが描かれていた。加えて「掃除は毎週月曜日」といった具体的な運営方法までが考えられていた。さらに周囲の建物については、古い郵便局を移民のための郵便センターにしたり、高層建築の最上階に眺めの良いレストランをつくるなど、リノベーションによって新しく機能させることが構想されていた。リナはこの高架下の公園を、交通のためだけではなく、文化や生活のインフラストラクチャーとして位置付けた。このプロジェクトは、常に都市に意識を向けていたリナのエンジニア的、ランドスケープ・デザイナー的視点が見られると共に、壮大で思い切ったビジョンが感じられる貴重なものといえる。

アニャンガバウ渓谷。
Anhangabaú Valley.

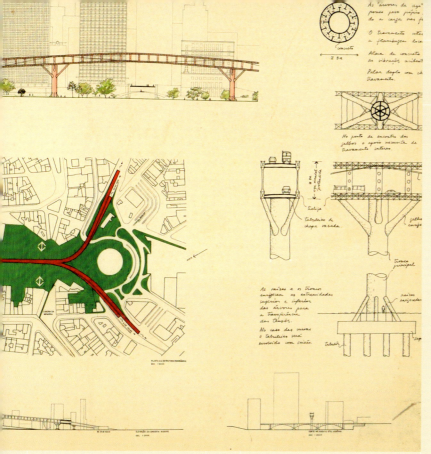

「アニャンガバウ」、提出された立面図・平面図・柱の詳細図。
丘のように波打つ道路、高架下の緑地計画、柱の構造が分かる。(1981年)
A detailed blueprint of the elevation, floor plan and columns submitted for "Anhangabaú". You can see the undulating, hill-like road, the greenery area plan for under the elevated road, and the structure of the columns. (1981)

could express it in concrete form without losing a poetic sense characteristic of the region. Unfortunately, her plan was not accepted by the project's parent company and thus it never materialized.

Rethinking Urban Transportation

As an urban scale project, the most remarkable one was probably the city planning draft for the "Anhangabaú Valley Project" in the central part of São Paulo City in 1981. Anhangabaú is the name of a district surrounding a small river that cuts across the city of São Paulo, and it was once the heart of São Paulo. But due to the population explosion in the 1950's, the city structure underwent a sudden change, and this caused the city center to move to Paulista Avenue where the "São Paulo Museum of Art (MASP)" (p. 036) was located. This project was undertaken as a large-scale public competition proposal to redevelop Anhangabaú, which was gradually falling into ruin. The winning team submitted a plan that would see them move transportation underground, but Lina attempted to create a dynamic excitement in the city by entirely opposite means.

The team led by Lina built an elevated road to serve as a road that would separate pedestrians and vehicles, and they submitted a plan to have the entire area beneath it serve as a park exclusively for pedestrians. With a width of nine meters overlapping above and below, the elevated road was supported by tubular metal pillars that resembled the shape of tropical vegetation appearing to be entwined by the horizontal metal grid-pattern structure they used. They added a natural path-like slope to the road and built a landscape resembling a hill. Lina did not aim to use natural materials as is but rather to fit an organic personality into man-made objects. According to the project draft, the lush green park below the road would only be open to pedestrians

「アニャンガバウ」、高架周辺地域の復興計画のドローイング。高架下の公園でくつろぐ人びとの視線の先にある建物は修復され、新しい機能が計画されていた。

Drawing of the "Anhangabaú Valley Project" a revitalization plan for the area surrounding an elevated road. There was the idea of adding new functionality through the renovation of buildings within sight of the people relaxing in the park below the road.

地方都市の復興

そして1987年、「サルヴァドール旧市街修復プロジェクト」(p. 118)では、既存の都市に複数の小さな手を加えるという手法が採られた。リナは、都市の歴史、人びとの暮らし、営まれる文化が密接に混ざり合うような計画を提案した。伝統的なアフロ・ブラジル文化と、地域の現代文化の両者を発信する施設となるよう、重要な建造物を修復して生まれ変わらせると共に、生活の基盤となる住居や商店をその近くに配置した。住民の暮らしを少し手助けするような、大らかで、明るく、楽しく、力強い都市の姿がデザインされていた。しかし、政権と自身の健康上の問題とで、完全な実現は果たせなかった。

土地を人びとへ取り戻す

リナは生涯都市プロジェクトを完成させることはなかったが、その態度からは、都市と建築に対する壮大な夢や希望が感じられる。歴史を重視しながらも、生活の中で生まれた問題を解決し、人びとがより豊かに暮らせるように手助けするためには、大胆に改修することをためらわなかった。そのビジョンの一端は「MASP」の「ベルヴェデーレ」から感じられる。高架下の公園で「人びとのセントラルパーク」を目指したように、都市の中に人びとが集い、憩い、語り合って楽しみ、自分たちの場所だという意識がもてる空間をつくり出すことで、市民の生活と精神を守り、街のアイデンティティを生成するように促し続けた。

also conceived of the idea of adding new functionality through renovations by, for example, turning an old post office into a mail center for immigrants, building restaurants with a nice view on the top floor of high-rise buildings, and so on. Lina positioned the park below the elevated road not only for the sake of transportation, but also as cultural and lifestyle infrastructure. In addition to showing Lina's engineering and landscape design perspective due to her habitual consciousness of the city, this project was valuable for allowing one to conceive her magnificent and bold vision.

The Revitalization of Regional Cities

And then, for the restoration of "The Historic Center of Salvador" (p. 118) in 1987, Lina used a technique that involved making several minor improvements to the existing city. She proposed a plan to closely blend together the city's history, the lives of people, and the culture they lived in. In addition to restoring important buildings through renovations to create facilities that would transmit both traditional Afro-Brazilian culture and contemporary regional culture, she arranged housing and shops nearby to serve as a foundation for

and, along with the pond that seemed to hint at the history of this place which used to be a river, stone benches were placed under tropical vegetation like gum trees and palm trees, and they had drawn things like outdoor stands that sold ice-cream and kebabs, used books and magazines, and toys. Moreover, they had even thought of specific instructions, such as "Cleaning will be done each week on Monday". Regarding the surrounding buildings, they

life. Lina designed an easy-going, bright, fun and strong cityscape to help the lives of residents a little. But, due to issues with the government and her own health, Lina was unable to fully realize this project.

Returning the Land to the People

Lina did not complete the city project during her lifetime but, from her attitude, we can sense her lofty hopes and dreams regarding the city and architecture. While she attached importance to historical context, she did not hesitate to make bold modifications in order to solve issues found within everyday life and to lend a hand in creating a more well-rounded life for people. A part of this vision is perceivable in the "MASP"'s "Belvedere". In the same way she aimed for a "Central Park for the people" at the park below the elevated road, she continued to defend the lives and spirit of citizens while encouraging the formation of an urban identity by creating a space inside the city for people to gather, think, enjoy conversing with each other, and develop a consciousness of the place as their own.

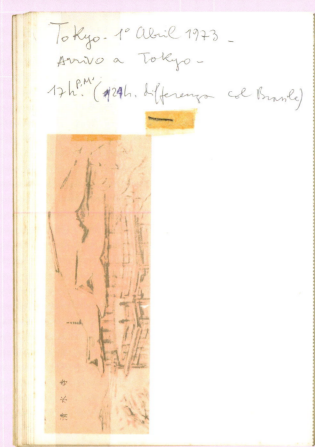 

日本滞在中のノート。
京都の寺院でのスケッチ。(1973年4月1日)
Notes taken during her stay in Japan. A sketch done at a temple in Kyoto. (April 1, 1973)

Around the Architecture

Lina in Japan
日本とリナ

A country of the Far East, more in line with the course of time, more connected to the results of scientific practice (and its results), and that after Hiroshima it could have reached the same scientific and technological results of the West, but with "lower cost".
Lina Bo Bardi

思い描くのは、極東にありながら時代の流れに乗り、
科学的実験（と、それによる成果）に関わり、「ヒロシマ」ののちも
西欧と同様の科学的・技術的成果を、「より効率良く」達成した国のことです。
リナ・ボ・バルディ

日本から持ち帰ったもの

リナは1973年4月と、「SESCポンペイア文化センター」（p.068）設計中の1978年10月（58歳と64歳の時）に日本を訪れている*1。1回目は京都を中心に、2回目は東京を中心に鎌倉・日光をまわり、建築や風景、食事、文化、そして人びととの交流を楽しんだ。建築家・丹下健三を訪ねたともいわれている。リナは旅先で多くのスケッチやメモを残しており、この旅はその後の生き方へも大きな影響を与えたことが伺える。食べ物や生活に対する向き合い方も変わり、一時はお酒や煙草をやめることも考えていたようだ。リナが日本を捉える視点には、西欧と地理的に離れ、独自の文化をもつブラジルとの共通点も含まれていた。ブラジルのあるべき姿を考え続けたリナにとって、日本は国が独自の文化を守りながら近代化を進めるための方法論を探す、よい対象でもあった。

この旅での経験は、デザインへも反映された。規格的でありながらさまざまな組み合わせが可能な畳や、日本の伝統的な建具の無駄のないシンプルな美しさに以前から興味をもっていたリナは、寺院や日本家屋、鎌倉近代美術館を訪れた。歌舞伎の鑑賞時には劇場設計の参考のためにメモを取っている。ブラジルに帰国後リナは「SESC」において、出発前は長方形にしていた窓の形を、曲線を用いた雲形に変更し真っ赤な格子戸を設けたり、鎌倉の寺院で見た側溝を敷地内の歩道脇に取り入れている。さらに1986年に自邸の敷地内に建てた小さなスタジオは、木造で引き戸が採用され、周囲にはたくさんの竹が植えられた。

*1　来日の主要目的は毎日新聞社主催の「MASP」のコレクション展のため。

「ガラスの家」敷地内に建てた自身のスタジオ。
Her own studio built on the site of the "Glass House".

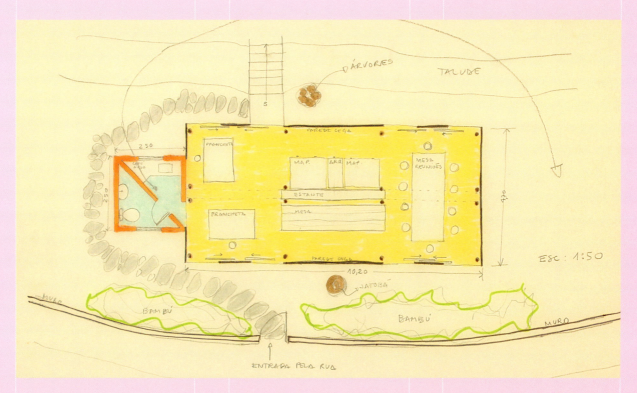

スタジオの平面ドローイング。竹林や石畳の歩道などが描かれているほか、木の柱による構造が分かる。（1986年頃）
A floor plan drawing of the studio. It depicts a bamboo forest and a stone-paved path. In addition, one can see a structure made of wooden pillars. (*circa* 1986)

鎌倉、円覚寺にてスケッチをするリナ。(1978年10月4日)
Lina sketching at Engaku-ji, Kamakura. (October 4, 1978)

Experiences Brought Back from Japan

Lina visited Japan in April of 1973, and during the design of "SESC - Pompéia Factory Leisure Center" (p. 068) in October of 1978. Her first trip focused on Kyoto, while her second trip focused on Tokyo, where she traveled to Kamakura and Nikko, enjoying the architecture and scenery, cuisine, culture, and her interactions with people. She is also said to have met with the architect Kenzo Tange. Lina made many sketches and memos here and there during her stay, and the trip can be seen to have had a significant impact on her future life. It changed the way she confronted food and life, and she even appeared to consider quitting alcohol and tobacco at one point. Lina's perspective on Japan also included points in common with Brazil, such as having an original culture and being geographically distant from the West. To Lina, who continuously thought about the state of things in Brazil, Japan would have been a good example of a country searching for a methodology to forward modernization while protecting its unique culture. Her experiences during this trip were also reflected in her designs. Having an interest since before in Japan's traditional techniques, such as standardized tatami mats with a variety of possible combinations and the economical beauty of traditional Japanese furniture, Lina visited temples, Japanese houses, and the Kamakura Museum of Modern Art. She took notes while watching kabuki to use as a reference for a theater design. After returning to Brazil, Lina changed what had been rectangular windows at "SESC" before her departure to "cloud window" openings using curved lines, and she also set up bright red lattice doors and incorporated the gutters she had seen at Kamakura temple into the curbs within the premises. Furthermore, when she built a small studio on the premises of her own home in 1986, she adopted wooden sliding doors and planted many bamboo shoots in the surrounding area.

*1   The main purpose of her visits to Japan was for the collection exhibitions of São Paulo Art Museum sponsored by Mainichi Newspapers.

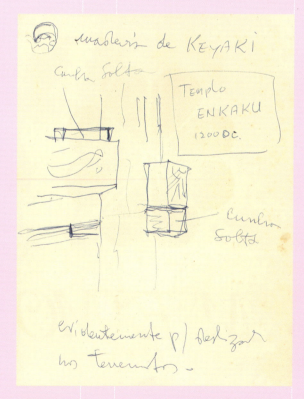

円覚寺で描いたスケッチ。
「地震」「ケヤキの木」などと書き込まれている。(1978年)
A sketch drawn at Engaku-ji. In it are written "Earthquake", "Zelkova Tree", etc. (1978)

リナの日記より
Entries from Lina's Journal

1978年9月27日　東京

午後5時に東京に到着。新しい成田空港に。世界中の多くの巨大な空港と似ている。周囲の風景はとても美しい。自然は人間の手で円満に変え得るという例だ。作物に応じて、緑、黄色、ベージュ、茶色といった色合いの四角い土地割りの群が規則的に並ぶ。そして大きな黒いかたまりは森だ。

Sep. 27, 1978 Tokyo

I arrive at Tokyo at 5:00 on the afternoon. New Narita Airport will agree with a world big anonymous airport. The neighboring scenery is very beautiful. Nature is the human example which can be changed peacefully by hand. The neighboring scenery is very beautiful. It is all green, and, depending on the crops, yellow, beige, groups of the square land at the rate of of the hue such as the brown line up regularly. It is all green, and, depending on the crops, yellow, beige, groups of the square land at the rate of of the hue such as the brown line up regularly. And the big black lump is a forest.

紅葉の押し花。
A pressed maple leaf.

1978年9月30日

私たちは安田という会社の本社ビル*¹に行った。（中略）その後私たちは最上階（52階）で開かれている展覧会を訪れ、東京を見渡した。サンパウロ美術館の絵画は、東京の風景に囲われていた。私は凍りつき、麻痺したようになり、サンパウロのことを、パウリスタ通りのことを考えた……。たったふた言が口から出た。これはアメリカだ。

*1　旧安田火災海上本社ビル（現損保ジャパン日本興亜本社ビル）と思われる。

Sep. 30, 1978

Then we went (...) to the Japanese Yasuda Company headquarters(...) Then we visited the art exhibition on the top floor (52nd) and watched Tokyo. The paintings of the Museum were ensured by them. I was frozen, paralyzed, thinking about São Paulo, the Paulista Ave... I think I said no more than 20 words. It's the USA America.

*1　Thought to be the former Yasuda Fire and Marine Insurance Head Office Building (currently the Sompo Japan Nipponkoa Head Office Building).

植物のスケッチ。旅先で植物を記録するのはリナの習慣だった。
A sketch of the flora. It was Lina's custom to record the flora she encountered during her travels.

1978年10月1日　日光

日本文化には、身体が本来もっているエロティックな優美さに対する愛情が感じられる。これはギリシャにはないものだ。クリスチャンの西欧国で起きた身体への畏敬の念は、「私的な」自分勝手さと、お互いへの真の優しさの欠如に由来する。中国のマルキシズムは、(中略)クリスチャンの愛情とはまるっきり異なる。

　昨夜夕食の席で、私たち(妹のグラツィエッラと私)が母親に対して感情を爆発させていたことが恥ずかしくなった。ある家族がホテルのロビーに入ってきた。おそらく裕福な農家だろう。ボーイや豪華なテーブル、ウェイターたちを気にかけることもなく、背の高くたくましい息子が、母親をおぶっていた。彼のその背中はいつもバッグや荷物も運んでいるはずだ。彼は前のめりになっていた。母親の腕は彼の脚の前に垂れていた。小さな老婦人だったが、重いことは明らかで、彼女はグレイの着物に白い日本のサンダルをはいてその背中にだらりとぶら下がっていた。

　誰もそのさりげない魔法のような行動を、みじめとも素晴らしいともとらない。富士山のように、岩のように、木々のように、池のように当たり前のことだった。私の目には涙があふれた。しかし隣の木村*1を見ると、彼は静かに落ち着いていた。私は冷静になり、イタリアで先ほどのようなことがあったらと想像してみた。誰もが立ち上がって手伝おうとし、夕食での会話は目の前で起きた事実の話題になるのでは……などと。西欧では、年老いた母親はたいてい老人ホームに入れられる。老婦人への愛情と深い敬意は、ここでは自然への愛情と敬意と同じくらい強い(おそらくみごとな文明化達成の賜物なのだろう)。一方アフリカとアフロ・ブラジルには、偉大なる父*2と、偉大なる母*3がいる……。

*1　旅行に同行した友人のケイ・キムラ。

*2,3　アフリカ由来のブラジルの民間信仰カンドンブレの太陽の神オシャラと海の女神イエマンジャのこと。

October 1, 1978 Nikko

In Japanese culture, the affection for the erotic grace that the body originally has is felt. This is not in Greece. The reverence for the body that occurred in the West European countries of Christians comes from "self" selfishness and lack of true kindness to each other. Marxism in China shows (...) This is entirely different from the affection of Christian.

Last night I was ashamed that we (the younger sister, Graziella and I) were exploding their feelings towards their mothers at the dinner table. A family came into the hotel lobby. Probably it will be a wealthy farmhouse. Tall and rugged son, who had a mother, totally irrespective of the existence of a boy, a luxurious table, waiter and so on. His back should always carry bags and luggage. He was scooped down. My mother's arms were hanging in front of his legs. It is a small old lady, but it is obvious that it is heavy, she wears a white Japanese sandal in a gray kimono and hanging hanging on her back.

No one takes its casual magical behavior, not miserable either. Like Mt. Fuji, like a rock, like a tree, like a pond was a matter of course. Tears overflowed in my eyes. However, looking at the next Kimura*1, he calmed down quietly. I calm down and imagined that there was something like Italy in the past. Everyone got up and tried to help, and the conversation at dinner would be a topic of facts that occurred in front of me ... and so on. In Western Europe, old mothers are usually placed in nursing homes. Love and deep respect for old ladies are as strong as love and respect for nature here (perhaps it is the gift of achievement of amazing civilization). On the other hand, Africa and Afro Brazil have a great father*2 and a great mother*3.

*1　Ky · Kimra of a friend who accompanied the trip.

*2,3　Brazilian private faith derived from Africa About God of the sun of the sun of Candombre and the goddess of the sea Yemanja.

1978年10月4日

鎌倉へ行き、寺院と美術館*1を訪れた。寺院についてメモを取る。美術館では、館長に会い、坂倉事務所のチーフにインタビューをした。レポーターが記録や撮影などを行った。美術館は深い森に覆われた丘に寄り添うように建っている。夕方には、美術館の美しい庭へ行った。建物の周りに育っている蓮はダークブルーのように見えた。

　古い日本料理店へ夕食に出掛けた。私が子どもの頃に夢見ていた日本のすべてが、その古い家に集まっていた。緑、柔らかい芝、木々と花々、周りを囲む森。そのころには夕方になっていた。提灯の灯りだけが庭を照らしていた。コオロギが鳴いた。時々夜行性の鳥も。それは古き良き日本だった。着物で給仕をしてくれた女性たちはみんな年老いていた。甘く深いメランコリー。

October 4th, 1978

We went to Kamakura, visited the temples and the art museum. Took notes on the temples. At the museum, I was received by the director, had an interview with the chief architect of the Sakakura group. The reporter recorded, photographed, etc. In the evening I went to the beautiful garden of the Museum which leans on a hill covered by dense woods. The lotuses growing around the building were dark blue. We went out for dinner at an old Japanese restaurant. Everything I dreamed about Japan when I was a child was gathered in the old house. The green and soft grass, the trees and the flowers, the woods all around. By now it was evening. Only a lantern illuminated the garden. The crickets sang. Occasionally a nocturnal bird. It was the ancient Japan. The ladies who served in kimono were all old. Sweet and deep melancholy.

*1　神奈川県立近代美術館鎌倉館（坂倉準三設計）のこと。

鎌倉にて。（1978年10月4日）
At Kamakura (October 4, 1978)

神奈川県立近代美術館、庭の蓮池。（1978年）
The garden lotus pond at the Museum of Modern Art, Kamakura (1978)

雨の中、鎌倉の寺院。側溝による排水に注目し、帰国後「SESC」の歩道に採用している。（1978年10月）
Kamakura temple in the rain. Lina took note of the drainage gutter and adopted it for the path at "SESC" after returning to Brazil. (October 1978)

*1　The Museum of Modern Art, Kamakura (designed by Junzo Sakakura).

1978年10月6日
3時までに、毎日新聞社の方が私たちを成田へ車で送ってくれた。雨で、何もかも灰色で悲しい。本当に出発の日だ。さあサンパウロへ戻るのだ。

でも何もかも変わらなければ。去年と同じではいけない。日本茶が恋しい。シンプルな和食が恋しい。サンパウロでの食生活も変えてみよう。

On October 6, 1978
Mainichi Shimbun drove us to Narita on Friday by Tokyo 3:00. I am sad with all gray because of rain. It is really the departure date. Well, I come back to Sao Paulo.
But all must change. It is the same as last year and is wrong. I yearn for Japanese green tea. I yearn for simple Japanese food. I will change the eating habits in Sao Paulo.

おでんを描いたドローイング「出汁のなかで泳ぐ大きな貝と生き物たち」。食べ物に対する日本人の姿勢はリナの印象に深く残っていた。(1978年10月4日)
A drawing of oden. "Large shellfish and living things swim inside the broth". Japanese people's attitude towards food left a deep impression on Lina. (October 4, 1978)

坐禅のように座るリナ。
日本への旅から帰宅後、「ガラスの家」にて。(1978年)
Lina sitting in a zazen-like pose. This was taken at the "Glass House" after she returned from her trip to Japan. (1978)

対談　妹島和世×塚本由晴
Interview
Kazuyo Sejima &
Yoshiharu Tsukamoto

進行
和多利恵津子(ワタリウム美術館館長)
＋
周防貴之(建築家)

Conducted by
Etsuko Watari
(WATARI-UM, The Watari Museum of Contemporary Art)
&
Takashi Suo (Architect)

都市へのあざやかなアプローチ

——おふたりが訪れたなかで印象に残った作品からお話を伺いたいと思います。

妹島——ワタリウム美術館でのリナ・ボ・バルディ展(2016年)の準備のために、和多利さんや会場デザインを担当した周防さんと一緒にブラジルに行きました。見たのは、「ガラスの家」(p. 012)と「サンパウロ美術館(MASP)」(p. 036)、「SESCポンペイア文化センター」(p. 068)、「サンタ・マリア・ドス・アンジョス教会」(p. 106)、「テアトロ・オフィシナ」(p. 140)、「ヴァレリア・P・シレル邸」(p. 156)などだったと思います。

一番印象に残っているのは「MASP」ですね。エレベーターで上がって、見終わって上の展示室から外の階段に出た瞬間、下のピロティにいる人たちとバスと大通りがパッと視界に飛び込んでくるというのが一番の衝撃でした。もうひとつは「サンタ・マリア・ドス・アンジョス教会」です。赤い土の小道を抜け、階段を上って教会の正面に向き直った瞬間、奥の祭壇とトップライトが突然見える。

このふたつは、配置図や建物の構造から予想できているつもりでしたが、いきなり場所と建物がドッキングして、驚くべき体験で、とても面白いと感じました。

塚本——僕は「MASP」はリナの作品のなかでは異質な感じがしています。「SESC」や「テアトロ・オフィシナ」が一方にあって、もう一方に「MASP」があって、間に「ガラスの家」があると捉えています。

でも、どちらも"人びと"というものに対する想像力がいいんです。建築というのはこんなに"人びと"をイメージさせるのか、喚起させるのかと。しかもリナ自身もその"人びと"の一部となっていて、決して「あの人たちのためにサービスする」感じではない。そういうところにずっと感動しています。

それはブラジル社会独特のものかもしれないし、1950年代から70年代ぐらいまでの、第2次大戦後の世界がもっていた、世の中をつくり直すんだという希望の表れかもしれないのですが、なんだかうらやましくもあります。

妹島——「MASP」はどう思いました? 私は前にも行っていて、1回目に行った時は中に入れなくて、ピロティの下に行ってみただけだったので、大きな広場をつくったくらいにしか認識していなかったんですね。でも2回目に行った時、展示室から外に出た瞬間に、展示室と街がひとつに連続してすばらしいと思いました。ああそうか、と腑に落ちました。ピロティでもち上げたからこそ、塚本さんが言った人びとのこととか、人と街、その場所がつながっている感じとか、建築が都市の一部をつくっていることが体験できるようになっている。本当にリナのつくり方は面白いと思います。

——リナ展のデザインの際に妹島さんから「建築のデザインだけでなく、設計のアプローチの大胆さを見て分かるようにしたほうがいい」と言われたのが印象に残りました。

塚本——僕は「MASP」には最初はパウリスタ通りから行きました。2回目はパウリスタ通りから下がっていく斜面にある植物園を下から登ってパウリスタ通りに出たんです。すると、いきなりピロティ越しに街の向こう側が見えました。すごく印象的なシークエンスでした。そういう都市構造との関係が意識されていますね。

「リナ・ボ・バルディ」展 (2015年、ワタリウム美術館) 展示風景。
View of the "Lina Bo Bardi" exhibition (2015, WATARI-UM, The Watari Museum of Contemporary Art).

「アンジョス教会」。扉が開くと、階段から内部の祭壇まで見通せる。
"Santa Maria dos Anjos Chapel". One can see from the stairs all the way in to the altar when the door is open.

広場にふさわしい美術館

妹島——リナの建築は、ラディカルでありながら、いろいろな既存のものと関係があったり、材料も地元の土を使ったりして、周辺の環境に馴染んでいるんですが、「MASP」だけは、建築がちょっと街のスケールから浮いて見えるようなところがありますね。

塚本——「MASP」は施設建築に対するアプローチとしては建築家らしいあり方。そこで想起される人びととは市民という一般性をもっている。他のものは、デザインやつくるプロセスが、使う人、住む人にもっと近い感じがして、もう少し具体的な人びとに向き合っている。

妹島——そうですね。リナ展の時に上映していたビデオのなかで、リナは「MASP」に関わりはじめた頃の話をしていますが、もともと市長はあの広場に公園と公衆トイレをつくろうと計画していたようですね。それを「あそこは素晴らしい場所なのだから、美術館にするべきだ」と言って、相当政治的に動いている。だから、市民を驚かせるような、巨大で存在感のあるものをつくろうという意識は強くあったと思います。

「MASP」のピロティでいろんな集会や展示が行われている写真を見ると、人びとというより、もうちょっと抽象的な、"民衆"みたいなものまで含まれている感じがしますね。

塚本——公共の施設としてのあり方を引き受けていますからね。でも施設型の建築は権威的になったり、管理が優先されて冷たい感じになりがちだけど、リナの場合そうはならない。展示の仕方、都市空間に対する大胆な構えなどに、人間的な配慮が重ねられているからでしょうね。ただそういうことのできる建築家は他にもいるでしょう。でも「MASP」以外の作品の、あの施設ではない感じで建築をつくれる建築家は、今もだけど特にあの時代は少なかったと思います。リナ・ボ・バルディのすごさをそこに見ています。

妹島——「MASP」を設計しているときのドローイング(p. 200)を見て感じるのは、リナにはアートはみんなのもので、美術館のなかに後生大事に閉じ込めておくものではないという意識があって、アートをピロティにも展示しよう、一緒に街のなかに飛び出していこう、見ている人が触ってもいい、そういう思いがリナのドローイングから感じられますね。

塚本——そういえば、「MASP」の初期案のドローイング(p. 210)って、外壁がガラスじゃなくて、植物が描かれていませんでした?

妹島——わざわざ外壁に植物を入れていました。でも土壁では重すぎるというので、最終的にはガラスに決まったんですね。

壁から解放されたアート

塚本——「MASP」は展示方法が面白いですね。

妹島——面白いですね。だいいち展示壁がないですからね。

塚本——この手法は、妹島さんもルーヴル・ランスでも参考にされていますね。

妹島——あれは不思議な経過を辿りました。最初はたしか展示壁をアイランド形式でスタディしていたんですよ。そうしたらランスのキュレーターがこれはどうかと言って「MASP」の展示室の写真を持って来たんですね。こんなことを本当にやっていいのかなあと半信半疑でスタディしているうちに、そのキュレー

「MASP」内部への階段から「ベルヴェデーレ」を見晴らす。
Looking onto the "Belvedere" from the stairs to the interior of the MASP.

ターがいなくなってしまった（笑）。それで「MASP」案は却下されて、また壁を立てるなど紆余曲折があった後、展示壁をアルミでつくるという提案をした時に、館長が「展示壁にアルミを使うのはもしかしたら面白いかもしれない」ということになり、パリのルーヴル内にモックアップをつくってみたらすごく美しかった。それでアルミでやることになり、結果的に、アルミ壁から展示を解放して、現在のような展示方法になりました。

──絵を壁から解放して展示するというのは、今までと相当違う話ですよね。

妹島──すごく違いますね。自分でアートを自立させて見せる手法を実際にやって本当に驚いたのは、展示物を室内に並べ出したら、見ている自分と展示物との距離がすごく近くなってしまうんですよ。壁だったら、いくら近づいても「こっち側は展示物ですよ」「私は見ていますよ」という関係が自然にできているけれども、あんなに近いと壊そうと思ったら壊せるし、施工が進んでいる時、少し怖かったですね。

塚本──この展示方法が面白いなと思うのは、広場にいっぱい人がいるのと同じ状況を歴史的な絵画や彫刻も含めてつくろうという話ですよね。以前、植田実さん*1の展覧会のデザインをしたときに、『都市住宅』誌と住まいの図書館の本を1冊ずつ立たせて並べたのですが、本一つひとつが独自の人格をもっているように見えて面白かった。

妹島──本当に近くなりますね。自分で距離を調整することになるので、思わず後ろを振り返ってみたりしました。

塚本──「MASP」の展示では、モディリアーニの絵の後ろに女性が立っている、この写真（p.061）も面白いですね。

妹島──面白い。それに、リナは絵画を掛ける部分をガラスにしているでしょう。ガラスにしたことで、鑑賞している人との距離がもっと近くなっていますね。

塚本──しかも、これはコンクリートとガラスと木でつくっていますからね。地震がないところは、いいねぇ（笑）。

妹島──そういうラディカルなことができるというのも、やっぱりリナがイタリア人というのがすごく大きいのだろうと思います。

塚本──あと、リナ特有の民主主義の考え方みたいなものがありますね。どこまでを仲間に入れるか。その境界は閉じることはなく、しかもその対象は生きている人間だけではない。そういう広がっていく感覚があったのではないでしょうか。

妹島──だから、リナはおばけみたいなものとかいろんな変わったものも集めるんでしょうね。自邸（「ガラスの家」）に、いろんなものが置いてありました。

塚本──限られた人たちのためだけじゃない民主主義を考えていたのだと思います。今の世の中は、制度や産業の仕組みが、想定する人びとの自画像やメンバーシップを押し付けてくるようなところがあるから、リナのパースペクティブは今こそ有効ですよ。

"貧しい演劇"を支える"貧しい建築"の多様性

──塚本さんは「テアトロ・オフィシナ」を絶賛されていましたね。

塚本──「テアトロ・オフィシナ」は、劇団員がほとんど住むように活動しています。鉄骨足場でできたバルコニーが積層していて、2、3階は観客席だけど、さらに上の階は楽屋になり、天井のフレームには舞台衣装がびっしり掛けられています。屋根がガ

*1　1935年〜。編集者。1968年に『都市住宅』を創刊し編集長として活動。

ラス張りの所に連れて行かれて、真上から演劇を見せることもあると説明を受けました。ホームベースなので長時間の演目も可能です。

　ユートピア的な演劇空間かもしれないけれど、それが本当に美しく具現化した事例が「テアトロ・オフィシナ」だと思う。建築家も劇団のなかに居場所があるぐらい、深く関わっています。倉庫を劇場に転用するという説明では済まない、何か根本的に違う社会的な事件が起こっているようです。

妹島――使うところまでも一体化していますね。

塚本――リナ自身もしばらくの間、そこでほとんど劇団の一員のような感じで打ち合わせをしながらつくっていったと聞いたんですが、そういうところが本当に面白いですね。

妹島――そうですね。

――「テアトロ・オフィシナ」は、イギリスのガーディアン紙が選ぶ「世界一アバンギャルドな劇場」のなかに入っていますが、劇場に入ると、長い通路があるだけで客席が見当たらなかったのには、どうなっているんだろうと驚きました。

塚本――この劇団は、ブラジルの人たちが、貧しい土地で大変な苦労をして農地を開墾してきたことや、内戦が続いた時期の流血のストーリーなど、現代ブラジル史の壮絶なドラマを上演してきました。通路のようなそのステージは「ストリート」なのです。だから脇に木が生えていたり、噴水があったりする。私はリハーサル中に、ストリートの下にあるトレンチに入れてもらいました。それは下水道から突然兵士が出て来て戦う演出のためだと聞きました。

　一般的に劇団の人たちは、脚本、演出、役者、美術などさまざまな要素をひとつのパッケージにしているので、いろんな場所で上演したい。演劇はそもそも旅をしながら上演していくものでもあるので、劇場の方はむしろ融通の利く、ユニヴァーサルであることが求められてもいるわけですね。それに対して建築家は実験劇場を構想しがちで、結構演劇人からは疎んじられているのですが。

妹島――実験劇場だと、そこでしか上演できないですからね。

塚本――ところがここは奇跡的に両者の意図が一致しています。ポーランドの劇作家イェジー・グロトフスキが1965年に提唱した「貧しい演劇」への共感があったようです。それは演劇を文学、音楽、美術、衣装などの総合芸術ではなく、それらを差し引いてむしろ貧しくすることによって浮かび上がる、俳優と観客の間の関係を探求する演劇だそうです。「アルテ・ポーヴェラ（貧しい美術）」にも通ずる思想ですね。

妹島――でも、「テアトロ・オフィシナ」という箱の中がただ貧しかったら本当に貧しい感じになってしまうけれども、太陽の光が入ってきたり、水が流れていたり、植物があったりと、いろいろなものを取り込むようにしていることで、すごく多様な演劇空間がつくられる。

塚本――そう思います。

設計事務所をもたない建築家

塚本――リナは家具もたくさんデザインしていますね。「SESC」の劇場のごつい椅子いいですよね。現場でつくったとどこかで読みましたが。

妹島——「サンタ・マリア・ドス・アンジョス教会」の椅子も、並べるだけでつながっていく感じがすごくいいですね。

塚本——リナは事務所をもたず、現場に入り込んで職人や利用者と一緒に考えていたようですね。なかなか職業建築家には難しいことですが、それができるのはうらやましいです。

妹島——それにしても事務所がなくてどうやってつくっていたんだろう（笑）。

塚本——現場がはじまったら、現場事務所で一緒にやっていたんじゃないかな。

妹島——だから家具もああいうものがつくれたんでしょうね。今の私たちだったら、どうつくるかというのを図面で置き換えて考えていきますが、リナは家具の組み立てと同じように、建築も現場で、たぶんこうやって組み立てていけばつくっていけるんじゃないかというふうに考えてつくっていっているようなところがある。「MASP」で使われているガラスのイーゼルとか。現場でいろんなものができ上がったんだと思いますね。

塚本——大きいものでも手づくり感があります。

妹島——デザインしたものをどうやってつくるかという時に、現場でものを組み立てるように考えていくから、特別な技術をもった人がいなくてもある程度つくっていけるみたいなところがある。だからある意味でとても現代的と言えると思います。

塚本——工業化が進展していく時代に、建設産業からのサービスとは一線を画していた感じがします。だから、実際のふるまいからデザインができる。リナの建築ってふるまいに対する配慮や、発想にあふれているので、勝手にビヘイビオロロジー（建築のふるまい学）の師と崇めています。日本では、吉阪隆正とか象設計集団が近い思想をもっていました。象設計集団も名護市庁舎のコンペを勝った後は、市庁舎の敷地にテントを張って暮らし、1日の気候の変化を感じながら設計していたと聞きました。そういう建築への巻き込まれ方から生まれる建築の質がありますね。

ブラジルの民衆・民俗エネルギーとの出合い

妹島——塚本さんが最初に言ったような、第2次大戦後の、この時代は、「民衆のための建築はこういうもの」という上から目線じゃなくて、民衆と一緒に考えてものごとを推し進めていくような時期だったこともあって、リナ自身も、この時代の風潮に興味をもったというか、思想的にも傾倒していったということと、彼女がイタリア人だったこと、イタリアからブラジルに来たこと、いろいろなことが混じり合ってリナの建築がつくられていったのかなと思います。

彼女の建築はすごくイタリア人的で、ものすごくラディカルにものをつくっていると思います。一方でブラジルに来て、ブラジルの民芸的なもの、風土的なものが好きになった。だから思想的にも、その両方をやるべきだという思いをもっていたんでしょうね。

塚本——リナはコミュニストだったんですよね。イタリアは共産党が政権をとっても、第2次大戦の敗戦国なのでアメリカのコントロール下にあったようです。イタリアのコミュニズムというのは、表面上は盛り上がっているように見えるのですが、自分たちの考える社会の仕組みをつくろうとすると、必ずアメリカの横やりが入る。第2次大戦の敗戦が尾を引いているわけです。それで建築家の間にもラディカリズムの表現が出てきます。

「MASP」建設現場にて、施工者と語り合うリナ。
（1965年）
Lina at the "MASP" construction site, talking with a construction worker. (1965)

妹島——ラディカルにやらざるを得ないという感じでしょうね。
塚本——資本主義の膨張に対する懸念や疑問が共有されても、決して社会システムには実装されない。その反動がスーパースタジオやアーキズームなどラディカリストのユートピア的表現を生んだそうです。リナもイタリアに残っていればそうなったかもしれない。けれどブラジルに来て、人びとのエネルギーに触れたことで、空間の実践が花開いたのかもしれません。
妹島——リナはローマで生まれて、大学卒業後、ミラノのジオ・ポンティの事務所でインテリアデザインをしたりイラストを描いていた時に、爆撃で街や自分の事務所が壊されて、戦争に対していろんな思いをもっていたんでしょうね。そんな時にピエトロ・マリア・バルディと結婚して、彼がサンパウロ美術館の館長になったので、リナも一緒にブラジルに移住する。ピエトロは著名な美術評論家で目利きのアートディーラーだったから、その影響も相当にあったと思います。
塚本——戦前、ジオ・ポンティとルドフスキーとともに『ドムス』をつくるんですよね。
妹島——すごいトリオですね。ブラジルに行かなかったら、リナは全然違っていたんじゃないかと思いますね。

「歴史」と「構造」、「空間」と「場」の混在する時代

塚本——当時は文化人類学が知識人の間で支持された時期でもあったと思うんです。それまでは歴史的弁証法が支配的だった。たとえば日本の丹下健三は、西洋のモダニズム（正）と、日本建築の伝統というまったく異なる背景をもつもの（反）の対立を止揚し、統合しようとした（合）。「正・反・合」によって「歴史」が動くという考え方。実はそうやって歴史を動かさなければならない必然性があった。

産業革命が人間社会の生産性を異常に高めてしまったからです。長距離の移動も可能になり、土地に縛りつけられないモノや人も爆発的に増えました。しかし定常社会ではその能力を使い切れません。「社会とは更新されるものだ」というパースペクティブをつくるのに、「歴史」という概念が必要だったとは考えられないでしょうか。

それに合わせて変容を迫られた建築が活路を見出した概念が「空間」ではないか。空間に依拠することで、建築は移動可能、再現可能、計量可能なものとしての性格を強めることができます。それは土地やコミュニティが事物を繰り返し産出する「場」に対するオルタナティブになります。人口も安定したところで、身の回りの資源を使って、毎日の生活を均衡させているのが定常社会です。ヴァナキュラーな建築はその結果と言えます。未開の社会はずっとそうですが、定常社会で大事なのは均衡を支える「構造」です。事物の連関が見えていて、いろいろなタブーや制約が閉じたメンバーシップで運営されることで資源がマネジメントされる「場」です。近代は手に入れた生産性や、流動性を生かすために、その均衡やメンバーシップの閉鎖性を破る「歴史」と「空間」を必要としたのではないでしょうか。

リナが活動した時期は、ヘーゲルとかマルクスとかの歴史的弁証法に対して文化人類学が「構造」というオルタナティブを出してきた時期に重なります。どうやったらもう一度均衡状態を生み出せるかというのは、現代的な関心でもあります。リナは

文化人類学者的なところがあって、いろいろなところに行って、どういう資源を使い、どういう背景のもとに人びとが暮らしをしているかに興味があったからこそ、フォークロアのオブジェを集めていたのでしょうね。そういう感覚の人が、歴史的弁証法をどう見ていたのか聞いてみたかったですね。

　実は文化人類学的建築家像というのを考えるのは容易ではありません。でも、歴史弁証法的建築家像との対比はできると思います。歴史的弁証法の問題は、「正・反・合」ができる、丹下健三のような天才を求めてしまうこと。しかも天才である以上、答えはひとつでなきゃいけない。

妹島——なるほど。

塚本——そうであることが普遍性を獲得するために不可欠とされた時代があったと思います。今でこそ、そういう価値観を少し引いて見られるようになったけれど、リナの時代にそこから引きをとるのは並大抵のことではなかったはず。リナの建築にはすごく親近感も、シンパシーもあるけれど、今の感覚だけで理解したつもりになってはいけない気がします。

人びとを勇気付けるラディカルさ

妹島——今塚本さんが言われたことは、リナの建築のあり方をすごく変えていますね。リナの建築は既存のものに新しいものを足したりとか、建ち方が完結していないじゃないですか。たとえば坂につくった家はずるずると庇が出て、階段を上がったらそれがそのまま屋根のところで擁壁になったりとか。どこまでが建築かが曖昧になっていく。

それから、建築のなかに人だけでなく動物からおばけまで、いろいろ入れていくというのもすごく面白いですね。

塚本——建築で「空間」という場合、どこかで境界を切らないとなかなか成立させにくい。リナの建築は、もっと「場」に懸けている感じがする。そのなかで一番カチッとしているのが「MASP」かな。他の作品は、どこまでが彼女がつくったもので、どこまでがその場に備わっているものか、区別が付きにくいですね。

妹島——ラディカルな骨組みがどこかに絶対あるので、だらだらいくと"状況"だけのようになってしまうおそれがあるのに、そうならないですね。

塚本——そのラディカルさも、そこにいる人たちとか場所と関係ないわけではなくて、すごく勇気付けるというか、応援するようなラディカルさとでも言えばいいでしょうか。

妹島——勇気付けていても、ただやさしいだけでもないですよね。「ついて来れるなら、ついて来なさい」みたいな感じがありますよ（笑）。

塚本——東日本大震災以降よく使われるようになった言葉が「寄り添う」です。それは大事なことだけれど、リナの場合はおしりをたたきながら寄り添っていく感じ（笑）。

——「みんなの家」と言う時に、その「みんな」のなかに建築家自身が入っているかどうかということが、今日本で突きつけられているところだと感じます。

妹島——日本では今どちらかというと寄り添いすぎて、距離感が分からなくなってしまっているところがありますね。そういう意味では、リナの立ち位置というのは、これからの日本にとってヒントになるものがあるような気がします。建築家はいろいろな

「民衆文化伝承館」展示室へのアプローチとなるブリッジ。
A bridge serving as the approach to the "Solar do Unhão – Popular Art Museum".

人の意見を聞くのは重要だけれど、ただの御用聞きになってもしょうがないから、その辺はすごく難しい。

塚本——御用聞きとして受け入れてもらえればまだいいですよ。実際の復興の現場では、建築家は相手にすらされなかったという厳しい現実も忘れてはなりません。距離感を取るためにも、厳しい現実を見詰めるためにも、さっきの「歴史」とは違うのですが、独自の歴史観をもたないといけないと思います。

多様性がつくり出す豊かなエコロジー

——ブラジル建築に共通する特徴などはありますか。

塚本——ブラジルの建築家の作品はコンクリートを用いた造形に特徴があります。サンパウロ州やリオ・デ・ジャネイロ州は年間の温度差が少ないので、鉄と複合されるコンクリートの弱点である膨張収縮が抑えられる理想的な環境です。コンクリートの可能性を考えると、面内剛性だけに重力を担わせるシェル構造や、現場でつくることができる大きな梁や柱を用いたキャンチレバーや橋のような構造は、物質の重量感と空間の軽やかさの対比が魅力的です。オスカー・ニーマイヤーは一気に全体をつくるシェルやキャンチレバーの面白さを追求し、パウロ・メンデス・ダ・ローシャは重厚なボリュームを橋のようにふわっと浮かぶ。「MASP」と「ガラスの家」を除けば、リナは一気に全体のかたちが決まるようなアプローチは取らないですね。

妹島——どちらかというと線の組み合わせ。面よりは、柱を組み立てて、そこから庇とか材料を付けていきますね。

塚本——今の言葉で言えば、エコロジカルな感覚に長けていたと思うんです。それは建築の材料の選び方にまで反映されています。適材適所という言葉がありますね。強いものは表に出し、弱いものは内に引っ込める。雨に弱い材料は軒裏に使う。昔の建築は強いものと弱いものを組み合わせるので適材適所にならざるを得なかったのが、近代になると強い材料でつくるようになるので、一体的で面一な表現が増えます。材料の種類が少ないほうが純粋に見えるので好まれたのでしょう。対してリナの場合、いろいろな材料が「みんないていいよ」みたいな感じ。

第2次大戦でミラノも爆撃を受けるのですが、日本と違って石造りの建築、れんが造りの建築が多いから、爆弾も日本に落とされた木造建築を延焼させていくようなナパーム弾じゃなくて、衝撃力で建物をぶっ壊すダイナマイト的な爆弾なんですね。

妹島——リナの手記にも「家が全部崩壊してバラバラになった」と書いてあります。

塚本——それでミラノの街は歯抜け状態になってしまう。その歯抜けになった所を50年代になるとジオ・ポンティ、アスナゴ＆ヴェンダー、カッチャ・ドミニオーニといった建築家たちが再建していくわけですが、その隣に建っている建物は200年前300年前のパラッツォ建築だから、それに合わせた新世代のパラッツォ建築がデザインされます。ところが材料のエコロジーに関しては対照的なアプローチが見られます。ドミニオーニはいろいろな材料を適材適所に使うので、そのファサードは陰影に富んでいます。それは同時に石屋、左官屋、木サッシュ屋、ブロンズ職人、鉄の職人、いろいろな職人がひとつのファサードに関わるということでもある。それに対して、アスナゴ＆ヴェンダーは、下から上まで大理石で、それと同じ面にアルミサッシュが納まるよう

「シレル邸」。
石や木材、屋上庭園など、
様々な要素が集まる。
"Valèria P. Cirell's Home".
There are various
elements gathered
such as stone, lumber, a
rooftop garden, etc.

な合理的なつくり方を好みました。だからファサードに関わる職種は石屋とアルミ製窓屋に限られたかたちになっています。

妹島——近代は大量生産型になってきたから、工種を限定したほうが安いということもありますね。だけど、建築をもっと大切に使い続けようとした時に、使われている材料が適材適所であれば傷んだ所だけ直せば済むところを、全部同じものでできていると全部やらないと直せませんよ、みたいなことにもなってしまう。

だからいろんなことが関係していると思います。リナの建築は多様性をすごく大切にしているから、いろんな人が面白いとかいいなと思うものを許容できるだけの力をもっている。現場でいろんな職種の職人さんと話しながら決めていくというのは、建築を見ても実感できるところがありますね。

エコロジーの結節点としての建築

塚本——リナは展覧会のデザインやキュレーションも手掛けていますね。美術館の空間には、建築による空間だけでなく、人と展示物の関係性によってつくられる空間もあります。そういうセンスが抜群にいい。それが建築の設計をする時にも生かされています。

妹島——そうですね。リナは、家具とか展示だけでなく、衣装やプールのタイルまでデザインしているし、書籍の編集もやっている。デザインの対象がかなり広範囲にわたっていますね。

塚本——人のふるまい全般に興味があったのでしょうね。でも自分ですべてデザインしないと気が済まないわけではない。ユーゲント・シュティールみたいに、住宅の建築からティーカップ、スリッパまでデザインしたすごい時期もありましたが、それではないですよね。彼女の場合は、デザインする対象の向こう側にいる人や背景までが手繰り寄せられ、建築に豊かなエコロジーが結び付けられていく感じでしょうか。そういうふうに建築を捉えられるといいですね。

「アンジョス教会」の前で。
妹島和世（左）、西沢立衛（右）。
In front of "Santa Maria dos Anjos Chapel". Kazuyo Sejima (left), Ryue Nishizawa (right).

A vivid approach to the city

— Please tell us about the works that stood out for you during your visit.

Sejima — To prepare for the Lina Bo Bardi exhibition (2016) at WATARI-UM, The Watari Museum of Contemporary Art, I traveled to Brazil with Ms. Watari and Mr. Suo, who was in charge of venue design. I think that we saw the "Glass House" (p. 012), "São Paulo Art Museum (MASP)" (p. 036), "SESC-Pompéia Factory Leisure Center" (p. 068), "Santa Maria dos Anjos Chapel" (p. 106), "Oficina Theater" (p. 140), and "Valéria P. Cirell's Home" (p. 156).

The thing that struck me the most was "MASP". Going up the elevator, and then, after seeing everything, the moment you step onto the outdoor stairs from the exhibition room, the way the people, buses, and main street jump into view around the pilotis below had the greatest impact on me. The other one was "Santa Maria dos Anjos Chapel". Breaking away from the red earthen path and climbing the stairs, the altar in the back and top light suddenly become visible when you turn to face the front of the church.

Regarding these two, I more or less expected how they would be from the structure of their layouts and buildings, but the sudden communion of these places and buildings was a surprising experience that I found quite interesting.

Tsukamoto — For me, "MASP" feels like something different compared to the rest of Lina's works. The way I see it, on the one hand you have "SESC" and "Oficina Theater", and on the other hand you have "MASP", and then the "Glass House" is somewhere in between. But they each have their own sense of imagination when it comes to "people". Can architecture really evoke a sense of "people" or be stirring to this extent? Moreover, Lina herself was a part of these "people" and certainly didn't seem to feel as though she was "doing a service for those people". This is the thing that always impresses me.

It may be something unique to Brazilian society, or the sense of hope towards rebuilding the world after World War II that existed between the 1950s and 1970s, but I feel somehow envious.

Sejima — What did you think about "MASP"? I had been there once before. The first time I went I couldn't enter inside. I just went beneath the pilotis and was simply aware that they had created a large plaza. But when I went the second time, I thought it was amazing how the exhibition room and city connected as one the moment I stepped outside of the exhibition room. That's when I understood. I think that the experience mentioned by Mr. Tsukamoto about people or people and the city, the way the place feels connected, and how the architecture creates a part of the city is possible precisely because the whole thing is held up by the pilotis. I think Lina's building method is quite interesting.

— When I was designing the Lina exhibition, I particularly remember being told by Ms. Sejima "you should make obvious at a glance the audacity of not only the architectural design but also the design approach".

Tsukamoto — I first went to "MASP" from Paulista Avenue. The second time I made my way to Paulista

「リナ・ボ・バルディ」展
（ワタリウム美術館）展示風景。
View of the "Lina Bo Bardi" exhibition (WATARI-UM, The Watari Museum of Contemporary Art).

Avenue by ascending from the lower end of the botanical garden located on the slope that descends off of Paulista Avenue. It was then that the other side of the city suddenly came into view through the pilotis. This was a very memorable moment. There is an awareness of its relationship with the urban structure.

A museum suitable for a plaza

Sejima — Lina's architecture is radical but at the same time it has a relationship to things that already exist, and materials consist of earth and such from the local area, so it feels right at home in the surrounding environment. But only the architecture of "MASP" appears in some ways to stand out slightly from the scale of the city.
Tsukamoto — As an approach to building facilities, "MASP" seems like the work of an architect. The people that it brings to mind are city residents, where there is a sense of commonness. Other things feel as though their design and building process is closer to users or people who live there, so they are suited to a somewhat more specific group of people.
Sejima — Right. In the video that was shown during the Lina exhibition, Lina talks about the period when she began getting involved with "MASP". The city mayor had originally planned to build a park and toilets in that plaza. Lina said "That is a wonderful place so a museum should be built there", and she got quite politically involved. So I think that's why she was strongly conscious of building something large with a real presence that would surprise local city residents.
When I see photos of various meetings and exhibitions taking place at the pilotis of "MASP", I feel that, more than just people, it includes a more abstract sense of the masses.
Tsukamoto — Because it inherited its nature as a public facility. But facility-type architecture has a tendency to feel authoritarian and cold because priority is given to its management, but in Lina's case, it is different. This is because there is a human sense of consideration added to the exhibition method and bold stance towards the urban space. But there are other architects who can do this, right? When looking at works other than "MASP", I think that the number of architects who can make architecture without it feeling like a facility-type building must have been small, especially in those days. We are witnessing the greatness of Lina Bo Bardi there.
Sejima — What I feel when I see the drawing that shows the design of "MASP" is that Lina had an awareness that art was for everybody and it shouldn't be stuffed inside a museum like some kind of treasure. Displaying art on the pilotis, having it spring out into the city, allowing people to touch it, and so on. These are the ideas that I sense from Lina's drawings.
Tsukamoto — Speaking of the early draft drawing of "MASP" (p. 210), weren't the outer walls depicted as vegetation and not as glass?
Sejima — They intended to place vegetation on the outer walls but the earthen walls were too heavy so they decided on glass in the end.

Art freed from walls

Tsukamoto — "MASP" uses interesting display methods.
Sejima - It certainly does. Most importantly, there is no display wall.
Tsukamoto — This method also served as a reference for you at Louvre Lens, right?
Sejima — That followed an odd course. I believe they first studied an island format for the display wall. Then the curator of Lens brought a photo of the "MASP" display wall and asked how that would be. As I wondered doubtfully whether it would really work, that curator disappeared (laugh). That's why the "MASP" draft was rejected and, after some twists and turns such as once again building a wall, the director said "using aluminum for the display wall might be interesting" when I proposed making a display wall with aluminum. And when I built a mockup inside the Louvre in Paris, it was really stunning. So it was decided that we would use aluminum and, as a result, the display was freed from the aluminum wall and it turned into the kind of display method used now.
— Freeing paintings from walls to display them was something extremely different from the norm up till now, right?
Sejima — It's very different. The thing that really surprised me when I actually tried that display method by making art independent was, if you line up display items inside a room, the distance between yourself and the display item gets very close. If it's a wall display, it naturally creates a relationship that says "This side is for display items" and "I am looking at you". But when you are really close up, you could even break it if you wanted to, and this made me anxious when the construction was going on.
Tsukamoto — What I find interesting about this display method is that you are trying to build something identical to a plaza packed with people that includes historic paintings and sculptures. Previously, when I was designing the exhibition show for Makoto Ueda[*1], I stood and lined up the book "Toshi Jutaku" (Urban Housing) and a book by SUMAI Library Publishing. It was interesting because each book appeared to have its own character.
Sejima — It really gets close. I was able to adjust the distance so I found myself unintentionally turning around and whatnot.
Tsukamoto — This photo taken at the "MASP" exhibition that shows a woman standing behind a painting by Modigliani is also interesting. (p. 061)
Sejima — It's interesting. On top of that, Lina uses glass for the part to hang the painting, right? By choosing glass, she makes the distance with viewers seem even closer.
Tsukamoto — And the fact that she made this with concrete, glass and wood. They're fortunate to have no earthquakes (laugh).
Sejima — I think that Lina being Italian probably played a large part in her being able to do something so radical.
Tsukamoto — Lina also had something of a uniquely democratic way of thinking. To what extent would she involve her fellows. She did not create boundaries, and her target was not only living people. She must have had this broad perspective.

*1   1935-. Editor. Launched "Toshi Jutaku" (Urban Housing) in 1968 and worked as editor-in-chief.

Sejima — So, Lina also collected things like monsters and other oddities, right? She placed a lot of different things inside the "Glass House".
Tsukamoto — I think her idea of democracy was not limited to a select group of people. In today's world, Lina's perspective is particularly valid because the mechanism of systems and industries seems to force assumptions regarding the self-portraits of people and membership.

The diversity of "poor architecture"
that supports "poor theater"

— Mr. Tsukamoto, you have a fascination for "Oficina Theater", don't you?
Tsukamoto — At "Oficina Theater", company members practically live on the spot because of their work. The balconies made of steel scaffolding are laminated, and while the first and second floors are occupied by seats, the higher floor is a dressing room where stage costumes hang closely packed from the ceiling frame. The roof leads out onto glass windows, and I was told that the plays can be seen from directly above. Since it's their home base, even lengthy programs are possible.
This may be a utopic theater space, but I think an example that really beautifully embodies this is "Oficina Theater". The architect is nearly a member of the theater company because of how closely that architect is involved. It's not enough to say they are diverting a warehouse into a theater; it seems like there is some kind of fundamentally different social happening taking place.

Sejima — Even the location used is integrated.
Tsukamoto — I heard that Lina herself was almost one of the theater members for a while when she was involved in meetings while supervising construction. That kind of thing is really interesting.
Sejima — Right.
— "Oficina Theater" was placed on the list of the "world's most avant-garde theaters" by the British newspaper The Guardian. I was shocked and wondered what was going on when I entered the theater and there was just a long aisle with no seats in sight.
Tsukamoto — This theater company has presented magnificent dramas based on modern Brazilian history, including stories about how the people of Brazil went through great hardships to reclaim agricultural land from the poor soil, and stories about the bloodshed during a time of continuous civil war. The aisle-like stage is a "street". That's why there are trees growing on the side as well as a fountain. I was taken to the trench under the "street" during their rehearsals. I heard that was for the sake of the performance where soldiers suddenly come out of the sewers to fight.
The theater company members generally make one package from various elements such as a script, performance, actors, and art, and then they perform it at various locations. Some plays are designed to be performed while traveling in the first place, so the theater is expected to be flexible and universal. Architects have a tendency to conceive of experimental theater, and they often face a cool reception from the theater members.

「テアトロ・オフィシナ」の花壇。
木が外部へ飛び出ている。
The "Officina Theater" garden.
The vegetation protrudes outside.

Sejima — If it's experimental theater, it can only be performed at that location.
Tsukamoto — But this time both parties are miraculously in agreement. It appears they sympathized with the "poor theater" that was advocated in 1965 by Polish playwright Jerzy Grotowski. This is not a comprehensive art kind of theater with literature, music, art, and costumes but, by subtracting those elements to make it poor, it is said to become theater that pursues a relationship between actors and spectators that emerges.
This is an idea that has common ground with "Arte Povera (poor art)".
Sejima — But if the interior of "Oficina Theater" was truly poor, it would just feel really poor, but a very diverse theater space is created through incorporating various elements like sunlight, running water, and vegetation.
Tsukamoto — That's how I feel.

An architect without a design office

Tsukamoto — Lina also designed a lot of furniture. I like those sturdy chairs in the theater at "SESC". I read somewhere that she built those on the spot.
Sejima — The way the chairs from "Santa Maria dos Anjos Chapel" seem to connect when you line them up is also really nice.
Tsukamoto — Lina Bo Bardi was the kind of person who had no office and got involved onsite while consulting with craftsmen and visitors. This is fairly difficult to do as a full-time architect, so I'm envious towards people who can do this.

Sejima — Even so, how did she build everything without a studio? (laugh)
Tsukamoto — Once a site was setup, I guess she would have done everything at a kind of onsite studio.
Sejima — So that's how she built that kind of furniture. For us here today, we would think about how to build something using a blueprint, but Lina probably figured she could put together architecture onsite in the same manner she put together furniture onsite, and this is reflected in the way things were built. The glass easels used at "MASP", and so on. I think a lot of things were built onsite.
Tsukamoto — Even the large objects feel handcrafted.
Sejima — When thinking about how to build a design, I think that you can build to a certain extent even without specially-trained craftsmen because there is this idea to build things onsite. In a sense, that's why I think you can call this very modern.
Tsukamoto — In an age of advancing industrialization, it feels like she drew a line from the construction industry. So she could actually create designs from human behavior. Lina's architecture shows great consideration and imagination with regards to behavior, so I personally revere her as a master of behaviorology (architectural behavior studies). In Japan, Takamasa Yoshizaka and Zosekkeishudan (Atelier Zo) had similar ideas. After winning the Nago City government building competition, I hear that Zosekkeishudan put up tents on the grounds of the city government building and set to work on design as they felt the various changes in weather throughout the day. Involvement in this kind of architecture can create a

「MASP」にあるガラスのイーゼル。
A glass easel at the MASP.

certain quality of architecture.

Encountering the energetic people and folk customs of Brazil

Sejima — Like you mentioned before regarding the period following World War II, it was not about looking down on people from above like "This is architecture for the masses", but rather a period when you shared ideas with people and things moved forward in that way. Lina herself also held an interest in the trends of this period and was committed to it ideologically. I also think that Lina being Italian and having moved from Italy to Brazil were part of the elements that mixed together to form the foundation of Lina's architecture.

I think her architecture is very Italian, and the way she builds things is incredibly radical. On the other hand, she came to appreciate things influenced by Brazilian folk art and the local climate after moving to Brazil. So, ideologically-speaking, she probably thought she should do both.

Tsukamoto — Lina was a communist. Even though the communist party held power in Italy, the country was defeated during World War II so it came under the control of the U.S. Italian communism appeared to be doing well on the surface, but whenever they thought about creating a mechanism for the kind of society they envisioned, the U.S would step in and interfere. Their defeat during World War II had a lasting effect. And that's why the expression of radicalism can be seen among architects.

Sejima — It feels like they had to do things radically.

Tsukamoto — Even if they shared a sense of apprehension and doubt about the expansion of capitalism, they definitely didn't implement this inside the social system. That reaction gave birth to the utopian expressionism of radicals like Superstudio and Archizoom. Lina may have become like that had she remained in Italy. But by moving to Brazil and coming into contact with the energy of the people, her practical use of space may have bloomed.

Sejima — Lina was born in Rome and, while she was doing interior design and illustrations at Gio Ponti's company in Milan after graduating, a bombing campaign destroyed the city and her office so she must have had her own thoughts in regard to war. It was at this time that she got married to Pietro Maria Bardi and moved together with him to Brazil because he became the director of the São Paulo Art Museum. Pietro was a well-known art critic and an expert art dealer so I think this had a considerable influence on Lina.

Tsukamoto — Before the war, she launched "Domus" together with Gio Ponti and Rudofsky.

Sejima — What an incredible trio. If she hadn't gone to Brazil, I think Lina would have turned out completely different.

An age in which "history" and "construction", "space" and "place" intermingle

Tsukamoto — At the time, I think that it was a period when cultural anthropology was supported by intellectuals.

「ガラスの家」にある
リナの民芸品コレクション。
Lina's folk art collection in the "Glass House".

Historical dialectic had been dominant up until then. For example, Kenzo Tange from Japan attempted to negate the opposition between, and then integrate, Western modernism and traditional Japanese architecture, which are two things with entirely different backgrounds. It's a way of thinking about "history" moving through thesis-antithesis-synthesis. In fact, it was an inevitability that history would be moved in such a manner.

That was because the industrial revolution abnormally raised the productivity of human society. Long-distance travel became possible, and there was an explosive increase in things and people that were not tied to the land. But in a stable society, you can't make full use of that capability. Don't you think that a concept of "history" was required to create a perspective that "society is something that gets updated"?

In line with this, wouldn't "space" be the concept in which architecture found new life after being confronted with transformation? By relying on space, architecture can strengthen its personality as something that is movable, reproducible, and measurable. This is an alternative in regard to the "place" where a land and community repeatedly produces things. In a place where the population is stable, a stable society is one in which we use surrounding resources to balance our everyday lives. You could say that vernacular architecture is a result of that. An uncivilized society is always like that, but the important thing in a stable society is the "structure" that supports balance. The relation between things is visible, and there is a "place" where resources are managed by closed membership operating various taboos and restrictions. In modern times, I imagine it was necessary for a "history" and "space" that broke that balance and the closed nature of the membership to make use of the productivity and mobility that we had acquired.

The period in which Lina was active overlaps with the period in which the alternative of cultural anthropology as a "construction" was proposed in regard to Hegel and Marx's historical dialectic. The question of how to once again create a balanced state is also a topic of interest today. Lina was something of a cultural anthropologist herself, and it was precisely because she had an interest in visiting many places, and in seeing what kind of resources were used and what kind of backgrounds formed the basis of peoples' lives, that she collected folklore objects. I would have liked to ask a person with such sensibilities what they thought of historical dialectic.

In fact, it's not easy to think of the image of a cultural anthropologist architect. But I think you can make a comparison to the image of a historical dialectical architect. The problem with historical dialectic is that it requires a genius like Kenzo Tange who is capable of thesis-antithesis-synthesis. As long as it requires a genius, there must only be one answer.

Sejima — Right.

Tsukamoto — I think there was a period where that was necessary in order to gain universality. Nowadays, we can step back and look at such a sense of values from a distance but it would have been no easy task to do that during Lina's generation. There is a great sense of intimacy and sympathy in Lina's architecture, but I feel that we mustn't pretend to understand it based only on our current sensibilities.

A radicalism that encourages people

Sejima — What you mentioned now is something that really alters Lina's way of architecture. Lina's architecture adds new things on to existing things. Doesn't her way of building seem incomplete? For example, the house built on a hill has eaves slipping out and stairs that lead directly to a retaining wall where the roof is. It becomes unclear to just what extent it is her architecture. And it's also very interesting how she places not only people but also everything from animals to even monsters inside her architecture.
Tsukamoto — In the case of "space" in architecture, it's hard to establish anything without setting boundaries somewhere. I feel that Lina's architecture is more focused on "place". In that sense, the thing that clicks the most for me is "MASP". In her other works, it's hard to distinguish how much she built herself and how much was provided for by the place in question.
Sejima — There is definitely a radical framework somewhere in there, so it might become only a set of "circumstances" if it was done lazily, but it obviously didn't turn out this way.
Tsukamoto — That radicalism is not unrelated to the local people and places. You might say it's a kind of radicalism that gives great encouragement and support.

Sejima — Even if it's encouraging, it's not just kind. It also gives off a feeling like "if you can follow, then follow". (laugh)
Tsukamoto — One word that came into frequent use following the Great East Japan Earthquake is "yorisou" (to cozy up). This is something important, but in Lina's case it felt like she would cozy up while spanking your behind. (laugh)
— When we talk about "Home for All", I feel that whether the architects themselves are included with "everyone" is a question now being confronted in Japan.
Sejima — In Japan, if anything, it feels like we cozy up too much and have lost our sense of perspective on distance. In that sense, Lina's position may give us a hint for the future of Japan. It's important for architects to ask the opinions of various people, but that can turn into just making the rounds so it's quite difficult.
Tsukamoto — It's still okay if it's perceived as making the rounds. We shouldn't forget the tough reality that architects were given the cold shoulder and ignored on the actual renovation sites. In order for us to gain a sense of distance and face the harsh reality, I think that we need to possess an original historical viewpoint that is different from the "history" mentioned earlier.

A rich ecology produced by diversity

— Are there features common to Brazilian architecture?
Tsukamoto — The works of Brazilian architects are characterized by the use of concrete in molding. Since there is little annual temperature gap in São Paulo and Rio de Janeiro, it creates an ideal environment where the

「シレル邸」周囲に
向かい延びる主屋の庇。
The eaves of the main building extending towards the surroundings of "Valéria P. Cirell's Home".

weak points of steel and concrete composite, such as expansion and contraction, can be suppressed. Thinking about the possibilities of concrete, structures such as a shell structure that bears gravity solely with plane stiffness and cantilevers and bridges using large beams and columns that can be made onsite create an attractive contrast between the sense of weight of materials and the lightness of the space. Oscar Niemeyer pursued his interest in shells and cantilevers that would build everything at once, while Paulo Mendes da Rocha imposing volumes float weightlessly like a bridge. Aside from "MASP" and the "Glass House", Lina didn't take an approach where the overall form would be decided at once.

Sejima — It was more like combining lines. Rather than the front, she would set up columns and from there go on to attach materials like eaves.

Tsukamoto — To put it in modern terms, I think that she excelled in an ecological sense. This is reflected even in her way of choosing construction materials. It's about using the proper materials in the proper place. The strong ones come to the front, and the weak ones withdraw inside. Materials susceptible to rain were used behind the eaves. Traditional architecture combined the strong and the weak, and it naturally adopted the idea of the proper material in the proper place. However in modern times because things came to be built with stronger materials, constructions were integrated and flat. Fewer varieties of materials made things look more pure so this was preferred. In response to this, it seemed Lina felt that various materials were "perfectly acceptable together as they were".

Milan would also be bombed during World War II but since it differed from Japan with its prominence of stone architecture and brick architecture, the bombs used were not like the napalm bombs dropped on Japan that spread fire to wooden buildings but rather dynamite-like bombs that would utterly destroy buildings with their impact force.

Sejima — Lina even wrote in her notebook that "the houses had all collapsed and pieces were lying all over the place".

Tsukamoto — This is how the city of Milan was rendered toothless. During the 1950s, those toothless areas would be rebuilt by architects like Gio Ponti, Asnago and Vender, and Caccia Dominioni. The adjacent buildings were 200 or 300 year old Palazzo buildings so they designed a new generation of Palazzo buildings that would conform to them. However, you can see a contrasting approach regarding the ecology of the materials. Dominioni used various materials that were well-suited for the purpose, so the façade is richly shaded. That also meant there were a variety of craftsmen simultaneously involved in that one façade, including stone masons, plasterers, carpenters, bronze craftsmen and iron craftsmen. In response to this, Asnago and Vender preferred a logical way of building that used marble from top to bottom and seemed to fit everything within an aluminum sash on the same side. So the job types of those involved in the façade were limited

「ベナンの家」中庭にあるベナン共和国風の小屋。
A hut from the Republic of Benin found in the courtyard of the "House of Benin".

to stone masons and aluminum window makers.
Sejima — These days it's all about mass production so limiting the kinds of construction employed is also cheaper. But when it comes down to using architecture with care, it's easy to fix a spot if proper materials were used in the proper spots. But if everything was made with the same materials, then that means you can only fix it by redoing the whole thing.
That's why I think a lot of things are related. Lina's architecture really values diversity so it has the power to allow all kinds of people to think it's interesting or good. I truly feel like even just seeing the architecture gives me a sense of how she talked with various craftsmen onsite while making decisions.

Architecture as an ecological node

Tsukamoto — Lina also worked at designing exhibitions and curation. Inside the museum space, space is not only created through architecture but also through the relation between people and the items on display. She had an outstanding sense for that kind of thing, and she also made use of it when designing architecture.
Sejima — Right. Lina designed not only furniture and exhibitions but also things like costumes and even pool tiles. She also edited books. The object of her designs was quite broad in scope.
Tsukamoto — She must have taken an interest in everything related to human behavior. But she didn't seem to be obsessed with designing everything by herself. Similar to Jurgendstil, there was a crazy period when she designed everything from home architecture to teacups and slippers but that was not her style. In her case, she pulled in people and scenery from the opposite side of the object of her design. This made it feel as though a rich ecology was tied to her architecture. This is a good way of grasping architecture.

「SESC」ラウンジ。
リナデザインの椅子に座って
憩う人びと。
The "SESC" multi-use space. People sitting and resting in chairs designed by Lina.

リナ・ボ・バルディの生涯
The Life of Lina Bo Bardi

自伝　1914〜51年

——リナ・ボ・バルディ

　私はローマのプラティ・ディ・カステッロで生まれた。ローマがイタリアの首都になってからできた郊外の地域だ。

　私は若くありたいなんて決して思わなかった。私が本当に欲していたのは、自分だけの歴史をもつことだった。25歳の時に回顧録を書きたいと思ったけれど、私にはまだ書くための材料がなかった。

　私の守護天使は兵士だ。ステファノ・ポルカーリ通りにあるピアンチアリ小学校に通っていた時、先生は私たちにこう言った。「1週間授業はお休みです。兵隊さんたちがここにお泊まりになるのです。」そして兵士のジョカルデッリが私たちの学校にやって来た。それ以来何十年もずっと彼が私の守護天使だった。

　私は子どもの頃、フランスとの国境にあり、ニースやカンヌに接しているボルディゲーラの街をよく訪れた。ときどき母方の祖父の住むアブルッツォに連れて行かれることもあった。祖父は医者で、タリアコッツォにある古くてとてもかわいい家に住んでいた。また時には、ローマ近くにあるオスティアへ行き、ビーチを訪れたりもした。

　10代の頃、私は母の言いつけを破って、よくバラエティーショウを観に行っていた。ジャーナリストの伯父が連れて行ってくれたのだった。そこで、ペトロリーニ[*1]といった俳優たちを知るようになった。また、行ける限り映画も観に行ったものだ。ドイツやアメリカ、フランスの素晴らしい映画を鑑賞した。当時のイタリア映画は遅れていて、私たちにとってはつまらないものだった。

　私はローマ大学の建築学部を卒業した。グスターヴォ・ジョヴァンノーニ[*2]やマルチェッロ・ピアチェンティーニ[*3]といった教授陣により、大学の教育は建築史を重視する方向に向かってい

---

*：　この文章は、リナ・ボ・バルディによるいくつかの文章のコラージュである。
　　　出典：Marcelo Carvalho Ferraz(ed.), *Lina Bo Bardi*, São Paulo, Instituto Lina Bo e P. M. Bardi, 1993, pp.9-12.

*1　1898年ナポリ生まれ。イタリアの喜劇俳優。

*2　1873〜1947年。ローマの建築家。

*3　1881〜1960年。ローマの建築家。

妹のグラツィエッラ（左）と。（1928年）
With sister Graziella (left) (1928)

Literary Curriculum
—written by Lina Bo Bardi

I was born in Rome, in Prati di Castello, a suburb created after the city became the capital of Italy.

I never wanted to be young. What I really wanted was to have History. At the age of twenty-five I wanted to write memoirs, but I didn't have the materials.

My guardian angel was a soldier. At Stefano Porcari street, in the Pianciari Primary School, our teacher had announced that "there will be no classes for one week. The soldiers are going to be billeted here". So soldier Giocardelli was allocated to the School. He was a guardian angel and stayed with us for a number of years.

When I was a child, I used to go to Bordighera, on the border with France, Nice, Cannes. Sometimes I would be taken to Abruzzi to visit my maternal grandfather. He was a doctor and lived in Taliacozzo, in an old, very pretty house. Other times we would go to the beach, in Ostia, near Rome.

When I was a teenager I used to go to variety shows, against my mother's wishes. I had an uncle who was a journalist, and he would take us. We got to know the actors, such as Petrolini.[*1] I would also go to the movies as often as I could. I saw great German, American and French films. In those days Italian cinema was very backward and we used to find it tedious.

I graduated from the College of Architecture, Rome University. The College – whose principals were Gustavo Giovannoni[*2] and Marcello Piacentini[*3] – gave more

幼少期の水彩画。(1920 年代)
Childhood watercolor painting. (1920's)

幼少期の水彩画。(1925 年 9 月 25 日)
Childhood watercolor painting. (September 25, 1925)

* : This quote is a collage of several quotes by Lina Bo Bardi. Source: Marcelo Carvalho Ferraz(ed.), *Lina Bo Bardi*, São Paulo, Instituto Lina Bo e P. M. Bardi, 1993, pp.9-12.

*1 Born in Naples in 1898. An Italian comedian.

*2 1873-1947. A Roman architect.

*3 1881-1960. A Roman architect.

Literary Curriculum

雑誌『ベレーザ』掲載のイラスト。(1942年)
Illustration published in *Belleza* magazine (1942)

幼少期の水彩画。
おとぎ話の一場面や植物をよく描いていた。(1920年代)
Childhood watercolor painting.
Lina often painted scenes depicting fairy tales and plants. (1920's)

た。建築の構成より建築史の方が大切だと考えられていたのだ。ローマは古典文化の中心地のひとつであるため、学生たちは古代のモニュメントを学ぶことにほとんどの時間を費やしていた。

私は美術高校出身である。そこでは4年間、陰影の法則や幾何学的なドローイングなど、建築とアートの教育を受ける。ローマ大学内だけでなく、ローマのアカデミック界全体にはびこっていた優雅な「ノスタルジア」スタイル*4の流行に嫌気がさし、私はミラノへ移った。ファシストによって復活した古代の廃墟から逃げ出したのだ。ローマは停止した街、そしてファシズムが台頭する街だった。ミラノを除くイタリア全土が、どういうわけか停止してしまっていた。

ミラノでは「実践する」ために、私は高名な建築家ジオ・ポンティのオフィスに入所した。彼はイタリアの職人たちの地位向上を目指す運動*5のリーダーでもあり、ミラノ・トリエンナーレや雑誌『ドムス』のディレクターも務めていた。彼はすぐに、私へ向

かって「君に給料は払わない、君が僕に払うんだ。」と言った。

私は、朝8時から深夜まで、休みもなく働いた。仕事は、ティーカップや椅子のデザイン、ファッション、つまりは衣服から、「アバノ」(ヴェネト州のスパリゾート)といった都市プロジェクトにまで及んだ。オフィスでの活動は「モンテカティーニ」*6の建設から、装飾芸術のトリエンナーレ*7の運営や雑誌の編集まで多岐にわ

* 4 当時のイタリアの建築教育は、歴史と美学的な視点を重視するローマ(ジョヴァンノーニやピアセンティーニら)、工学と美術双方を重視するミラノ(ジオ・ポンティやカミッロ・ボイトら)、工学を重視するトリノと、代表的な3都市で潮流の違いがあった。

* 5 ジオ・ポンティはリチャード・ジノリ社との協同製作、『ドムス』創刊、後述のミラノ・トリエンナーレの開催など、工芸を近代産業に適応するように転換・再定義する活動を行っていた。

* 6 1935年、ジオ・ポンティがミラノに設計した「モンテカティーニ・ビル」。建物に合わせてデスクや照明などインテリアの細部まで設計し、同名の椅子はイタリアモダン家具の名作として名高い。

attention to Architectural History courses, considered to be more important than Composition. Since Rome was one of the centres of classical culture, students dedicated most of their time to the study of ancient monuments.

I came from the Artistic Lyceum, four years of architectural-artistic education, Theory of Shading and Geometric Drawing. The stylist-courtly "nostalgia" trend[*4], not only at the University but also in the Roman academic environment as a whole, made me go to Milan. I ran away from the ancient ruins that were being restored by the fascists. Rome was a city that had stopped, it was where fascism was. All Italy somehow stopped. Except for Milan.

In Milan, to "gain practical experience", I joined the office of celebrated architect Gio Ponti, leader of the movement promoting Italian craftsmanship[*5], director of Milan Triennials and of magazine "Domus". He said right away, "I'm not going to pay you, you have to pay me". Work was from 8 in the morning to midnight, Saturdays and Sundays included. The work ranged from the design of teacups, chairs, fashion, that is, clothing, to urban projects such as the "Abano" (a spa in Veneto). Office tasks extended from the construction of "Montecatini"[*6] to organising the Decorative Arts Triennials[*7] and editing magazines. In this way, I came into direct contact with the real problems of the profession.

Gio Ponti described himself as the "last of the humanists". His enemies, on the "Casabella" side, lead by architect Giuseppe Pagano[*8], would say, "certainly the last". The outbreak of war, right after the 1940 Triennial – in which I participated anonymously as Ponti's assistant-, presented other problems: one could no longer build, and the field of "Practice" was replaced by "Theory". I had my own professional office in Milan, but the small number of jobs, which had become problematic due to air raids, led me to also take up the activity of illustrator for important Milan's magazines and newspapers, among

ミラノのスタジオの庭で。(1940 年)
In the garden of her own studio in Milan. (1940)

them the magazine "Stile", founded by Gio Ponti, who at that time had left the management of *Domus*.
From 1941 to '43 I had an intense journalistic career, contributing to popular weekly magazines such as *Tempo*, *Grazia* and *Vetrina*. I also edited the *Quaderni di Domus*, collections in which I was engaged in research and study activities on craftsmanship and industrial design. And I

*4 Architectural education in Italy at the time was divided between three different currents embodied by three representative cities; Rome (Giovannoni, Piasentini *et al.*), which emphasizes history and aesthetic viewpoint; Milan (Gio Ponti, Camillo Boito *et al.*) which emphasizes both engineering and art; and Turin which emphasizes engineering.

*5 Gio Ponti worked in collaboration with Richard-Ginori, launched "Domus", held the Milan Triennale described later, and converted and redefined crafts to adapt them to modern industries.

*6 Gio Ponti designed the Montecatini Building in Milan in 1935. He designed everything down to the interior details such as the desks and lighting to complement the building. The chair of the same name became famous as a masterpiece of Italian modern furniture.

*7 The Milan Triennale. Gio Ponti was one of those involved in the launch.

*8 1896-1945. An Italian architect. He presided over the editing of the "Casabella" architectural magazine.

たった。そこで私は、自分の仕事上の問題の核心に直面することになったのである。

　ジオ・ポンティは自身を「最後のヒューマニスト」と称した。彼の敵、『カーザベッラ』を主催した建築家・ジュゼッペ・パガーノ*8らも、「間違いなく彼が最後のヒューマニストだ」と言っていた。

　1940年のトリエンナーレ——私はジオ・ポンティのアシスタントとして匿名で参加した——の直後に戦争がはじまり、新たな問題が発生した。もはや建築を建てることはできず、「実践」に代わり「理論」が台頭していった。私はミラノに自分のオフィスをもっていたが、そこでの数少ない仕事も空襲により次第に難しくなっていった。しかしそれらの仕事は、私をイラストレーターとしてミラノの重要な雑誌や新聞での活動に導いてもくれたのだ。当時『ドムス』のディレクターをすでに退いていたジオ・ポンティが創刊した雑誌『スティーロ』も、それらの仕事のひとつとして引き継いだ。

　1941年から43年まで、私はジャーナリストとしての活動に打ち込み、『テンポ』、『グラツィア』、『ヴェトリーナ』といった人気の週刊誌に寄稿した。また『クァデルニ・ディ・ドムス』シリーズを創刊し、工芸とインダストリアル・デザインに関する調査とスタディに没頭した。そして雑誌『イッルストラツィオーネ・イタリアーナ』での仕事をはじめた。当時は、プリンシペ・デ・サヴォイア・ホテル*9で暮らしていた。

　1943年の夏、ファシズムが崩壊した。8月13日の爆撃で私はオフィスを失った。私はジオ・ポンティの素晴らしいスタジオ・オフィスから離れようとしていたが、ポンティから『ドムス』の経営をやらないかと誘われた。私がその仕事を受けたのは第2次世界大戦最中のドイツ占領下でのことだった。

　サロ共和国*10から出版停止を命じられるまで、戦時中に『ドムス』の本社があったベルガモで、古い出版物を参考にひとりで雑誌をつくっていた。

　戦時中の1年は、50年にも相当する。そして人びとは、後世のための判断をした。爆弾とマシンガンの嵐の中、私は状況を吟味し、大事なのは無傷で生き抜くことだと判断した。でもどうやって？　唯一の方法は、客観性と合理性をもつことだと感じた。ほとんどの人が、文学的で郷愁的な「落胆」を選ぶなか、客観性をもち、かつ合理的にことを進めるのは難しいことだった。

雑誌『ドムス』誌面。（1943年）Page from *Domus* magazine (1943)

私は、世界はまだ救われ得ると、よりよくなると信じていた。そう信じることが、生きる上で価値のある唯一の務めであり、生き抜くためのスタート地点だったのだ。私は、レジスタンスや共産党

* 7 　ミラノ・トリエンナーレ。ジオ・ポンティは立ち上げに関わったひとりである。
* 8 　1896～1945年。イタリアの建築家。建築雑誌『カーザベッラ』の編集を主宰。
* 9 　1927年に創業したホテル。ミラノのランドマークで、歴史的有名人が多く宿泊したことでも知られる。第二次世界大戦終盤はドイツ軍、のちにアメリカ軍の本部として使われた。リナが滞在していたのはその前のことであろう。
* 10 　イタリア社会共和国に同じ。イタリア降伏後、ムッソリーニによってイタリア王国から分離する形で建国され、2年近く北部・中部イタリアを支配した。北イタリアの町サロに政府を置いたため「サロ共和国」とも呼ばれる。

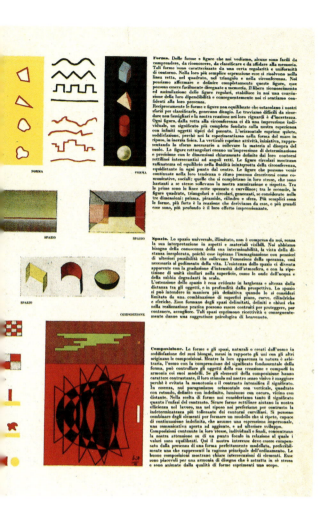

judgement of men is a judgement for future generations. Among the bombs and machine guns, I took stock of the situation, and decided that the important thing was to survive, preferably unscathed. But how? I felt that the only way was that of objectivity and rationality, an extremely difficult to take when the majority of people opt for literary and nostalgic "disappointment". I felt that the world could still be saved and improved, and that this was the only task worth living for. The starting point to be able to survive. I joined the Resistance, the clandestine Communist Party. I saw the world around me only as an immediate reality and not as an abstract literary exercise.

The house of Man collapsed. In Italy, along Aurelia and Emilia. In Sicily and Lombardy. In Provence, in Britanny. The house of Man collapsed in Europe. We did not expect that it would disappear this way. It was solid. It was a "bastion". Was there ever anything "stronger" than the house? It had been there for years. Every year there was a change. A daughter that would get married. A new generation that arrived. The 1800's velvet fringed armchair that disappeared giving way to the "English" piece of furniture in mahogany and sky-blue-satin. "Opaline" lamps were substituted for large gilded-metal chandeliers. Then, the grandchildren wanted to make changes. They wanted to renovate, following that latest fashion, which mixed old and modern pieces. And the Louis Philippe[11] chaise longue

began to work for "Illustrazione Italiana". At that time I lived in the Principe de Savoia Hotel[9].
July 1943. Fascism fell apart. In the August 13th bombings I lost my office. I left Ponti's great studio, and was invited to run *Domus* magazine. I took on the job in the middle of the World War during the German occupation.
In Bergamo, where *Domus* had its wartime headquarters, alone, with the help of old publications, I organised the magazine issues until the Republic of Saló[10] ordered its suspension.
In wartime one year corresponds to fifty years, and the

[9] A hotel founded in 1927. It is also known as a landmark in Milan where stayed many historical celebrities. Towards the end of World War II it served as the headquarters of the German army, and later the U.S. army. Lina supposedly stayed there before the occupation.

[10] Same as the Italian Social Republic (RSI). After the kingdom of Italy capitulated, Mussolini formed the RSI from its remains and exercised sovereignty in Northern and Central Italy for nearly two years. Also known as the Republic of Saló from the town of Saló in Northern Italy where its government was headquartered.

[11] An antique style prevalent in France around the middle of the 19th century. Characterized by a simplicity with consideration for ease of use.

雑誌『グラツィア』誌面。同僚のカルロ・パガーニと共に手掛けたイラスト。（1941年）
Page from *Grazia* magazine. Illustration made in collaboration with colleague Carlo Pagani. (1941)

の秘密結社に参加した。私は、自分の周りの世界を抽象的で文学的な動きとしてではなく、直接的な現実としてのみ理解しようとしていた。

　人びとの家は崩壊した。イタリアのオーレリア通りとエミリア通りで、シチリアとロンバルディアで、プロヴァンスとブリタニーで。ヨーロッパ全域で家が崩壊した。こんなふうに消えるなんて思ってもいなかった。それは頑丈な「要塞」だったからだ。「家」より強いものなんていったい存在するのだろうか？　それは何年もそこにあり、毎年変化があった。結婚する娘。生まれる新たな世代。マホガニーとスカイブルーのサテンでできた「イギリス風」の家具に取り替えられて消えてしまった1800年製のフリンジつきの豪華なソファ。ぴかぴかの金属でできたシャンデリアに取り替えられた「オパールのような」ランプ。その後、変化を求めた孫が改修したがった。最新の流行に合わせた、アンティークとモダンの融合だ。ルイ・フィリップ様式*11のソファは、白く塗られた錬鉄製のモダンなランプとしっくり合う。セメンタイトの壁と2枚のシュルレアリストの絵画も同様に。一家まるごと

しゃれた界隈に引っ越してから、もっとモダンな建物にしようと、フランスの最新流行を追ったアーモンド・グリーンのシルクのドレープカーテンと、白いバロック風の化粧漆喰をフランシスコがオーダーした。そのため家はいくぶん「退廃的」に、建築家の言う「現代的」なものになってしまった。それでも何も問題ない。ここにはスタイルがある。友人たちは誉めたたえるし、世間の雑誌でも紹介された。

　こんなふうに終わるなんて思ってもみなかった。ある朝起きてみると、私たちの家はすでに無かった。縞模様の白い漆喰の欠片があった。それは、バラ色のランプの小さな破片だ。でも奇妙なことに、とても奇妙なことに私たちの愛しい家はいっさい残っていないのだ。他と区別する何もかもがない！　すべては灰となった。塵の山だ。かつて家であったはずの他の灰色の山とまったく同じ。それらは決して、私たちの家ほど美しくなどなかったのに。

　その後、爆弾が無慈悲にも人間の遺産を粉々にした時、私た

* 11　19世紀中期頃フランスで流行したアンティーク様式。使いやすさが考慮されたシンプルさが特徴。

would go very well with the white-lacquered wrought iron modern lamps. As would the walls in cementite and the two surrealist paintings. At one point the whole house was moved to a posh neighbourhood, to a more modern building. And it was then that Francisco ordered the great almond-green silk curtains that draped according to the latest French fashion, and the white baroque-styled stucco: thus rendering the house slightly "decadent" as an "à la page" architect once put it. But it was doing well. It had its style. It was much admired by friends. And it was even featured in a worldly magazine.

I swear I never thought it would end up like this. And, on that morning, when our house was no longer there, I found a piece of veined white plaster, and noticed that it was a small fragment of a rose tint lamp. But how odd, how very odd that nothing remained of our lovely house. Nothing that could distinguish it from the others! It was all ashes. All dust. All like the other pile of ashes that had been houses. All of which surely less beautiful than ours had been.

It was then, while the bombs mercilessly destroyed the work and the work of Man, that we understood that the house should be for the "life" of Man. It should serve. It should comfort one. And it should not reveal, as in a theatrical performance, the unnecessary vanities of the human spirit. We then understood why the houses were collapsing, as were the stuccoes, the "mise en scène"[*12], the satins, the velvets, the fringes, the coats of arms: because in the morning everything was nothing but small desolately identical grey piles. In Italy, the houses collapsed, along Italian roads. In cities, the houses collapsed. In Europe, the houses collapsed. And for the first time men would have to rebuild the houses. So many houses in the center of big cities, along country roads, in villages. And for the first time "man think about the Man", rebuilds for the Man. The war destroyed the myth of "monuments". Also in the

雑誌『A』誌面。（1946年）
Page from A magazine. (1946)

『A』3号表紙。「すべての人が幸せな生活をつくるために、始まりへ、Aの文字へ戻らなければ。」「建築は終わりではなく（目的でもなく）、理解し、生活を変えるための道具である」（1946年）
Cover of third issue of A magazine. "We must go back to the beginning, to letter A, to build a happy life for everyone. (...) One in which architecture is not the end (nor the purpose), but the instrument by which one may understand and change life." (1946)

*12 Meaning "direction".

Literary Curriculum

ちは家が人間にとって「生命」であるべきだということが分かったのだ。家は、人に仕え、慰めてくれるべきもの。わざとらしいパフォーマンスのように、役に立たない人類のうぬぼれた精神を見せるべきものではない。私たちは、化粧漆喰、「ミザンセーヌ」*12、サテン、ベルベットやフリンジ、紋章の付いた家が、どうして崩壊したのかを理解した。イタリアの高速道路沿いて家が崩壊する。ヨーロッパで家が壊れる。そして人びとは初めて、家を建て直さなければならなくなったのだろう。大都市の中心に、田舎の道沿いに、村々に、とてもたくさんの家を。そして、初めて「人間は人間について考え」、人間のために再建する。戦争は「モニュメント」の神話を破壊した。家の中でも同様に、モニュメンタルな家具はもはや存在しない。それらもいくばくかは、戦争の勃発に手を貸したのだ。家具は人に「仕える」べきものなのだ。椅子は座るために、テーブルは食事をするために、アームチェアは読書とリラックスのために、ベッドは眠るためにある。家とはもはや不吉なふるさとではないだろう。それは人間の盟友であり、すばやく、盲従し、そして人間と同じように死ぬこともある。*13

1944年、仮設のスタジオにミラノの建築家たちはよく集まったものだった。サロ共和国の警察から隠れて、新しいシンジケートの職業組合の創設を話し合うために。この「建築家連合組合」は、のちに「建築研究運動（Movimento Studi Architettura）」となる。

太陽と青空と幸福にあふれるはずだった数年間、組合員は爆弾とマシンガンから逃れるためのシェルターを運営し、地下に隠れていた。ナチス・ドイツが北イタリアを占領していた1944年、「地下の人びと」への「愛」は絶頂に達した。ドイツ人（一方では完璧なシティ・プランナー）は、地下街のプロジェクトを開始した（原子爆弾をかけたレースに勝つと考えていた最後のその時まで）。その時、命とヒューマニティの敵、ナチス・ドイツは地下に

*12 「演出」の意。

*13 Lina Bo Bardi, "In Europe the house of Man fell down", *Rio*, p. 92(February 1947)

『A』誌面。(1946 年)　Page from A magazine (1946)

house, monumental pieces of furniture should no longer exist. They too may, in part, precipitate wars. Furniture should "serve": chairs are for sitting on, tables for eating at, armchairs for reading and relaxing, beds for sleeping. And therefore the house will no longer be an everlasting and ominous home, but an ally to man, agile and serviceable, and that can, like man, die[*13].

1944. The architects of Milan used to meet at a temporary studio, hidden from the Saló police, in order to discuss the establishment of a new syndicate and professional organisation, the "Organisation of Associated Architects", later transformed into the "Movimento Studi Architettura".
The years that should have been of sunshine, blue skies and happiness, I spent underground, running and taking shelter from bombs and machine guns. The "love" for the "underground men" reached its climax in 1944 during the nazi-fascist occupation of Northern Italy. The Germans (perfect city planners, for the other side) launched a project for underground cities (up until the end they thought they would win the race for the Atomic Bomb). Now the nazi-fascist were underground, the traitors of life and humanity. Far better to defy fate and death on the rooftop of some building watching the fireworks show of searchlights and airplanes' machine guns. One article I wrote (an urban architecture criticism) for a *Domus* magazine editorial caught the attention of the Gestapo. I escaped by a miracle… underground!
Every minute alive was a victory. When hiding, we would listen to the BBC broadcast from London. It would start the international broadcast every day with Beethoven's Fifth Symphony. I listened carefully to the latest news about the heroic resistance at Stalingrad[*14]…
1945. The War ends. The hope of building instead of destroying encourages everyone. Everything was in our hands: we leftists and centre-leftists were happy. Shortly after the armistice, together with a reporter and a photographer, I worked on a newspaper report in the areas affected by the war. We travelled all over Italy, documenting the situation of the country. We felt that something had to be done to get architecture out of that dead end. We then began to think about a magazine or a newspaper that would be available to all and that would point out the most common mistakes made by Italians… To bring up architecture to everyone's life, so that anyone could come to a conclusion and decide on the house they should live in, the factory they should work at, the streets they should walk along.

Modern architects, the INTRANSIGENTS, that is, those who work in silence and who see in the new architecture a way towards cleanliness and the salvation of humanity, should be depicted as certain saints of the past, with armour and a flaming sword – the sword that combats the countless multitude of incompetents and ignorants who pester us with their false crystals, false gods, twisted god's and lion's paws, satin curtains, taffeta curtains, damask curtains, fringes and frills, large and small moors, stucco of all types, coats of arms without weapons, real or fake Baccarat chandeliers, quilting, matelassés, chinaware (especially chinaware), cords, paints coloured green or almond, pink, cream coloured, sugar candy white, sky blue, purples and violets, tassels and pompons.
Of course we have a great deal of respect for all things antique, the real ones, and we also have them in our home, but as relics and sometimes they are put away in cupboards. But to deface an era by imposing upon it plaster and cardboard stuffed animals, means to be unaware of the tiring and painful progress of humanity, during which incompetence, dilettantism and ignorance make it slide

[*13] Lina Bo Bardi, "In Europe the house of Man fell down", Rio, 92(February 1947).

[*14] Now Volgograd. A city located in the western part of Russia, the stage for the "Battle of Stalingrad" (1942-1943), where Soviet troops defeated the Axis forces led by Germany.

いた。どこかの建物の屋上で、サーチライトと飛行機からのマシンガンがつくる花火のショーを観ながら、運命と死に反抗する方がずっといいだろう。私が『ドムス』の社説に書いた都市建築批評が、ゲシュタポの目に入った。私は不思議にも助かった……地下にいたおかげで！

　生きている毎秒が、一つひとつの勝利だった。隠れながら、私たちはロンドンからのBBCの放送を聞いたものだった。BBCは毎日ベートーベンの交響曲第5番と共に国際放送をはじめていた。私はスターリングラード*14での勇ましいレジスタンスに関するニュースを注意深く聞いていた……。

　1945年、戦争が終わった。破壊に代わる建築への希望は、すべての人を元気付けた。すべては私たちの手中にあった。私たち左翼と半左翼の人びとは幸福だった。

　休戦後まもなくして、私は記者とカメラマンと共に、戦争で被害を受けた地域に関する記事の執筆に取り組んだ。私たちは、イタリア中を旅してこの国の状況を記録した。建築を行き詰まった状況から脱却させるために、やらなければならないことがあると感じていたのだ。その後、イタリア人がしてしまう典型的な間違いを指摘する、誰にでも手に入る雑誌や新聞について考えはじめた……建築の問題を多くの人の生活にもち込むことで、誰もが結論に辿り着き、住むべき家を、働くべき工場を、歩くべき道を決めることができると考えた。

　現代建築家という妥協をしない人びと、すなわち、静かに働き、新しい建築に清潔さとヒューマニティの救済を見出す人びとは、甲冑と燃えるような剣を身に付けた、信頼できる古代の聖者として描かれるべきだ。その剣は、偽物のクリスタル、偽物の神、ゆがんだ神とライオンの足、サテンのカーテン、タフタのカーテン、ダマスク織のカーテン、フリンジとフリル、大小の荒れ地、あらゆるタイプの化粧漆喰、兵器のない紋章、本物だか偽物だか分からないバカラのシャンデリア、キルト、マトラッセ、陶磁器、コーデュロイ、グリーンやアーモンド、ピンク、アイスクリーム色、砂糖菓子の白、スカイブルー、紫、すみれ色の絵画、飾り房や玉房……などによって私たちを悩ませる、無知で無能な数えきれない人びとと戦うためのものだ。

　もちろん私たちはアンティークや本物の品にも多大な関心を抱いているし、家にもあるが、それらは時に遺物として戸棚に投げ捨てられてしまう。しかし、動物模様にあふれた漆喰や段ボールを用いることで時代に背くのは、疲弊したヒューマニティのわずかながらの進歩をも無視することを意味する。ヒューマニティが進歩のための努力によって、何とか1センチを守っているのと同時に、無能、素人芸、無力がそれを数キロメートル後退させているのだ。*15

　ローマではブルーノ・ゼーヴィ*16に会った。彼は有名な建築批評家で、人種的な理由からイタリアを離れたが、ローマに「有機的建築連合」を立ち上げるためにアメリカの第5軍と共に戻って来たのだった。私たちは『A－生活の文化』という建築週刊誌を創刊することに決めた。雑誌は『ドムス』と同じ制作会社によって、ミラノでつくられた。これを機に、私は建築批評家として日刊紙『ミラノ・セーラ』での仕事と、「国家復興議会」に参加するよう誘われた。

　1946年、古い亡霊が戻って来た。古い名前が戻って来た。そしてキリスト教民主主義が権力を握った。それと共に、旧政府の人物や、永久に追放されたと思われたすべてのものが権力を握った。

　私はピエトロ・マリア・バルディと結婚した。彼は、私がローマの美術高校に通っていた10代の頃から憧れていた人だ。ピエトロは影響力をもち、現代的でアートを推進しており、最も優れたイタリア人ジャーナリストだった。私たちはデートをして、その後結婚した。同年、私たちは南アメリカへ旅行をした。ピエトロはすでにその地をよく知っていたのだ。

　船でリオ・デ・ジャネイロ市に到着したのは、10月のことだ。眩しい。海から渡って来た人びとにとって、保健教育省*17の建物は空に向かって進む巨大な白とブルーの船のように見えた。

*14　現ヴォルゴグラード。ロシア西部に位置する都市で、ドイツ率いる枢軸国軍にソ連軍が勝利した「スターリングラード攻防戦」（1942～43年）の舞台となった。

*15　Lina Bo Bardi, "A chair of grumixaba and boards is more moral than a divan of frills", Diário de São Paulo, November 13, 1949.

*16　1918～2000年。ローマ生まれの建築史家、建築評論家。

*17　ブラジル旧教育保健省庁舎（1943年）。ル・コルビュジエ、ルシオ・コスタ、オスカー・ニーマイヤーら設計。ブラジル現代建築のランドマーク。

リオに向かう船の上で。(1946年)
On the ship heading to Rio. (1946)

ローマにて、リナとピエトロの結婚式。(1946年8月24日)
In Rome, on Lina and Pietro's wedding day (August 24, 1946)

　それは、第二次世界大戦勃発後初めての、平和へのメッセージだった。想像もできないような国に来たと感じた。ここでは何もかもが可能だ。私は幸福を感じた。リオは廃墟となってはいなかったのだ。

　初めてリオに来たヨーロッパ人にとって、ブラジルはどう映ったのか？　飛行機から見えたスラムと現代建築のコントラストは、洒落た家々ではなく標準化された高層ビルに対するブルジョワジーの憤りというよりもむしろ、社会の混沌を表しているようだった。船から見ていると、コパカバーナ*18のビーチと、教育保健省やその他の建物が並ぶ入江が突然現れ、それらは船上まで届くほど強く香る森へ寄りかかっているかのように見え、小さなポルトガル風のコロニアルハウスよりも高層ビルのほうが優れているのかと考える間もないほどに、人びとの冒険心が表れていた。

　背景となる資料について。ニューヨーク近代美術館の書籍『ブラジル・ビルズ』は、まさに、抽象的な意味ではなく、毎日の希望だった。建築的解決の明快さと、人類からの呼びかける声は、遠くかけ離れた世代にとっては未知の内容だった。戦争直後には、死の土地を輝かせる灯台のようだった……それは素晴らしいものだった。

　ブラジル建築家学会（IAB）のリオ支部での出会いについて。ルシオ・コスタ、オスカー・ニーマイヤー、ロシャ・ミランダ、ロベルト兄弟、アトス・ブルカォン、ブーレ・マルクスといった人びととの出会い。コスメ・ベリョ*19では、ポルチナーリ、彫刻家のランドゥッチ、マルコス・ジャイモヴィッチらにも出会った。皆、オスカーの旧友だ。リオ支部は、ブラジル初の国際的な前衛の場だった（ふたつ目はブラジリアだろう）。知的で明快な、人間としての器の眩しさ。中産階級が存在せず、たったふたつの偉大な上流階級があるのみという、信じられない国の眩しさ。土地とコーヒーとサトウキビと……そして、人の眩しさ。

*18　リオ・デ・ジャネイロ市南東部に位置するリゾート地。

*19　リオ・デ・ジャネイロ市南東部の町。

back kilometres for every centimetre it has managed to secure in its struggle to go forward.*15

In Rome I met Bruno Zevi*16, a well-known architecture critic who had left Italy for ethnic reasons and returned with the American 5th Army. He had returned to establish, in Rome, the "Association for Organic Architecture". We then decided to start a weekly architecture magazine named "A Cultura della Vita". The magazine was printed in Milan by the same company that published *Domus*. I was also invited to work as an architecture critic for the daily newspaper "Milano Sera" and to take part in the "First National Meeting for Reconstruction".

1946. The old ghosts were back. The old names reappeared, and Christian Democracy rose to power. Along with it, figures from past governments. All that we thought had been forever overthrown.

I married P. M. Bardi, whom I had admired ever since I was a teenager in Rome Artistic Lyceum. Pietro was important, modern, promoted the arts. He was the greatest Italian journalist. We dated, then married. That same year we travelled to South America, already familiar to Pietro.

Arrival in Rio de Janeiro, by ship, in October. Dazzle. For those arriving by sea, the Education and Health Ministry building*17 advanced like a great white and blue ship against the sky. The first message of peace after the flood of the Second World War. I felt myself in an imaginary country, where everything was possible. I felt happy, and Rio was not in ruins.

* 15 Lina Bo Bardi, "A chair of grumixaba and boards is more moral than a divan of frills", Diário de São Paulo, November 13, 1949.

* 16 1918-2000. An architectural historian and architectural critic born in Rome.

    The former Brazilian Ministry of Education and Health Building (1943).

*17 Designed by Oscar Niemeyer et al. A landmark of Brazilian modern architecture.

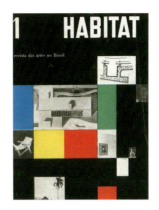

雑誌『アピタ』1号表紙。(1950年)
Cover of the first issue of *Habitat* magazine. (1950)

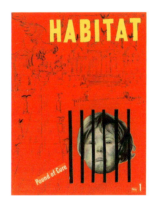 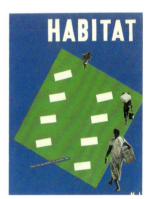

『アピタ』1号、表紙のデザイン案。(1950年)
Preliminary design for the cover of the first issue of *Habitat* magazine. (1950)

『アピタ』誌面。
Page from *Habitat* magazine.

（左）孔雀石のネックレス。
(leftmost) Malachite necklace.
（中）石、青いトパーズ、金のネックレス。
(second from left) Blue topaz lapidated on rough stone, mounted in gold.
（右）石英のネックレス。
(left) Rose quartz necklace.

さまざまな石を用いたブローチ。
幼少期から石を集めるのが趣味だったリナは、
ブラジルの石を使ったアクセサリーを制作した。
Broach set with various stones. Lina loved collecting stones from when she was a child. She went on to create accessories using Brazilian stones.

1947年、シャトーブリアン[20]が、ピエトロにブラジルでの美術館設立と経営の話をもちかけた。リオかサンパウロのどちらかという話で、私はリオを希望したが資金はサンパウロにあった。私はピエトロに、ここに残りたいと伝えた。戦時中の夜に浮かんでいた希望に、もう一度出合いたいのだ、と。そして、私たちはブラジルに残ることになった。

1951年、私はブラジル市民に帰化した。生まれる時、人はその場所を選択することができない。たまたま生まれるだけだ。私はブラジルに生まれはしなかったが、この地で生きることを選んだ。だからブラジルは、第2の母国になった。ブラジルは私の「選んだ国」であり、私はこの国の全都市の市民であるような気さえする。カリリ[21]からトリアングロ・ミネイロ[22]まで、田舎から国境まで。

* 20 アシス・シャトーブリアン。1892〜1968年。ブラジルの実業家。
* 21 カリリ・ド・トカンティンス。ブラジル中部の町。
* 22 ミナスジェライス州。ブラジル南東部に位置する。

IABのカーニバルのダンスパーティにて。
自身がデザインしたネックレスを着けている。（1948年）
At a dance during the IAB carnival. Wearing a necklace she designed herself (1948)

What is Brazil like for a European arriving for the first time in Rio de Janeiro? From an airplane, the contrast between slums and modern constructions suggests social chaos rather than the bourgeois resentment over the standardised skyscrapers that were replacing stylish houses. From a ship, Copacabana[*18] beach and the bay beyond, with the Ministry of Education and other buildings suddenly appearing in the background, almost leaning against the forest, from where the smell that came on board emanates, give the impression of a human enterprise that has no time to ponder whether the skyscraper is better than the little Portuguese colonial house.

Background documentation: the Museum of Modern Art's book Brazil Builds represented a real, almost palpable, daily hope, not a metaphysical one. The simplicity of the architectural solutions, the human "call-outs" were unknown to a whole generation that arrived from very far away… At that time, right after the war, it was like a lighthouse shining over a field of death… It was something marvellous.

Reception at Rio's branch of IAB (Architects Institute of Brazil): Lúcio Costa, Oscar Niemeyer, Rocha Miranda, the Robertos, Athos Bulcão, Burle Marx and others. In Cosme Velho[*19], Portinari, sculptor Landucci, Marcos Jaimovitch, all old friends of Oscar. This was Brazil's first international vanguard (the second would be Brasília). Overwhelmed by the intelligent simplicity and personal capacities. Overwhelmed by an incredible country with no middle class, just two great aristocracies: that of the land, of Coffee, of Sugar Cane, and… the People.

1947. Chateaubriand[*20] invites Pietro to set up and run an Art Museum in Brazil; either in Rio or in São Paulo. I much preferred Rio, but the money was in São Paulo. I told Pietro that I wanted to stay, that I had again found the hopes of the nights during the war. We thus stayed in Brazil.

1951. I was granted Brazilian citizenship. When one is born, one chooses nothing, one just happens to be born. I was not born here, but I chose this country to live in. For this reason, Brazil is my country twice times over, it is my "Country by Choice", and I feel like a citizen of all its cities, from Cariri[*21] to the Triângulo Mineiro[*22], the cities in the countryside and the ones on its borders.

*18 A resort area located in the southeastern part of the city of Rio de Janeiro.

*19 A town in the southeastern part of the city of Rio de Janeiro.

*20 Assis Chateaubriand. 1892-1968. A Brazilian businessman.

*21 Cariri do Tocantins. A town in central Brazil.

*22 State of Minas Gerais. Located in the southeastern part of Brazil.

旧サンパウロ美術館でのディオールのファッションショーにて。
左端がピエトロ、右から2番目がリナ。（1951年）
At the Christian Dior fashion show held at the former MASP. Pietro (leftmost) and Lina (second from the right). (1951)

リナ・ボ・バルディ関連年表

	リナ（＊は実現せず）	建築界の動き	社会の動き（ブラジルの動
1914	0歳 ■ローマにて誕生	■ドミノ・システム／ル・コルビュジエ	■第一次世界大戦勃発（-1918）
1915			
1916			
1917			■ロシア革命
1918			
1919		■ヴァルター・グロピウスが国立バウハウスの初代校長に就任	
1920			
1921			
1922			
1923			
1924		■シュレーダー邸／ヘリット・リートフェルト	
1925			
1926			
1927			
1928			■イタリアでファシスト独裁体制成立
1929		■バルセロナ・パビリオン／ミース・ファン・デル・ローエ	■世界恐慌 バルセロナ万国博覧会
1930			■ヴァルガス政権成立
1931		■サヴォア邸／ル・コルビュジエ	■満州事変
1932		■インターナショナル・スタイル展／ニューヨーク近代美術館	

リナ・ボ・バルディ、2歳。（1916年）
Lina Bo Bardi at age 2. (1916)

リナ、4年生。ローマの小学校でクラスメートたちと。
リナは前列、右端に立っている。（1923年）
Lina in 4th grade. With her classmates
in her elementary school in Rome.
Lina is standing at the right end of the front row. (1923)

	リナ（*は実現せず）	建築界の動き	社会の動き（ブラジルの動き）
1933		■第4回CIAM会議で「アテネ憲章」採択（ピエトロ・マリア・バルディも出席）	■ナチス政権獲得
1934	20歳 ■ローマ大学建築学部に入学		
1935		■落水荘／フランク・ロイド・ライト ■カサ・デル・ファッショ／ジュゼッペ・テラーニ	
1936			
1937			
1938			
1939	25歳 ■卒業制作「妊婦と幼児のためのケアセンター」で大学を卒業	■ル・コルビュジエのブラジル初訪問（1943年に2度目の訪問） ■ニューヨーク万国博覧会ブラジル館／ルシオ・コスタ、オスカー・ニーマイヤー	■第二次世界大戦勃発
1940	26歳 ■ミラノへ移り、ジオ・ポンティに師事（-1943） ■カルロ・パガーニと共にスタジオを開く	■パンプーリャ・コンプレックス／オスカー・ニーマイヤー	■日伊独三国同盟
1941			
1942			
1943	29歳 ■パガーニと共に建築雑誌『ドムス』の副編集長に就任 ■ミラノ空襲で事務所が破壊 ■レジスタンス活動に参加	■ブラジル教育保健省／ルシオ・コスタ、オスカー・ニーマイヤーら ■ブラジル・ビルズ展／ニューヨーク近代美術館	■イタリア無条件降伏
1944			
1945	31歳 ■イタリア各地の戦争被害を記録 ■雑誌『A：現実、建築、住居、アート』発行		■広島、長崎に原爆投下 ■第二次世界大戦終結 ■ポピュリズモ時代スタート（-1964）
1946	32歳 ■美術評論家のピエトロ・マリア・バルディと結婚 ■リオ・デ・ジャネイロに移住		■パリ講和会議
1947	33歳 ■サンパウロへ移住 ■「サンパウロ美術館（MASP）」をオープン ■美術館のためビルのフロアを改修 ■ブラジルの宝石を使ったジュエリーをデザイン	■バラガン自邸／ルイス・バラガン	■パレスチナ戦争勃発（-1949）
1948	34歳 ■インダストリアル・デザイン会社「ダルテ・パルマ」を設立		■マハトマ・ガンジー暗殺
1949		■グラスハウス／フィリップ・ジョンソン	■中華人民共和国成立 ■西独・東独成立
1950	36歳 ■夫と共に雑誌『アピタ』刊行	■ファンズワース邸／ミース・ファン・デル・ローエ	■朝鮮戦争勃発（-1953）
1951	37歳 ■「ガラスの家」建設 ■ブラジルに帰化 ■クリスチャン・ディオールのファッションショーを開催／MASP ■IAC（現代美術研究所）にインダストリアル・デザインコースを設立・運営 ■「海沿いの美術館」計画*		■旧日米安全保障条約締結
1952			

年	リナ（*は実現せず）	建築界の動き	社会の動き（ブラジルの動き）
1953		■オスカー・ニーマイヤー邸／オスカー・ニーマイヤー	■ヨシフ・スターリン死去
1954		■イビラプエラ公園／オスカー・ニーマイヤー ■ニュー・ブルータリズム提唱／スミッソン夫妻	
1955	41歳 ■サンパウロ大学都市建築学部の講師を務める（-1957）		■クビチェック政権成立
1956			■チベット動乱
1957	43歳 ■建築論の教授職に論文『建築論教育序論』で応募するも不採用 ■北イタリアのカントゥで行われた家具デザインコンペティションに参加 ■「サンパウロ美術館」計画スタート		■ソ連人工衛星の打ち上げ成功 ■ブラジリア空港開港
1958	44歳 ■「ヴァレリア・P・シレル邸」建設 ■バイーア州立大学での講義を担当し、以降約6年間主にサルヴァドールで活動 ■「シャメシャメ邸」（現存せず）を建設 ■サルヴァドールの新聞で連載をもつ	■雑誌『モデュロ』創刊／オスカー・ニーマイヤー	■欧州経済共同体（EEC）発足
1959	45歳 ■マルティム・ゴンサルヴィスとの共同展示「バイーア・イン・イピラブエラ」展を計画／第5回サンパウロ・ビエンナーレ ■バイーア現代美術館（MAMBA）の館長に就任	■ブラジリア建設開始（-1960）	■キューバ革命 ■フランスでヌーヴェルヴァーグの流行 ■文化面での黄金期（ボサノヴァの流行、シネマ・ノーヴォ）
1960	46歳 ■「三文オペラ」の舞台美術と衣装を担当	■ニューヨークグッゲンハイム美術館／フランク・ロイド・ライト ■CIAMの終焉, Team Xの台頭	■アフリカ各国が独立 ■ブラジリア落成
1961	47歳 ■演劇「カリギュラ」（マルティム・ゴンサルヴィス監督）の舞台美術と衣装を担当		■ソ連とアメリカが有人宇宙飛行に成功 ■ベルリンの壁建設
1962		■ブラジル司法省、ブラジル外務省／オスカー・ニーマイヤー	■キューバ危機 ■『沈黙の春』出版／レイチェル・カーソン
1963	49歳 ■「民衆文化伝承館」が「北東」展でオープン		■ケネディ大統領暗殺
1964	50歳 ■軍による「民衆文化伝承館」の占拠 ■サンパウロに戻る	■国立代々木競技場／丹下健三 ■建築家なしの建築展／ニューヨーク近代美術館	■クーデター勃発、軍事政権の成立 ■芸術活動への弾圧が強まる
1965	51歳 ■「ブタンタン研究所」の美術館*を計画 ■リオ・デ・ジャネイロのラージェ公園の展示パビリオン*を計画 ■イタマンプカ海岸のリゾート計画*を計画	■ソーク生物学研究所／ルイス・カーン	■ベトナム戦争が激化
1966	52歳 ■「サンパウロ美術館」計画再開	■『建築の多様性と対立性』／ロバート・ヴェンチューリ	■中国、文化大革命（-1977）
1967	53歳 ■「道ばたの椅子」制作	■オスカー・ニーマイヤー、パリに亡命（-1985）	■欧州共同体（EC）発足 ■ブラジル連邦共和国成立 トロピカリア・ムーブメント
1968	54歳 ■「サンパウロ美術館」完成		■「プラハの春」 パリ5月革命 キング牧師暗殺
1969	55歳 ■演劇「都市のジャングル」の美術と衣装を担当 ■「ブラジル人の手」展開催／MASP		■アポロ11号月面着陸 ■高度経済成長「ブラジルの奇跡」
1970	56歳 ■映画「プラタ・パロモレス」のアートディレクターと美術を担当	■日本万国博覧会（大阪万博）ブラジル館／パウロ・メンデス・ダ・ローシャ ■ブラジリア・メトロポリタン大聖堂／オスカー・ニーマイヤー	■日本万国博覧会（大阪万博） ■ペレの活躍でブラジルがFIFAワールドカップ3度目の優勝
1971			
1972		■キンベル美術館／ルイス・カーン	■日中国交正常化

	リナ（*は実現せず）	建築界の動き	社会の動き（ブラジルの動き）
1973			
1974	61歳 ■「レパッソス」展／MASP ■「カミュリュピン・コミュニティ・プロジェクト」*計画		■第一次石油危機
1975			■ベトナム戦争終結
1976			
1977	63歳 ■「ラストロ香水工場」*計画 ■「SESCポンペイア文化センター」設計開始（-1986年）	■ポンピドゥー・センター／ レンゾ・ピアノ，リチャード・ロジャース	■アマゾン横断道路が完成
1978	64歳 ■「サンタ・マリア・ドス・アンジョス教会」建設	■ニーマイヤーがブラジル民主主義 センターを創設，代表に選任	
1979		■ゲーリー自邸／フランク・O・ゲーリー ■ラ・ヴィレット公園／ベルナール・チュミ	■ソ連のアフガニスタン侵攻 ■イラン革命，第二次石油危機
1980		■ジュセリーノ・クビチェック大統領記念館 ／オスカー・ニーマイヤー	■イラン・イラク戦争（-1988） ■ジョン・レノン暗殺
1981	67歳 ■「美しいもの，そして醜いものが持つ権利」展を開催／SESC		
1982	68歳 ■「エスピリト・サント・ド・セラード聖霊教会」建設 ■「アニャンガバウ渓谷高架プロジェクト」*計画 ■「ブラジルのデザイン：歴史と現実」展を開催／SESC		■フォークランド紛争
1983	69歳 ■「ブラジルの子どもたちに1000のおもちゃを」展を開催／SESC	■つくばセンタービル／磯崎新	
1984	70歳 ■「カイピラス，カピアウス：パウ・ア・ピッケ」展を開催／SESC		
1985	71歳 ■「子どものための幕間」展を開催／SESC ■演劇『ユビュ王』（カサ・ロセット監督）の舞台美術と衣装を担当		■サルネイ政権成立，民政が復活
1986	72歳 ■「ポリテアマ・ジュンディアウ劇場」の修復開始（-1995） ■「サルヴァドール旧市街修復プロジェクト」開始 ■「グレゴリオ・デ・マトス劇場」完成	■ブラジル彫刻美術館設計開始（-1995） ／パウロ・メンデス・ダ・ローシャ	■ソ連チェルノブイリ原発事故
1987	73歳 ■「ベナンの家」完成 ■「ミゼリコーディア坂歴史的地区」の修復		■ブラジリア世界遺産登録
1988	74歳 ■「オロドゥムの家」「LBAコミュニティセンター」建設 ■「アフリカ・ネグラ」展を開催／MASP ■リスボンの「ベレーム文化センター」コンペティション*に参加	■オスカー・ニーマイヤー， プリツカー賞を受賞	
1989	75歳 ■「テアトロ・オフィシナ」建設 ■「ピエール・ヴェルジェ財団」*「ブラジルの家」*計画 ■野外劇場「ダス・ルイナス劇場」*計画		■天安門事件 ■ベルリンの壁崩壊
1990	76歳 ■「カンピーナス州立大学文化センター」*計画 ■「サンパウロ・シティ・ホール」設計開始	■東京都庁舎／丹下健三	■東西ドイツ統一
1991	77歳 ■「セビリア万博ブラジル館」コンペティションに参加（佳作）* ■古い映画会社を文化センターに変えるプロジェクト*を計画	■ニテロイ現代美術館設計開始（-1996）／ オスカー・ニーマイヤー	■ソ連崩壊 湾岸戦争勃発（-1991） ■日本でバブル経済の崩壊 ■ユーゴスラヴィア内戦
1992	78歳 ■3月20日，「ガラスの家」で生涯を終える		

Chronology of Lina Bo Bardi

	Events in Lina's Life (projects marked with an asterisk * are unrealized)	Events in the Architectural World	Events in the World (Braz...
1914	0 ■ Birth in Rome	■ Dom-Ino system / Le Corbusier	■ World War I (-1918)
1915			
1916			
1917			■ Russian Revolution
1918			
1919		■ Walter Gropius becomes first director of Bauhaus School	
1920			
1921			
1922			
1923			
1924		■ Rietveld Schröder House / Gerrit Rietveld	
1925			
1926			
1927			
1928			■ Establishment of fascist dictato... in Italy
1929		■ Barcelona Pavilion / Mies van der Rohe	■ Great Depression Barcelona International Expos...
1930			■ Establishment of Vargas regim...
1931		■ Villa Savoye / Le Corbusier	■ Manchurian Incident
1932		■ "International Style" exhibition / New York Museum of Modern Art	

夫ピエトロ・マリア・バルディを描いたドローイング。(1988年9月27日)
Drawing of husband Pietro Maria Bardi. (September 27, 1988)

	Events in Lina's Life (projects marked with an asterisk * are unrealized)	Events in the Architectural World	Events in the World (Brazil)
1933		■"Athens Charter" adopted at the 4th CIAM Conference (P. M. Bardi also attended)	■Establishment of Nazi regime
1934	20 ■Admitted to the Faculty of Architecture, University of Rome		
1935			
1936		■Fallingwater / Frank Lloyd Wright ■Casa del Fascio / Giuseppe Terragni	
1937			
1938			
1939	25 ■Graduates from university Graduation thesis titled "The Maternity and Infancy Care Center"	■Le Corbusier visits Brazil (the second visit in 1943) ■Brazil Pavilion at the New York World's Fair / Lúcio Costa, Oscar Niemeyer	■Outbreak of World War II
1940	26 ■Moves to Milan to study under Gio Ponti (-1943) ■Opens a studio with Carlo Pagani	■Pampulha Modern Ensemble / Oscar Niemeyer	■Tripartite Pact
1941			
1942			
1943	29 ■Begins working as associate editor for architecture magazine "Domus" together with Pagani ■Offices destroyed during the Bombing of Milan ■Participates in resistance activities	■Ministry of Education and Health Building / Lucio Costa, Oscar Niemeyer et al. ■"Brazil Builds" exhibition / New York Museum of Modern Art	■Italy surrenders unconditionally
1944			
1945	31 ■Chronicles the ravages of war across Italy ■Publishes magazine: "A: Attualità, Architettura, Abitazione, Arte (A: News, Architecture, Housing, Art)"		■Atomic bombing of Hiroshima and Nagasaki ■End of World War II ■Beginning of the Era of Populismo (-1964)
1946	32 ■Marries art critic Pietro Maria Bardi ■Emigrates to Rio de Janeiro		■Paris Peace Conference
1947	33 ■Moves to São Paulo ■Opens São Paulo Museum of Art ■Performs building floor renovation for MASP ■Designs jewelry using gems from Brazil	■Luis Barragán House and Studio / Luis Barragán	■Outbreak of Palestine War (-1949)
1948	34 ■Establishes industrial design company "Studio d'arte Parma"		■Assassination of Mahatma Gandhi
1949		■Glass House / Philip Johnson	■Establishment of People's Republic of China ■Establishment of West Germany / East Germany
1950	36 ■Co-founds magazine "Habitat" with husband	■Farnsworth House / Mies van der Rohe	■Outbreak of Korean War (-1953)
1951	37 ■Construction of the "Glass House (Casa de Vidro)" ■Becomes naturalized Brazilian citizen ■Christian Dior fashion show held at MASP ■Establishes / operates industrial design course IAC (Inter Arts Center) ■Planning of "Museum on the Seashore"*		■(Former) Japan-US Security Treaty concluded
1952			

Year	Events in Lina's Life (projects marked with an asterisk * are unrealized)	Events in the Architectural World	Events in the World (Brazi
1953		■Canoas House / Oscar Niemeyer	■Death of Joseph Stalin
1954		■Ibirapuera Park / Oscar Niemeyer ■New Brutalism theory / Alison and Peter Smithson	
1955	41 ■Works as lecturer at Architecture and Urbanism College, University of São Paulo (-1957)		■Establishment of Kubitschek government
1956			■Tibetan uprising
1957	43 ■Publishes thesis titled "Propaedeutic contribution to the teaching of architectural theory" to become professor of architecture, but is rejected ■Participates in furniture design competition held in Cantù, northern Italy ■Planning of "São Paulo Art Museum (MASP)" begins		■Soviet Union launches Sputnik ■Brasilia Airport opens
1958	44 ■Construction of "Valéria P. Cirell's Home" ■Became lecturer at Federal University of Bahia, and was mainly active in Salvador for the next 6 years ■Construction of "Casa do Chame-Chame" (no longer exists) ■Begins to write regularly for a newspaper of Salvador	■Magazine "Módulo" begins publication / Oscar Niemeyer	■Establishment of European Econ Community (EEC)
1959	45 ■Joint exhibition with Martim Gonçalves titled "Bahia in Ibirapuer" / 5th São Paulo Biennale ■Becomes director of Bahia Museum of Modern Art (MAMBA)	■Construction of Brasilia begins (-1960)	■Cuban Revolution ■Nouvelle Vague movement in Fra ■Cultural Golden Age (popularizat Bossa Nova / Cinema Novo
1960	46 ■Performs stage / costume design for "The Threepenny Opera"	■New York City Guggenheim Museum / Frank Lloyd Wright ■End of CIAM, rise of Team X	■African countries declare indepe ■Inauguration of Brasilia
1961	47 ■Performs stage / costume design for "Caligula"(directed by Martim Gonçalves)		■Successful manned space flights Soviet Union and United States ■Construction of Berlin Wall
1962		■Ministry of Justice, Ministry of External Relations / Oscar Niemeyer	■Cuban Crisis ■Publication of "Silent Spring" / Rachel Carson
1963	49 ■Opens "Solar do Unhão – Popular Art Museum" with "Northeast" exhibition		■Assassination of President Kenn
1964	50 ■Military occupation of "Solar do Unhão – Popular Art Museum" ■Returns to São Paulo	■Yoyogi National Gymnasium / Kenzo Tange ■"Architecture Without Architects" exhibition / New York Museum of Modern Art	■Military coup, Establishment of military regime ■Suppression of artistic activities inte
1965	51 ■Planning of "Butantã Institute" museum* ■Planning of Exhibition pavilion in Parque Lage, Rio de Janeiro* ■Planning of resort off the coast of Itamambuca	■Salk Institute for Biological Studies / Louis Kahn	■Intensification of Vietnam Wa
1966	52 ■Resumes designing of MASP	■"Complexity and Contradiction in Architecture" / Robert Venturi	■Cultural Revolution, China (-19
1967	53 ■Production of "Roadside Chair (Cadeira de Beira de Estrada)"	■Exile of Oscar Niemeyer in Paris (-1985)	■Establishment of European Commu ■Establishment of the Federative F of Brazil, Tropicalia Movement
1968	54 ■Completion of "São Paulo Art Museum"		■"Prague Spring" ■Social revolution of May 1968, F ■Assassination of Reverend Mart Luther King Jr.
1969	55 ■Performs art / costume design for "In the Jungle of Cities" ■"The Hand of the Brazilian People" exhibition / MASP		■Apollo 11 lunar landing ■Period of high economic growth "Brazilian Miracle" (-1974)
1970	56 ■Performs art direction / artwork for film titled "Prata Palomares"	■Brazil Pavilion at the Japan World Exposition(Osaka Expo) / Paulo Mendes da Rocha ■Cathedral of Brasilia / Oscar Niemeyer	■Japan World Exposition (Osaka ■Pelé helps the Brazilian selectio the FIFA World Cup for the 3rd
1971			
1972		■Kimbell Art Museum / Louis Kahn	■Normalization of Japan-China re

	Events in Lina's Life (projects marked with an asterisk * are unrealized)	Events in the Architectural World	Events in the World (Brazil)
1973			■ First oil crisis
1974			
1975	61 ■ "Repassos" exhibition / MASP ■ Planning of "Camurupim Community Project"*		■ End of Vietnam War
1976			
1977	63 ■ Planning of "Rastro Perfume Factory"* ■ Design of "SESC Pompéia Leisure Center" begins (completed in 1986)	■ Pompidou Centre / Renzo Piano, Richard Rogers	■ Completion of Trans-Amazonian highway
1978	64 ■ Construction of "Santa Maria dos Anjos Chapel"	■ Oscar Niemeyer establishes Brazilian Democracy Center, appointed as representative	
1979		■ Gehry Residence / Frank Owen Gehry ■ Parc de la Villette / Bernard Tschumi	■ Soviet invasion of Afghanistan ■ Iranian Revolution, Second oil crisis
1980		■ President Juscelino Kubitschek Memorial / Oscar Niemeyer	■ Iran-Iraq War (-1988) ■ Assassination of John Lennon
1981	67 ■ "Beauty and the Right to the Ugly" exhibition / SESC		
1982	68 ■ Construction of "Espírito Santo do Cerrado Church" ■ Planning of "Anhangabaú Valley Project"* ■ "Design in Brazil: History and Reality" exhibition / SESC		■ Falklands War
1983	69 ■ "A Thousand Toys for Brazilian Children" exhibition / SESC	■ Tsukuba Center building / Arata Isozaki	
1984	70 ■ "Caipiras, Capiaus: Pau-a-Pique" exhibition / SESC		
1985	71 ■ "Intermedio for Children" exhibition / SESC ■ Stage / costume design for "Ubú" (directed by Cacá Rosset)		■ Establishment of Sarney government, Restoration of civil government
1986	72 ■ Restoration of "Politeama – Jundiaí – Theater" begins (-1995) ■ Restoration of "The Historic Center of Salvador" begins ■ Conpletion of "Gregório de Mattos Theater"	■ Design of "Brazilian Museum of Sculpture" begins (-1995) / Paulo Mendes da Rocha	■ Chernobyl nuclear accident, Soviet Union
1987	73 ■ Conpletion of "House of Benin" ■ Restoration of "Misericórdia Slope"		■ Brasilia designated World Heritage Site
1988	74 ■ Construction of "House of Olodum" and "LBA Community Center" ■ "África Negra" exhibition / MASP ■ Entry for the "Cultural Centre of Belém"* competition	■ Oscar Niemeyer wins Pritzker Architecture Prize	
1989	75 ■ Construction of "Oficina Theater" ■ Planning of "Pierre Verger Foundation"* and "House of Brasil"* ■ Planning of Outdoor theater "Theater of Ruins"*		■ Tiananmen Square Massacre ■ Fall of the Berlin Wall
1990	76 ■ Planning of "Centre for Living Together" for Campinas University* ■ Design of "São Paulo City Hall" begins	■ Tokyo Metropolitan Government Building / Kenzo Tange	■ German reunification
1991	77 ■ Entry for the "Brazil Pavilion at the Universal Exposition of Seville" competition (honorable mention)* ■ Planning for project to transform an old movie studio into cultural center*	■ Design of Niterói Contemporary Art Museum begins (-1996) / Oscar Niemeyer	■ Collapse of Soviet Union ■ Gulf War (-1991) ■ Collapse of the Japanese economic bubble ■ Yugoslav Wars
1992	78 ■ Lived the rest of her days at the Glass House where she died on March 20th		

あとがき

私がリナ・ボ・バルディの建築を初めて知ったのは妹島和世さんが総合ディレクターをされた2010年のヴェネチアビエンナーレ国際建築展だった。彩色された美しいドローイング、写真、それに白いボードで作られたシンプルな模型が展示されていた。すぐに「SESCポンペイア文化センター」の模型に目が止まり、よく見ると壁に開いた不揃いな穴が窓になっていて、それはいわゆるきちっとした建築とは違う、自由で伸びやかな空気を放っていた。それから数年後に妹島さんにお会いした時、当時の感想を伝えると、「近々ブラジルへ行くので、興味があるなら一緒に行きましょう」、と誘っていただいた。いつでも、事のはじまりはそんな風で、私は「百聞は一見に如かず」と即座にブラジル行きを決心した。

サンパウロに到着すると「サンパウロ美術館(MASP)」「SESCポンペイア文化センター」「テアトロ・オフィシナ」「サンタ・マリア・ドス・アンジョス教会」などの代表作を一気に見て回った。それらは赤土から芽を出して、ブラジルの太陽を受けて大きく成長する植物のように、のびのびと、不思議な存在感があった。ただ、処女作の自邸「ガラスの家」だけは、ヨーロッパのモダニズムの要素がそのまま表れた、洗練された建築だった。

2015年12月より開催されたワタリウム美術館での展覧会からおよそ2年半を経て、ようやく本書の出版が実現した。書籍では展覧会では伝えきれなかったリナの人間像、思想、建築以外の活動などを加えたが、ここで少し言及したい。

> 記憶のための場所？ それとも有名なミイラを納める墓？ 人類の遺産をしまっておくための倉庫？ いいえ、そうではないのです。これからの美術館は、扉を開け放ち、フレッシュな空気と光を採り入れるべきなのです。
> リナ・ボ・バルディ　1952年

リナ・ボ・バルディの思想のなかでも、アートに関する見識の高さや態度の先進性は群を抜いている。おそらく夫君のピエトロ氏が大変な目利きでありアートに精通していたことも関係しているだろうが、「扉を開け放す」ことが現在でもどれほど難しいことか。本書では「キュレーション」の頁（p. 190）で、〈作品を壁から解放する〉〈市場のように展示する〉〈舞台のような展覧会〉

リナ・ボ・バルディ、71歳。サンパウロにて。（1985年）
Lina Bo Bardi, age 71. In São Paulo. (1985)

〈アートをみんなの手に〉といったいくつかの手法と思想をまとめた。彼女がアートや演劇といったクリエーションにこだわったのは、クリエーションこそが、すべての人びとに自由と希望をもたらすと深く信じていたからであり、リナの思想の根源であったからだと思う。その思想の根源は建築設計においても大きな柱となって彼女を支えていたに違いない。

そしてもうひとつお伝えしたいのは、リナ自身が「MASP」建設の内幕について語った映像記録の内容だ。美術館の敷地はサンパウロの目抜き通り、パウリスタ通りにあり、もともとサンパウロを一望できる歴史的な見晴台「トリアノン」があった場所だ。実は市は見晴台を壊してここに公園と地下公衆トイレをつくる計画を推進していた。それを知ったリナは、こう叫んでいる。

  何ですって？　中央駅にあるような公衆トイレをここに？
  まったくのナンセンスだわ。
  ここは街にとって大切な場所なのに。
  私はここに美術館を建てたい。

リナはすぐさま、行政を動かすために大作戦を立て行動する。ブラジルのメディア王や大統領候補者、夫のピエトロ、そして後にこの美術館の所蔵品の基礎となる美術品を提供した大物コレクター、シャトーブリアンまでもがこの作戦に巻き込まれていく。もちろん作戦は成功し、現在の見晴台の機能を備えたピロティ式の赤い「サンパウロ美術館」が実現し、美術館は今日もサンパウロのランドマークの役目を果たしている。これはあまり知られることのない裏話だが、彼女のエネルギーと行動力を知る記録である。

展覧会と出版実現のための3年にわたるリナ・ボ・バルディ・プロジェクトでは実に多くの方にお力添えをいただいた。駐日ブラジル連邦共和国大使で建築評論家のアンドレ・コヘーア・ド・ラーゴ氏をはじめ、企画を応援してくださった妹島和世さん、塚本由晴さん、展覧会で素敵な会場デザインを手がけてくださった周防貴之さん、「ガラスの家」のリナ・ボ・バルディ財団の皆様、そして清水栄江さんをはじめ親身に編集をお手伝いくださったTOTO出版の方々、デザインで新しいリナのイメージを創り出してくださったグルーヴィジョンズの原 徹さん、齋藤智仁さん、みなさまに感謝したい。

クリエーションは人びとの自由な世界をつくるためのものでなければならない、というリナ・ボ・バルディの揺るぎない哲学が今後のクリエーションの世界になんらかの参考になればと心から祈って最後の言葉としたい。

2017年9月
和多利恵津子（ワタリウム美術館館長）

Afterword

I first learned about the architecture of Lina Bo Bardi at the 2010 Venice Biennale International Architecture Exhibition where Ms. Kazuyo Sejima served as General Director. Beautifully-colored drawings, photos, and simple models constructed with white boards were on display. A model of the "SESC Pompéia Factory Leisure Center" immediately caught my attention and, when I looked closely, there were irregular holes in the walls acting as windows. This was different from so-called clean-cut architecture, and the piece gave off a free and unconstrained atmosphere. And then, when I met Ms. Sejima several years later, I related my impressions at the time and she responded with an invitation, saying "I'll be going to Brazil in the near future, so you should come too if you're interested". Things always seem to begin this way, and since "seeing is believing", I instantly made up my mind to go to Brazil.

After arriving in São Paulo, I toured Lina's most representative projects in one go, including the "São Paulo Art Museum (MASP)", "SESC Pompéia Factory Leisure Center", "Oficina Theater", and "Santa Maria dos Anjos Chapel". Sprouting from the red soil like plants growing big under Brazil's sun, they exuded a carefree and mysterious presence. And it was solely the "Glass House", which was her own house and maiden work, which stood as a refined piece of architecture, in which appeared elements of European modernism as is.

The publishing of this book was finally realized after some two and a half years had passed since the exhibition at WATARI-UM held in December of 2015. Details about Lina's human ideals, ideas and activities outside of architecture that we were not able to fully convey at the exhibition were added to the book, but I would like to

reference something here.

> A corner for memories? A tomb for illustrious mummies? A deposit or an archive for human works? None of this. The new museums should throw open their doors, let in the fresh air and light.
> Lina Bo Bardi, 1952

Even among Lina Bo Bardi's many ideas, her deep insight and innovative attitude regarding art was unmatched. Her husband Pietro being a serious connoisseur well-versed in art may have played a part, but even now the idea of "throwing open the doors" is exceptionally difficult. I gathered several techniques and concepts such as "freeing artwork from walls", "displaying works like in a marketplace", "realizing exhibitions with a theatrical flair" and "bringing art within everyone's reach" on the "Curation" page (p. 190) of this book. I think that the reason Lina paid close attention to creation through art and theater was because she sincerely believed that it was creation that brought freedom and hope to all people. This was at the root of her ideas, and it was the main pillar of her architectural design that surely served to support her.

And one more thing I would like to tell you about is the content of a video recording that talks about Lina's own account of building the "São Paulo Art Museum". The museum site was located on São Paulo's main street Paulista Avenue, which was originally the location of

"Trianon", the historic lookout that afforded a sweeping view of São Paulo. Actually, the city had been promoting a plan to destroy the lookout and build a park along with underground toilets on this location. Hearing of this, Lina exclaimed the following.

> What? Toilets like Central do Brasil? …
> It makes no sense.
> It's a wonderful plot…
> I want to do the museum building there.

Lina immediately set to work on a major strategy to move the local government. A Brazilian media mogul, a presidential candidate, and her husband Pietro, along with Chateaubriand, a major art collector who provided artworks that would later become the basis of this museum's collection, all became involved in her strategy. It goes without saying that this strategy succeeded, and the red, piloti-style "São Paulo Art Museum", providing a lookout function today, was realized. The museum serves as a São Paulo landmark even now. This is not a very well-known story, but it is a record that allows us to know about her energy and ability to take action.
I received considerable help from many people towards

the exhibition and publication of this book over the course of this three year Lina Bo Bardi Project. First and foremost, I would like to thank His Excellency Mr. André Corrêa do Lago, Ambassador of the Federative Republic of Brazil to Japan; Ms. Kazuyo Sejima and Mr. Yoshiharu Tsukamoto, who supported the project; Mr. Takashi Suo, who worked on the wonderful venue design for the exhibition; everyone from the "Glass House" Instituto Lina Bo e P. M. Bardi; Ms. Sakae Shimizu and the staff at TOTO publishing, who kindly assisted with editing; and Mr. Toru Hara and Tomohito Saito from Groovisions, who produced a new image of Lina for the design. My sincere thanks to all of you.

To conclude, I earnestly hope that Lina Bo Bardi's unwavering philosophy that creation must serve towards building a world where people can be free becomes something of a reference within the world of creation from here on.

September 2017
Etsuko Watari (Director, WATARI-UM, The Watari Museum of Contemporary Art)

作品データ　Project Data

凡例／Legend

1：所在地／Location
2：共同設計／Collaborator
3：面積／Area
4：着工年／Construction Start
5：竣工年／Completed

① ガラスの家 / The Glass House

1: São Paulo
2: Tulio Stuchi (computational engineer)
3: 540㎡(building); 7,000㎡(site)
4: 1950
5: 1951

② サンパウロ美術館 / São Paulo Art Museum

1: São Paulo
2: Figueiredo Ferraz (engineer)
3: 11,000㎡ (building)
4: 1957
5: 1968

③ SESCポンペイア文化センター / SESC-Pompéia Factory Leisure Center

1: São Paulo
2: André Vainer, Marcelo Carvalho Ferraz, Antonio Carlos Martinelli, Luis H. de Carvalho
3: 16,000㎡ (site);
   12,000㎡ (sport center);
   12,000㎡ (leisure center)
4: 1977
5: 1986

④ サンタ・マリア・ドス・アンジョス教会 / Santa Maria dos Anjos Chapel

1: São Paulo
2: Marcelo Carvalho Ferraz, André Vainer
3: 207㎡ (building)
4: 1978
5: 1978

⑤ サルヴァドール旧市街修復プロジェクト / The Historic Center of Salvador

1: Salvador
2: Marcelo Carvalho Ferraz, Marcelo Suzuki
3: over 30ha
4: 1986
5: March 1987

⑥ ベナンの家 / House of Benin

1: Salvador
2: Marcelo Carvalho Ferraz, Marcelo Suzuki
3: 706㎡ (building)
4: 1987
5: 1987-88

⑦ グレゴリオ・デ・マトス劇場 / Gregório de Mattos Theater

1: Salvador
2: Associates: Marcelo Carvalho Ferraz and Marcelo Suzuki
4: 1986
5: 1986

⑧ ミゼリコーディア坂 / Misericórdia Slope

1: Salvador
2: Marcelo Carvalho Ferraz, Marcelo Suzuki with João Filgueiras Lima and engineer Frederico Schiel
3: 11,364 ㎡ (building)
4: 1987
5: 1988

⑨ テアトロ・オフィシナ / Oficina Theater

1: São Paulo
2: Edson Elito
3: 993㎡ (building)
4: 1984
5: 1989

⑩ ヴァレリア・P・シレル邸 / Valéria P. Cirell's Home

1: São Paulo
3: 2,000㎡ (site)
4: 1957
5: 1958

⑪ 民衆文化伝承館 / Solar do Unhão — Popular Art Museum

1: Salvador
3: 1,038㎡ (building)
4: 1959
5: 1963

⑫ エスピリト・サント・ド・セラード教会 / Espírito Santo do Cerrado Church

1: Uberlândia
2: Marcelo Carvalho Ferraz, André Vainer
3: 1,404㎡ (building)
4: 1976
5: 1982

⑬ サンパウロ・シティ・ホール / São Paulo City Hall

1: São Paulo
2: André Vainer, Marcelo Carvalho Ferraz, Marcelo Suzuki
3: 8,000㎡
4: 1991
5: 1992

リナ・ボ・バルディ建築作品マップ　Architectural Works Map

ブラジル全域図　Map of Brazil

Brazil
⑤〜⑧ ⑪
⑫ Salvador
Uberlândia
①〜④ ⑨ ⑩ ⑬ São Paulo

サンパウロ広域図　Map of Metropolitan São Paulo City

③ São Paulo
④
① ⑩

サンパウロ市中心部　Map of the Center of São Paulo City

Memorial da America Latina
Pinacoteca do Estado de Sao Paulo
Shopping Patio Higienopolis
Shopping 25 de Marco
Galeria do Rock
Edificio Martinelli
⑬
Football Museum
São Paulo
② Avenida Paulista
⑨
Parque Ibirapuera

参考文献　Bibliography

西武美術館編『ジオ・ポンティ作品集＜1891〜1979＞』鹿島出版会、1986年
Seibu Museum ed. "The Collected Works of Gio Ponti – 1891-1979", Kajima Publishing, 1986

マルセロ・カルヴァリョ・フェラス「リナ・建築・ブラジル」『a+u』341号、1999年
Marcelo Calvalho Ferraz "Lina, Architecture and Brazil", a+u 341, 1999

ルイージ・メネゲッリ「アルテ・ポーヴェラ」『アルテ・ポーヴェラ展カタログ』児玉画廊、1992年
Luigi Meneghelli, "Arte Povera", in "Arte Povera Exhibition Catalog", Kodama Gallery, 1992.

泉勇佑「ミラノにおける「装飾芸術」の近代化：イタリアの建築教育制度と両大戦間期の建築雑誌に関する分析」、東京大学大学院工学系研究科修士論文、2017年、未公刊
Yusuke Izumi. "The Modernization of 'Decorative Art' in Milan: An Analysis of the Architectural Education System in Italy and the Architectural Magazines between the Two Wars", Master's Thesis at the University of Tokyo Graduate School of Engineering, 2017, unpublished.

Marcelo Carvalho Ferraz(ed.), *Lina Bo Bardi*, São Paulo, Instituto Lina Bo e P. M. Bardi, 1993

Jerzy Grotowski, *Towards a Poor Theater*, New York, Routledge, 2002

Daniel Bueno, "Saul Steinberg and Brazil: his time in the country, publications and influence on Brazilian artists", *Revista de História da Arte e Arqueologia*, 10 (2008), pp 117-148.

Lina Bo Bardi, *Lina por escrito: textos escolhidos de Lina Bo Bardi, 1943-1991*, São Paulo, Cosac Naify, 2009

Lina Bo Bardi, *Stones against Diamonds*, London, Architectural Association Publications, 2013

Zeuler R. M. de A. Lima, *Lina Bo Bardi*, New Heaven, Yale University Press, 2013

Cathrine Veikos, Lina Bo Bardi: *The Theory of Architectural Practice*, London, Routledge, 2014

Olivia de Oliveira, *Lina Bo Bardi: obra construída = built works*, Barcelona, Editorial Gustavo Gili, 2014

Renato Anelli, Anna Carboncini, and Maria Correia (eds.), *Lina Bo Bardi 100: Brazil's Alternative Path to Modernism*, Germany, Hatje Cantz Pub, 2014

Giancarlo Latorraca, *Maneiras de Expor: Arquitetura Expositiva de Lina Bo Bardi*, São Paulo, Museu da Casa Brasileira, 2015

Anna Carbonici and Tristan Bera, (2017) "Lina Bo Bardi, l'heureuse déracinée" in Emma Lavigne and Hélène Meisel(dirs.), Claire Bonnevie(ed.), *Jardin Infini: de Giverny à l'Amazonie*, Metz, Centre Pompidou-Metz, 2017

出典　Sources

p. 010
First published in Giancarlo Latorraca (ed.), *Cidadela da Liberdade*, São Paulo, SESC, 1986

p. 014
First published in *Habitat*, 10 (January – March 1953)

p. 038
First published in *Habitat*, 9 (1952)

p. 070
The original text is from an interview with Fábio Malavoglia, 1986

p. 106
The original text is from her personal notes, date unknown

p. 120
The original text is from her personal notes, date unknown

p. 138
The original text is from her personal notes, date unknown

p. 150
First published in *Domus*, 198 (June 1944)

p. 158
First published in *Diário de Notícias*, Salvador, 26 October 1958

p. 166
The original text is from her personal notes, date unknown

p. 174
The original text is from her FAU/USP lesson, São Paulo, 1989

p. 180
First published in *Habitat*, 2 (October – December 1951)

p. 182
The original text is from her personal notes, date unknown

p. 190
First published in *Mirante das Artes*, 5 (September – Octover 1967)

p. 202
The original text is from communication about restoration in Salvador, Évora, Portugal, 1989

p. 210
The original text is from Lina Bo Bardi, "Arquitetura e natureza ou natureza e arquitectura?" handwritten lecture notes, Salvador, September 27, 1958, ILBPMB

p. 218
The original text is from the presentation of the design, 1981

p. 230
The original text is from her personal notes, date unknown, ILBPMB

p. 254
The original text is from the transcript of VT documentary *Lina Bo Bardi*, São Paulo, 1993

「サルヴァドール旧市街修復プロジェクト」(pp. 118-135)はAna Carolina de Souza Bierrenbach博士の監修による。
pp. 118-135 "The Historic Center of Salvador" is under the supervision of Professor Ana Carolina de Souza Bierrenbach.

「植栽デザイン」(pp. 210-217)はリナ・ボ・バルディ財団によるテキスト（未公刊）を元に書き起こしたものである。
"Botanical Design" (pp. 210-217) is based on a text by the Lina Bo Bardi Foundation (unpublished).

「日本とリナ」(pp. 230-233)掲載のリナ・ボ・バルディの日記は、リナ・ボ・バルディ財団所蔵（未公刊）。
The diary of Lina Bo Bardi mentioned in "Lina in Japan" (pp. 230-233) is in the Lina Bo Bardi Foundation collection (unpublished).

作品データは、レナト・アネッリほか編著『Lina Bo Bardi 100: Brazil's Alternative Path to Modernism』（ドイツ、Hatje Cantz Pub、2014年）を参照した。
Project data is quoted from Renato Anelli et al. (eds.), Lina Bo Bardi 100: Brazil's Alternative Path to Modernism, Germany, Hatje Cantz Pub, 2014.

クレジット　Credits

写真　Photographs

Leonardo Finotti
pp. 012-013, pp. 022-037, pp. 046-059, pp. 065-069, p. 073, pp. 078-115, p. 124, pp. 128-147, pp. 156-169, p. 170 top and bottom, pp. 188-189, p. 204 left, p. 208, p. 212, p. 231, jacket of the book

周防貴之　Takashi Suo
p. 116, p. 155, p. 235 right, p. 236, pp. 241-243, p. 244 right, pp. 247-253

Marks Lanz
p. 125, pp. 148-154

Nelson Kon
p. 170 center, p. 171, pp. 175-178, p. 185, p. 186 left, p. 187

Rômulo Fialdini
p. 194 right

The Museu de Arte de São Paulo
p. 195

岡倉禎志　Tadashi Okakura
p. 235 left, p. 244 left

図版　Illustrations

The Museu de Arte de São Paulo
p. 190, p. 269 top and bottom

上記以外の写真・図版はInstituto Lina Bo e P. M. Bardi
Images / figures other than the above were provided by Instituto Lina Bo e P. M. Bardi

解説文、キャプション、年表
Project Explanations, Captions, Chronology

和多利恵津子＋杉山結子（ワタリウム美術館）　Etsuko Watari + Yuiko Sugiyama (WATARI-UM, The Watari Museum of Contemporary Art)

英訳　English Translation

川又勝利 Katsunori Kawamata

フランシスコ・ガルシア Francisco Garcia

ダニエル・マッキー Daniel Mackey

英文校正　English Proofreading

Miguel Falci
pp. 257-271

和訳　Japanese Translation

土居 純　Jun Doi
pp. 006-007

杉山結子（ワタリウム美術館）　Yuiko Sugiyama (WATARI-UM, The Watari Museum of Contemporary Art)
p. 010, p. 014, p. 038, p. 070, p. 106, p. 120, p. 138, p. 150, p. 158, p. 166, p. 174, p. 180, p. 182, p. 190, p. 202, p. 210, p. 218, p. 230, p. 254, pp. 256-270

協力　Cooperation

リナ・ボ・バルディ財団　Instituto Lina Bo e P. M. Bardi (ILBPMB)
　Carolina Tatani / Anna Carboncini / Marcella Carvalho

駐日ブラジル大使館　Embassy of Brazil in Tokyo

Ana Carolina Bierrenbach

編集協力　Editorial Cooperation

南風舎 Nampoosha

原田のぶ子 Nobuko Harada

「リナ・ボ・バルディ」展クレジット
"Lina Bo Bardi – Architecture for All" Credit

December 4 Fri, 2015 – March 27 Sun, 2016
Venue: WATARI-UM, The Watari Museum of Contemporary Art
3-7-6 Jingumae Shibuya-ku Tokyo 150-0001 Japan
Tel: 03-3402-3001 Fax: 03-3405-7714
Email: official@watarium.co.jp http://www.watarium.co.jp

Organizer: WATARI-UM, The Watari Museum of Contemporary Art / Bruno Taut Exhibition Committee / Ministry of Culture of Brazil / Embassy of Brazil in Tokyo
Subsidy: Japan Arts Fund
Exhibition Support: Instituto Lina Bo e P. M. Bardi

Superviser: Kazuyo Sejima
Exhibition Design: Takashi Suo
Architectural Model: noguchinaoto architect's
Graphic Design: groovisions
Installation Support: GREEN WISE Co., Ltd. / TOLI Corporation / Vidrotil Glass Mosaic Tiles / Arper SPA / Turkish Airlines / Base7
Video Cooperator: Tapio Snellman
Photo Cooperator: Ioana Marinescu
Cooperation: Noemi Blager / Marcelo Carvalho Ferraz / Andres Lepik / Naoko Sugiyama / Yuiko Sugiyama

リナ・ボ・バルディ──ブラジルにもっとも愛された建築家

2017年11月22日　初版第1刷発行
2023年12月10日　初版第2刷発行

監修　　　和多利恵津子（ワタリウム美術館）
協力　　　リナ・ボ・バルディ財団
発行者　　渡井 朗
発行所　　TOTO出版（TOTO株式会社）
　　　　　〒107-0062 東京都港区南青山1-24-3 TOTO乃木坂ビル2F
　　　　　[営業] TEL: 03-3402-7138　FAX: 03 3402 7187
　　　　　[編集] TEL: 03-3497-1010
　　　　　URL: http://www.toto.co.jp/publishing/
デザイン　groovisions
印刷・製本　大日本印刷株式会社

落丁本・乱丁本はお取り替えいたします。
本書の全部又は一部に対するコピー・スキャン・デジタル化等の無断複製行為は、著作権法上での例外を除き禁じます。本書を代行業者等の第三者に依頼してスキャンやデジタル化することは、たとえ個人や家庭内での利用であっても著作権上認められておりません。
定価はカバーに表示してあります。

© 2017 Etsuko Watari, Instituto Lina Bo e P. M. Bardi

Printed in Japan
ISBN978-4-88706-369-3